1996

BAD OBJECTS

BAD

OBJECTS

ESSAYS POPULAR AND UNPOPULAR

Naomi Schor

DUKE UNIVERSITY PRESS   Durham and London 1995

"Dreaming Dissymmetry: Barthes, Foucault, and Sexual Difference," previously appeared in Men in Feminism, ed. Alice Jardine and Paul Smith. Routledge, 1987, pp. 98–110.

"Devant le château: Femmes, Marchandises et Modernité dans Au Bonheur des Dames, previously appeared in Mimésis et Semiosis: Littérature et représentation, ed. Philippe Hamon and Jean-Pierre Leduc Adine. Nathan, 1992, pp. 179–187.

"Female Fetishism: The Case of George Sand," previously appeared in The Female Body in Western Culture, ed. Susan Suleiman, Harvard University Press, 1985, pp. 363–372.

"Fetishism and Its Ironies," previously appeared in Nineteenth-Century French Studies (1988-1989), 17: 89–97.

"Lanson's Library," previously appeared in French Literary Studies (1995) 23: 1–10.

"The Righting of French Studies: Homosociality and the Killing of 'La pensée 68'," previously appeared in Profession 92, pp. 23–34.

"This Essentialism Which Is Not One," previously appeared in differences 1.2 (1990): 38–58.

"The Portrait of a Gentleman: Representing Men in (French) Women's Writing, previously appeared in Representations 20 (Fall 1987): 113–133. Reprinted by permission of the Regents of the University of California.

"Triste Amérique: Atala and the Postrevolutionary Construction of Woman." Excerpted from Rebel Daughters: Women and the French Revolution, ed. Sara E. Melzer and Leslie W. Rabine. © 1992 The University of California Humanities Research Institute. Reprinted by permission of Oxford University Press, Inc.

Printed in the United States of America on acid-free paper ∞
Typeset in Joanna by Keystone Typesetting, Inc.
Library of Congress Cataloging-in-Publication Data appear
on the last printed page of this book.

For Elizabeth

Contents

L ike many authors of introductions, and perhaps especially of those intended to preface collections of their critical essays, I have been reading a lot of introductions lately. The ones that I have found most captivating are those that contain personal revelations. Lifting the veil of objectivity, they afford a tantalizing glimpse into the author's situation and an autobiographical context for her but also his—personal criticism is predominantly but not exclusively a form of women's writing—theoretical choices. Clearly, it is time for me to get personal, more personal than I have ever been in print, which isn't very. How had I become the reader that I am; what personal and professional forces came together to shape my practice as a critic of nineteenth-century French fiction and as a somewhat contrarian feminist theorist? To what degree has my trajectory, as I have reconstructed it, been idiosyncratic, hence of no interest to the general audience, and to what degree exemplary, which is to say banal?

My "story," which makes my experience both unique and typical, is that of the American-born, French-educated daughter of Polish Jewish refugees on the one hand and of an American—or better Franco-American—seventies feminist on the other. If there is any sort of originary matrix at work in my writings, it is my biculturalism and bilingualism. In this sense, the essay that seems most out of place in this volume, "Thème et Version," is in fact central; indeed it is the most personal of the heterogeneous texts collected here, for it is my first, and to date only, attempt to articulate my own skewed critical positioning. As some subjects oscillate between gender roles, I have throughout most of my life been divided between two languages and two cultures. My primary and secondary education was in French; in college I majored in English, but my graduate degree is in French. I began my career writing not only *on* but *in* French.

As the years have gone by I have become increasingly aware of the Frenchness of French theory—that which is most overlooked in its American reception. Only recently did I begin to understand that that Frenchness was bound up with universalism in a way that Americanness is not. Had I not unknowingly absorbed this essence of French national discourse while a student at the Lycée Français de New York—transforming myself from the not yet assimilated daughter of recent arrivals from what I used to call, in a dreadful set phrase, "war-torn Europe" into a direct heir to the glorious French revolution—I might never have become interested in the question of the universal that runs through several of the essays collected here and continues to mobilize my thinking.

Though French and English were the two languages and cultures that fashioned me as a divided self, I was in fact haunted by a third: Yiddish, with its legacy of laughter and unmournable loss. My biculturalism was complicated by my Jewish identity. When at the age of eight I was invited by a little playmate in the country to be her show-and-tell at school, I was asked to speak French, to answer such critically important questions as "How do you say ice cream in French?" I was delighted to show off my special knowledge. But when the teacher asked if there were anything I would like to say, I counted up to ten in Yiddish. I can only imagine how bewildered the second graders of Sayville, New York must have been by this inscrutable performance. Speaking French was absolutely natural for me—French was, after all, my first language—but counting up to ten in Yiddish was something I had had to learn how to do and, further, that I had learned from my father.

One might then describe my early linguistic situation as one of intense confusion; assimilation was for me a complicated task, but my double difference was also a source of inordinate and unjustified pride. I liked being different. Though challenging, my situation was by no means painful; indeed, my double allegiance as both an insider and an outsider in two cultures has provided me with a privileged or, at the very least, quirky perspective. Passing for French—the impossible dream of Americans in French—has never been my goal.

In the early sixties I arrived at Yale with only the slenderest theoretical baggage. The only ism I was even dimly aware of was the new criticism which had permeated the English department at Barnard College, where I had done my undergraduate work. I had no idea that in choosing to go to Yale—or rather in following my professors' recommendation that I go there—I had arrived at the capital of new criticism, but it didn't much matter because I was now back in French and as such was confronted by other isms. In the sixties, after Henri Peyre and before Paul de Man, the French department at Yale was a department in transition between thematic criticism, the so-called Geneva School—I read Jean-Pierre Richard, Jean Starobinski, and Georges Poulet with ease and some weird sense of recognition—and something newer, which was just beginning to make its way across the ocean, that was eventually known as structuralism. When I was casting about for a thesis topic, the thought of working on George Sand did cross my mind, but for all my childhood fantasies about being Florence Nightingale or the first (Jewish) woman lawyer— as I relate in the introduction of *George Sand and Idealism*—I was much too timorous to become a pioneering feminist critic. That work, my much deferred dissertation on Sand, did not appear in book form until 1993, almost a quarter of a century after I had left graduate school. Instead of writing on Sand, I embarked on a thematic analysis of several novels by Zola, who had, after all, been good for the Jews.

In the mid-sixties I spent two marvelous years in Paris on a Fulbright. I was in Paris in 1966, the annus mirabilis in twentieth-century French thought. But I might as well not have been there, as I was quite oblivious to what was going on around me. Because I had a boyfriend who was an American exchange student at the Ecole Normale Supérieure, I was not entirely out of the loop; indeed, I had access to the great figures then holding forth at the Ecole Normale. Probably my most significant memories from those days are of shaking Althusser's hand and being turned away at the door of one of Lacan's closed seminars. But when, on our nightly forays down to Maspero's, the legendary left-wing bookstore on the Boul Mich' which served as a rallying point for American opponents of the Vietnam war, my boyfriend looked over the latest theoretical and political publications, I whiled my time away in the more traditional literary criticism section. To read or not to read the latest works of theory seemed to me optional, and I chose not to. And this attitude was somehow obscurely aligned with sexual difference, though in those prefeminist days I lacked the categories and analytic tools to see this. Theory was for men.

When in the late sixties I arrived at Columbia, I quickly discovered that everything I had learned at Yale was irrelevant; I had arrived at a new Mecca, the Mecca of structuralist poetics. Shortly after my arrival I was asked to be on the defense of a thesis on Metaphor and Metonymy in Proust, and I realized for the first time that reading certain critics was not optional but the condition of my academic survival. So I learned all about tropes, Russian folktales, and shifters. I drew diagrams! This conceptual universe held no attraction for me, but ever the "bonne élève" (the good student), I went along. I attended countless lectures I did not understand, read *Poétique* and *Diacritics* from cover to cover, but I did not write. When, spurred on by the pressure to publish, I finally did begin to write, I read with enthusiasm the works of René Girard. He was one of the first theoreticians to provide me with two powerful notions—mediated desire and the scapegoat—that enabled me to read novels, and in particular Zola's fiction, differently. The influence of René Girard on a number of what were later to become influential feminist critics has never properly been acknowledged, though his indifference to gender has been roundly condemned.

And then came feminism. I joined a consciousness-raising group and went from faculty committee meetings against the bombing in Cambodia to marches in New York City and on Washington for abortion rights and the passage of the ERA. While in the many years since I have carried on love affairs with a multitude of isms (e.g., fetishism, realism, idealism, universalism), it is really only in feminism—where activism and criticism were joined—that I found an ism that made sense for me. I have often wondered what sort of career I might have had if feminism had not come along to give my intellectual and professional project meaning. Even Frank Capra could not make that a wonderful life.

The seventies were a heady time. I read Irigaray with passion, Derrida with immense profit, Foucault with great interest, and Barthes with and for pleasure. I can remember lying sprawled out in a pool of sunlight on the floor of a sublet on Morningside Drive around 1973—my troubled personal life had turned me into something of a nomad—reading Barthes's S/Z. It was a moment of sheer intellectual bliss.

A big urban university, Columbia did not exactly encourage contacts among its junior faculty on a university-wide basis. Or rather I lacked the confidence to teach in the only interdepartmental program that would have brought me into contact with my peers in other departments, Columbia College's vaunted and daunting Humanities course. My academic life was therefore limited to the fifth floor of Philosophy Hall, where, in the interstices of the imposing, anonymous institution, study groups were formed and some extraordinary lifelong friendships were forged among a talented and pioneering group of women in French. The diaspora from that time and that place—for not a one of us was kept on—are bound by a special camaraderie. It was only when I moved to Brown University (with tenure) that I discovered a different pleasure: that of being part of a transdisciplinary community of brilliant feminist scholars. The Department of French Studies was my disciplinary home, but I thrived on the constant exchanges with the feminist film theorists, historians, and literary critics who constituted a community the like of which I have never found anywhere since. We formed paper-reading groups and talked for hours over the telephone, endlessly dissecting the lectures we heard; eventually these and other activities came to be centered at the Pembroke Center for Teaching and Learning about Women, to which I remain linked to this day.

I moved to Brown in 1978; "Female Fetishism," the oldest essay I have reprinted here, was written in 1983. It was only the second "purely" theoretical essay I had written. (The first, "Female Paranoia: The Case for Psychoanalytic Feminist Criticism," is now included in *Breaking the Chain*). Throughout the eighties and even into the nineties I continued nevertheless to combine literary criticism and theoretical writing. Having been trained early on to do *explication de texte* in the best French tradition, my critical practice was to read closely and to think theoretically through literary texts, notably nineteenth-century French novels centered on female protagonists and/or written by women.

Around 1991—by this time I had moved to Duke—feminist literary criticism began to change quite dramatically, and the essays I have placed under the heading "Criticism" reflect some of these new developments, notably the marked shift from representation to construction. No ambiguity there. The more interesting part of the story is, however, ambiguous and must be read between the lines. Starting from a typically French feminist investment in psychoanalysis, I slowly came to see the limits of psychoanalysis: as constructionism reshaped my understanding of gender, psychoanalysis was displaced by history. The return of history is in the logic of constructionism: for once one truly ceases to view woman as a fixed identity existing prior to all social modeling and devoid of ideological function, then it becomes necessary to turn one's attention to the historical circumstances of certain representations. But the emphasis on the constructedness of gender that initially seduced me and eventually drew me into the orbit of cultural studies had in the long run a paralyzing effect on my activities as a feminist literary critic. Though I found the historicization of woman a welcome development, I could not get much momentum going from the dissolution of the identity of woman to which constructionism has led, for sexual difference was—indeed, I believe is—central to feminist literary criticism. In short, I could not accommodate the erasure of woman/women that the nineties have brought about.

But there is more: throughout the eighties, those brilliant feminist theoreticians who had been trained as literary critics repeatedly asserted their commitment to literary studies. In the nineties this claim rings—at least to me—hollow. Many of the most innovative and influential feminist theorists today were not trained as literary critics, which is not to say that they do not occasionally write about literature, since the boundaries between disciplines have become increasingly porous, not to say meaningless. This is a development with far-reaching consequences. Those feminists whose training was in literature must now contend with the forces working to undermine the study of literature—chief among them cultural studies, for when I speak of being drawn to cultural studies I mean being drawn away from the literary text. For those of us in French, who were in the catbird seat throughout the seventies and eighties, the nineties present other and increasingly ominous practical problems: diminishing enrollments and, at least at the institution where I currently teach, pressure from an administration which, on the one hand, lists "Internationalization" as one of the four criteria by which the faculty is judged and, on the other, nudges us in the direction of the universal language of English.

In the end I could not pursue my critical project with the same passion that had animated me since the early seventies. My theoretical work, which had so long been grounded in my readings, grew increasingly independent of literary texts and began to float free. My growing dissaffection from the very texts that had first drawn me because of the space for fantasy they offered and then excited me because of the rich cultural material they provided for feminist rereadings was in fact not an entirely idiosyncratic development, but related to larger, more pervasive critical trends. In the nineties, academic feminism became a victim of its own success; the rise of a growing number of identitarian communities spawned to a large extent by feminism weakened what many of those of my generation of feminists had treasured about feminism: a sense of commonality, of participating even as a footnote in perhaps the most successful peaceful revolutionary movement of our era. Anguished and legitimate claims to difference cannot, however, mask the perils of particularism and the dangers of separatism that are beginning to show through. The very possibility of dialogue between self and other(s) is negated by the rise of what I would call differences criticism—I realize that I coedit a journal by the same name—where sexual difference is viewed not as a privileged, because foundational, difference but simply as one difference among many, and where the interplay of these differences—which is accurately seen as an area of urgent concern—is viewed as more important than the struggle for female emancipation. What I am calling feminism and what some might prefer to call feminisms or feminism(s) is at a crossroad, and there are no clear signposts.

I remain a feminist, and I feel myself going back to literature as a feminist, but differently so. This may be my contrarian side speaking. The question for me is: will a *new* feminist literary criticism arise that will take literariness seriously while maintaining its vital ideological edge?

But what might my reader be asking him- or herself of my title? What do I mean by bad objects? Aren't bad objects secretly good objects anyhow? What I mean is simply this: at any given time, within the carefully policed precincts of the academy, some critical objects are promoted to the status of good objects (say, not so long ago, dead authors), while others are tabooed (say, in the old days, experience). I am drawn to what I perceive rightly or wrongly as the bad objects. What I am invoking, then, is something on the order of the female fetishism I once promoted, a sort of critical perversion. To deliberately make an object choice branded as bad is risky business at worst and at best a means to go beyond certain impasses, to read at an angle, to be an intellectual bad girl.

It would be difficult to thank all those who contributed by their invitations to bringing these essays to life: let me mention Howard Bloch, Leslie Rabine and Sara Melzer, Denis Hollier, Henri Mitterand, Catherine Gallagher, Ellen Rooney, and Marianne Hirsh. These essays conjure up happy memories of conferences in L.A., Washington, D.C., the Berkshires, Amsterdam, and the enchanting Urbino, where even the doctors in the emergency room I visited could give a perfect definition of semiotics. But more than an occasion to recognize my scholarly debts, these ritual acknowledgments allow me openly to declare my love for and gratitude to at least some of the devoted friends who have stood by me these past few years through a series of health crises: there was Nancy K. Miller, who came to Paris at a critical time, and Elizabeth Weed, the nurse's daughter, who called every night from Providence for the latest health bulletin and who seemed positively eager for the numbing details of my daily pre-op exams. It is to her that this book is dedicated. Since I cannot cite all those who wrote kind notes, sent beautiful bouquets, and called, I will mention only those who were the closest to hand: Catherine Porter and Philip Lewis, Danièle Haas-Dubosc, Christine Planté, Madeleine Goulaouic, and Jacques Derrida, who confirmed my sense of him as a real mensch. On the second go-around, my friend and colleague Eve Sedgwick transferred the ethics of care of which she herself had been a beneficiary to me, for which I am deeply grateful.

This book would never have existed if it were not for my friend and editor, Ken Wissoker. Not only was it his idea, but he patiently nursed it or me along during a dark period, putting up with my unseemly whining with tact and infinite patience. Anna Gilcher, my research assistant, took care of all the details with her usual competence and good cheer. And Andrew McQueen generously stepped in at a critical point in the manuscript's preparation. This introduction was the object of ministrations by Nancy K. Miller, Ken Wis-soker, and Margaret Waller, who gave me the inestimable gift of her truly inspired editorial suggestions.

As is customary in the case of collected essays, I have kept my revisions of the texts gathered here to the absolute minimum. I have, however, updated the footnotes, especially to take into account translations that didn't exist when I wrote certain essays and texts that were forthcoming and that are now in print.

Chapel Hill, fall 1994

BAD OBJECTS

I.

Universalism

French Feminism Is a Universalism

The dismantling of the universal is widely considered one of the founding gestures of twentieth-century thought. The notion that there might exist a universal human nature—and further that that human nature is rational—has been repeatedly called into question by a wide variety of modern thinkers who have emphasized pre-Enlightenment and post-Enlightenment universalism's dangerous tendency to slide from assertions of universal kinship to increasingly lethal forms of totalitarianism, ranging from the Spanish inquisition to the gulags and genocidal massacres of our own blood-soaked century. Following Horkheimer and Adorno, the Enlightenment leads to Auschwitz; after Auschwitz, the Enlightenment is a bankrupt, discredited, blighted dialectic.[1] Although for the most part I shall proceed in what follows as though the Enlightenment and universalism were synonymous, I think it crucial to any serious inquiry into universalism to unhook the two, as both Julia Kristeva and Ernesto Laclau do,[2] reminding us that universalism is an idea that predates the Enlightenment by many centuries, indeed that returns us to classical antiquity. In this historicized perspective, the Enlightenment is only one episode—albeit a very crucial one for our modernity—in the long history of Western universalism.

In a great number of writings on postmodernism, an increasingly ritualized and crude debunking of the Enlightenment targets universalism as postmodernism's despised binary opposite. Indeed I would characterize postmodernism as (among other things) an anti-universalism. And feminist postmodernism is deeply implicated in this condemnation of the universal, universalism, and universalizing.[3] Not only is the notion that there might exist some shared feminine nature anathema to feminist postmodernists, but even the notion that there might exist something like a transcultural feminist subject is strongly contested.

Now the relationship between feminism and universalism, not to mention between feminism and Enlightenment universal ideals, is rather more tangled than these recent feminist attacks on universalism would lead one to believe. For whereas first-wave feminism emerged in the context of the universalist French revolution (see Olympe de Gouges, *The Declaration of the Rights of Woman*, and Mary Wollstonecraft, *The Vindication of the Rights of Woman*) that promised to extend equal rights to all rational human beings, the rise of second-wave feminist theory and criticism was spawned by the growing disaffection of those social groups (women, blacks, people of color) whose very exclusion from the social contract made that contract possible. Lest this mapping I have just proposed not succumb itself to the very sort of erasure of differences that undergirds universalism, I want immediately to introduce a crucial qualification: when I speak of second-wave feminist theory and criticism, I mean by that *American* feminist theory and criticism. For despite the fact that all modern feminism is beholden to the Enlightenment, it will be my contention in what follows that what binds virtually all major *French* feminists from Simone de Beauvoir to Michèle le Doeuff is a common allegiance to the universal that contrasts starkly with the strenuous anti-universalism to be found among nearly all contemporary American feminist theoreticians. There is, then, nothing universal about the claim for access to the universal; in mapping the passage from the old universal, based on the Enlightenment model, to the new universal emerging at the close of the postmodernist era, and whose contours and contents remain to be defined, cultural specificities and contexts will have to be taken into account.

My comparison of American particularistic feminism and French universalistic feminism is not meant to be invidious, a tired replay of a familiar family spat. Nor, by the same token, is it meant to consolidate and privilege those two national entities, France and (North) America. Rather, it is meant to displace the question, the terms of the discussion. It is by now something of a cliché to assert that the importation of French feminism to the United States took little account of the historical and cultural differences between France and the United States, and one such neglected difference centers on the purchase of the universal in both national discourses and ideologies. Because I have dealt with this issue elsewhere (see below), I want to focus here on an illuminating recent paper on the issue of universalism by Pierre Bourdieu, for whom, in what I am arguing is a characteristically French fashion, speaking as an intellectual is to speak "with the ambition of the universal,"[4] which is to say with the ambition to overcome the historical and cultural differences that have traditionally divided European intellectuals and in so doing to access the universal. What is specifically French about Bourdieu's call for an "*International of intellectuals"* is the fact that for him the speaking position of the intellectual is obligatorily that of a universal or a would-be universal subject. In his brief essay "Two Imperialisms of the Universal," Bourdieu provides the most cogent analysis of the well-documented French identification with the universal, while at the same time contending that what characterizes the encounter between France and the United States is a face-off between two imperialisms of the universal, one on the decline, the other on the rise. That French culture, indeed French nationalism, is universalistic is the shared analysis of some of the most knowledgeable students of French identity.[5] That what Todorov calls "ethnocentric universalism"[6] is endemic to all Occidental imperialist nations is undeniable, but to deny the specificity of the French case is to fail to take the measure of an aspect of French culture that has a direct bearing not only on feminism, but also on a host of influential theoretical texts and movements that are embedded in this culture.[7] Bracketing for now the crucially important question of American universalism, let us consider the arguments Bourdieu makes in regard to France and its allegedly special claim on the universal. That claim is, not surprisingly, grounded in the myth of the French Revolution:

> France's heritage includes the universal Revolution par excellence. The French Revolution, the founding myth of the French Republic, is the universal Revolution and the universal model of all revolutions.[8]

This brings us to the paradox that lies at the heart of modern French universalism: it is a universalism without guilt, as it were. Whereas America, according to Bourdieu, stakes its claim to representing the universal on the moral superiority vested in it by God and the Constitution, France stakes its claim on its privileged historical relationship to the universal Revolution. Ringing the changes on the relationship of the particular and the universal, France's national particularity is precisely to embody the universal. Thus, in a passage cited by Derrida in his meditation on the crisis in European universalism, *The Other Heading*, the poet Paul Valéry remarks:

> our special quality (sometimes our ridicule, but often our finest claim) is to believe and to feel we are universal—by which I mean, *men of universality.* . . . Notice the paradox: to specialize in the sense of the universal.[9]

This deliberate confusion of France's particularity or specialty with its universalist mission has crucial implications for French imperialism. Legitimated by the founding myth of the Revolution, supremely confident in its unique claim on the universal, French imperialism can deploy itself in all good conscience in both the political and cultural fields: "to be French is to feel one is entitled to universalize one's particular interest, that national interest which has as its peculiarity to be universal" (p. 151). If, as Valéry and Bourdieu (among others) put it, the particularity of France is the sense of the universal, then French colonialism is represented as an act of generosity rather than of oppression, conferring upon its objects the privilege of participating in France's defining universalism. This is the logic that subtends French assimilationism: anyone—an Arab woman, a black man, a Jew—can acquire French identity providing they relinquish all claims to their cultural (religious, linguistic) differences. But the price to be paid for this access to the universal via the straight gate of Frenchness is not lost on France's colonial subjects. In the words of Léopold Sédar Senghor: "The Frenchman wants bread for all, liberty for all; but this liberty, this culture, this bread will be French. The universalism of this people is French."[10]

America's claim on universal morality will serve the same self-justificatory function in the national discourse, but—and this is the key to their difference—French universalism is paradigmatic, the original imperialism of the universal on which others, notably America's, is modeled.

French feminism is shot through with French universalism. But before going on to consider the universalism of two representative French feminists, Luce Irigaray and Monique Wittig, I want to rehearse some of the main stages in American feminism's abandonment or *attempted* abandonment—for the question can be raised: have they succeeded?—of the universal in the name of particularism, its embrace of resolutely post-Enlightenment philosophical stances.

I

In whose interests is it, exactly, to declare the abandonment of universals?
—Andrew Ross, "Introduction," *Universal Abandon*

The persistence of certain aspects of the Enlightenment model of the universal pervades both equality and difference feminists who followed in Beauvoir's wake. Or rather: the ambiguity built into the Enlightenment ideal of the universal produced the split between those feminists (e.g., Wollstonecraft and Beauvoir) who revindicated equal rights for women and unmasked femininity as a male construct and those (e.g., George Sand and Luce Irigaray) who, while sharing the same aspirations to education and economic independence as equality feminists, subscribe to the notion of an inalienable female difference.

Whereas Beauvoir's anti-patriarchal *politics* led her to question abstract Enlightenment universals, her humanist *aesthetics* constrained her to subscribe uncritically to the Kantian valorization of the universal. As Toril Moi puts it: "Radically contradicting her general political analysis, Beauvoir's aesthetics remain abstract and universalist."[11] The limits of Beauvoir's critique of patriarchy lie in her inability to question its aesthetic system of values and, notably, its privileging of the universal as a marker of artistic significance. Speculating on why it is that there have been to date, in her own words, "no great women writers," Beauvoir identifies woman's failed access to the universal as the grounds of her artistic second-rateness: " . . . it is very seldom that woman fully assumes the anguished tête-à-tête with the given world. The constraints that surround her and the whole tradition that weighs her down prevent her from feeling responsible for the universe, and that is the deep seated reason for her mediocrity."[12]

Woman's disqualifying failure to accede to the universal is due to a combination of factors: on the one hand, a deficiency in the capacity to generalize that traps woman in a world of minutiae, and on the other, a misogynist patriarchal system that blocks woman's access to the ennobling universal. Beauvoir writes as though woman suffered from a sensory deficiency that disables her vision, making her unable to generalize, to emerge out of a fog of clotted particulars into the sharp light of the universal: "Not accepting logical principles and moral imperatives, skeptical about the laws of nature, *woman lacks the sense of the universal*; to her the world seems a confused conglomeration of special cases" (p. 685; emphasis added). But on closer inspection, it emerges that this lack is enjoined upon women by patriarchy. Thus, elsewhere in the final section of *The Second Sex*, Beauvoir points the way to a far more significant reason for women's failure to assume the universal than their particularism, namely that, to date, women and other underprivileged groups have been historically excluded from this prestigious realm by institutionalized means. It is not because of some deficiency remediable by education that women shy away from a tête-à-tête with the "given," but because men have, to date, preempted this cozy dialogue. Access to the universal is restricted; it can only be achieved through struggle by those who have been historically excluded:

To regard the universe as one's own, to consider oneself to blame for its faults and to glory in its progress, one must belong to the caste of the privileged; it is for those alone who are in command to justify the universe by changing it, by thinking about it, by revealing it; they alone

can recognize themselves in it and endeavor to make their mark upon it.
It is in man and not in woman that it has hitherto been possible for Man to be incarnated.
(p. 793; emphasis added)

What is merely hinted at in Beauvoir—that heretofore Man has claimed
himself to be the sole incarnation of the Universal—has since become the
jumping-off point for a wide-ranging critique of Enlightenment universalism
in the writings of more recent feminists. As we have already noted, second-
wave feminism is a body of theory born of disillusionment with the promise
of the French Revolution to extend access to universal rights to all, a deep loss
of faith in the emancipatory promise of the Enlightenment ideal as such.[13] I
do not mean to suggest that women did not always feel excluded from the
Declaration of the Rights of Man and with good reason; what I do mean to
suggest is that there have been several stages in the grand narrative of feminism: in the first, feminist women attempted to prop up the Enlightenment
by making it more inclusive;[14] in the second stage—the one I am focusing on
here—the Enlightenment itself came under intense scrutiny. And the third
stage, which now seems to be looming on the horizon—what we might call
new wave feminism—seems to situate itself beyond the Enlightenment and its
universalism.[15]

Coming to terms with their banishment from the fraternal social contract
ushered in by the French Revolution led post-'68 feminists both in France and
the United States to a crucial insight: what had advertised itself for centuries
as the universal was in fact a false universal, a universal that appropriated the
universal for the white, male subject. Monique Wittig is particularly incisive
on this point:

. . . for all its pretention to being universal, what has been until now
considered "human" in our Western philosophy concerns only a small
fringe of people: white men, proprietors of the means of production,
along with the philosophers who theorized their point of view as the
only and exclusively possible one.[16]

The abstract form, the general, the universal, that is what the so-called
masculine gender means for the class of men who have appropriated the
universal for themselves. One must understand that men are not born
with a faculty for the universal and that women are not reduced at birth
to the particular. The universal has been, and is continually at every
moment, appropriated by men. (p. 66)

According to this widespread critique, what has passed for the universal since
(at least) the mid-eighteenth century in Europe is in fact nothing but a sham,

a fake, a phony, or, in Rosi Braidotti's feminist rendition, "an inflation of masculinity into cosmic transcendental narcissism."[17] While few would dispute this characterization of the old universal as false—of course man is not the universal subject—few grapple with the fact that to speak of a false universalism logically implies that there is such a thing as a true universal, unless, that is, one simply assumes that all universalisms are by definition false. And that in the final analysis is the question: for if there do exist true universals, then the entire feminist critique of universalism (not to mention others') needs to be rethought. What is certain is that whereas in American feminist theory there has been a tendency to extrapolate from the falseness of phallocentric universalism the notion that all universals are false, in French feminist theory the universal remains, despite all its misappropriations, a valorized category to be rethought and refashioned. Though French feminist theoreticians reject the imperialistic universalization of masculine particularity, like so many French intellectuals they remain wedded to the concept of the universal.

In rhetorical terms, we might say that the discredited form of universalism is a synecdoche masquerading as a metaphor. The false universal passes itself off as a whole (Mankind) standing for all its constitutive parts (Women, Children, Blacks, Queers), rather than recognizing that it is a mere fragment of the whole, which is to say man. "The universal is no more than a particular that has become dominant" is how Ernesto Laclau expresses this prevailing demystified view of modern European universalism.[18]

The universal whose cover we have blown is, then, an inflated particular. It should be added, however, that this wild, galloping inflation of the particular is not without its regulatory mechanisms. For, contrary to what Laclau suggests, it is not just any particular that arrogates dominance—women could not just be promoted to the status of the universal subject. Moreover, not all universals are overblown particulars. Indeed, speaking from a strictly logical perspective, particularity does not always *precede* universalization.

When one considers the tension between the universal and the particular from a point of view other than that of a demoted particular, one becomes aware that the scenario of implicit subordination leaves what is in fact a hierarchy discreetly veiled. The very distinction between the subordinated particular and the dominant universal does not necessarily operate according to the temporal sequence implied by Laclau's admittedly critical formulation. For, as Joan Scott notes, using a typical Foucauldian reversal to excellent effect, what is significant is not that particularity is puffed up into universality or even that universality depletes particularity; it is that what appears as a prior cause (i.e., particularity) is in fact a subsequent effect; it is that the very opposition between the universal and the particular is driven by a distinction that is embedded in the social, that is, sociopolitical discrimination; ultimately it is power that underwrites the hierarchy of the particular and the universal: "difference and the salience of different identities are produced by discrimination, a process that establishes the superiority or the typicality or the universality of some in terms of the inferiority or atypicality or particularity of others."[19]

Perhaps in no area of our social order is the efficacy of discrimination in producing the hierarchy of the universal and the particular more shamefully obvious than in the workings of racism, which preempts the valorized universal for whites and relegates blacks and people of color to the disdained and invisible margin identified with the particular. Thus, scarcely had white feminists shown up the white male face lurking behind the mask of universality, than American black feminists accused them in turn of being false universalists, simply promoting white feminists in the place of white patriarchs as all too particular paradigms of the universal. Just as the predominantly white feminists of the seventies accused men of preempting the universal, black feminists of the eighties accused white feminists of preempting feminism. Throughout the eighties, black feminist literary critics and theoreticians as different as bell hooks, Barbara Christian, and Hazel Carby denounced white feminists for presuming to speak for all women, for universalizing the category of white woman without taking into account the racial and class differences that distinguish and divide women.

It is worth noting that accusing racially and economically privileged feminists of rushing to occupy the site of the universal from which white men had only just been evicted does not signify for black feminists a complete rejection of the universal as an aesthetic ideal, nor of the historically emancipatory enlightenment model as a means of political empowerment. Quite the contrary. Just as certain pioneer feminists argued that burying the author was a premature gesture for those whose literature had only recently been disinterred, more than one black feminist has argued that it was premature to jettison the universal to which they had only recently struggled to accede.[20] Thus, in a brief, problematic but symptomatic 1983 article titled "Creating a Universal Literature: Afro-American Women Writers," Barbara Christian claims for a hitherto despised Afro-American women's writing the universality which allegedly characterizes canonic literature: "It is called 'political,' 'social protest,' or 'minority' literature, which in this ironic country has a pejorative sound, meaning it lacks craft and has not transcended the limitations of racial, sex, or class boundaries—that it supposedly does not do what 'good' literature does: express our universal humanity."[21] More recently, in her best-selling *Alchemy of Race and Rights*, Patricia Williams registers her dissent from Critical Legal Theorists by remaining wedded to the concept of rights: " 'Rights' feels new in the mouths of most black people. It is still too deliciously empowering to say. It is the magic wand of visibility and invisibility, of inclusion and exclusion, of power and no power. The concept of rights, both positive and negative, is the marker of our citizenship, our relation to others."[22]

More than the endless accusations of false universalisms advanced by each marginal or subaltern subjectivity struggling to emerge and assert its humanity, the most damaging aspect of the critique of the universal has, in recent feminist theoretical writings, arisen from the conflation of universalism with essentialism. One strand of the critique of essentialism, and not the least, is in fact directed at the idea of a universal human nature, for there is at least in one of its meanings a constant and repeated slippage between essentialism and universalism. As a corollary, the endless debates between self-acknowledged essentialists and anti-essentialists (or "constructivists," depending on the idiom) that consumed so much energy throughout the decade of the eighties have worked to obscure the issue of universalism versus particularism to dissimulate, for example, the not insignificant fact that whereas Beauvoir is, as we have just seen, in some formulations a somewhat conventional and typically French universalist, she is by no stretch of the imagination guilty of essentialism, that is, the ascription to widely different women of a cluster of unchanging, ahistorical, transcultural traits that constitute "patriarchal femininity,"[23] the Eternal feminine. It is only in the eyes of a global anti-humanist critique that universalism and essentialism can be so readily and unproblematically conflated and the complex relationship of universalism and particularism so thoroughly ignored. When universalism is not ignored but rather attacked, one observes a little-noted phenomenon: many of the arguments marshaled against universalism are in fact borrowed from the critique of essentialism; it is as though via universalism what is in fact (yet again) being targeted is essentialism. As Nancy Fraser and Linda Nicholson observe:

> Some theorists who have ceased looking for the causes of sexism still rely on essentialist categories such as gender identity. This is especially true of those scholars who have sought to develop gynocentric alternatives to mainstream androcentric perspectives but who have not fully abandoned the universalist pretensions of the latter.[24]

It follows that one of the most urgent goals of postmodernist feminists is to expose and expunge all lingering "vestiges of essentialism" (p. 33). Universalism is the last refuge of essentialism and as such must be rooted out. If, as I wish to do, one seeks to displace the question away from essentialism and on to universalism, it is necessary to proceed differently, to pry the two apart. For no more than universalism is coextensive with the Enlightenment does it neatly overlap with essentialism.

Denounced as lending itself to a false representation of the whole, unmasked as participating in a hierarchic paradigm, the universal is in this instance rejected as a prime example of the denial of historical and cultural difference(s). The assumption that essentialism and universalism are interchangeable is particularly damaging precisely because, according to Elizabeth Grosz, universalism is the least accommodating to differences between women of the chain of equivalent isms in which it is currently and I think often mistakenly inscribed:

> Unlike essentialism, biologism, or naturalism, in which not only the similarities but also the differences between women may be accounted for (race and class characteristics can also be explained in naturalist, biologist, or essentialist terms), universalism tends to suggest only the commonness of all women at all times and in all social contexts. By definition, it can only assert similarities, what is shared in common by all women, and what homogenizes women as a category.[25]

For all their legitimate attacks on an earlier unwitting feminist universalism, certain communities of feminist theorists could and under certain circumstances did accommodate universalizing moves. To build a countercanon of black women's writing, for example, entails some allegiance to the notion of the universal, although it is unclear at this time whether that notion is invoked from the standpoint of race or of gender, and whether the universality that is claimed is gendered or gender neutral. Is claiming that Toni Morrison embodies the universal subject the same as making such a claim— and both are made—for Ralph Ellison?[26] But if the assertion of discrete and distinct identities based on gender, race, class, ethnicity, sexuality, and so forth does as much to extend the purchase of the universal as it does to produce particularistic differences, anti-identitarian politics attempts to situate itself outside the particularism-universalism problematic altogether. The most powerful and brilliantly argued feminist anti-universalist critique is that recently mounted by Judith Butler, the preeminent postmodernist feminist theoretician, who seeks in *Gender Trouble* to undermine all forms of identity, and first and foremost the identity "women," which she sees as irremediably tainted by universalist foundationalist assumptions. For Butler there are in fact two interlocking and mutually supportive forms of universalism at work in feminism: patriarchy and essentialism.

The political assumption that there must be a universal basis for feminism, one which must be found in an identity assumed to exist cross-culturally, often accompanies the notion that the oppression of women has some singular form discernible in the universal or hegemonic structure of patriarchy or masculine domination.[27]

Butler's goal is to subvert what has remained most stubbornly immovable in this "fictive" universal dyad: the idea of a universal female subject, the features of which she sees as a product of heterosexuality, as excluding the homosexual—for it is the unfortunate property of all essential identities to exclude all others. Just as an earlier feminist anti-universalism targeted what Anne Phillips calls the "universalisms of humanity," Butler's critique targets the "universalisms of gender."[28] In order to do so, Butler directs her critique of essentialist, identitarian feminism at its point of maximum vulnerability: politics.[29]

Previous theorists with otherwise impeccable anti-essentialist, contextualist, deconstructionist credentials have always laid down their arms in the name of politics. Thus, Denise Riley, who paved the way for Butler's attack on the universalist conception of women, concludes her book with the following admission:

> Does all of this mean, then, that the better programme for feminism now would be—to minimize "women"? To cope with the oscillations by so downplaying the category that insisting on either differences or identities would become equally untenable? My own suggestions grind to a halt here, on a territory of pragmatism. I'd argue that it is compatible to suggest that 'women' don't exist—while maintaining a politics of 'as if they existed'—since the world behaves as if they unambiguously did.[30]

However much they may have disputed the assumption of a seamless, coherent, and ahistorical female subject, however much they may have called for a dissolution of the bondage of the binary, most eighties feminist theorists were willing to suspend their theoretical beliefs in order to effect urgently needed political and social change. Thus the challenge for Butler is to take on the apparently self-evident, hence unexamined, necessity of a hypothetical universal female subject for politics, and her wager is to demonstrate that politics can not only do without a universal category of women but can in fact draw new energy from getting rid of it, thereby undoing the grounds for the current euphemism for sexual difference, "gender." Translated into current political terms, what Butler questions is traditional coalitional identity politics, and what she proposes (but does not concretely elaborate on) instead is an "antifoundationalist approach to coalitional politics."[31]

As is immediately apparent, Butler carries constructionism within the sphere of feminist theory to its logical extreme, but, as is less apparent, she also articulates an extreme form of anti-universalism, and in so doing she instantiates a decisive rupture with the ideals of feminism as constructed around the Enlightenment conception of human universals. It would be difficult to overestimate the central role of Foucault in Butler's work; indeed, queer theory in general stands or falls on the axiom of discursive power. Power, to speak in somewhat dated terms, is the transcendental signifier in the field of queer theory. And yet on this precise point Foucault's role is curiously contradictory, or perhaps a certain ambiguity in Foucault is revealed. On the one hand Butler derives from Foucault's analytic of power the insight that the feminist subject is constructed by the very juridical power to which she addresses her claim to emancipation. In this instance Butler enlists Foucault as an ally in the anti-foundationalist project. And yet Foucault is not spared in her attempt to root out all lingering traces of the legacy of the Enlightenment. In her survey of several representative figures—notably Foucault but also Wittig—she is hardest on any manifestation in their writings of any shred of faith in Enlightenment conceptions of political emancipation.[32] In *Gender Trouble* there is no absolute outside, no simple before, no utter beyond, only repetition, for just as repetition constructs gender, so, too, does it deconstruct it.

It is to Butler's great credit that she has continued, in the aftermath of *Gender Trouble* and its immense success, to rethink her positions and has come in a relatively short time to recognize that identity is essential to politics and that the category of the universal cannot entirely be done away with. Thus, in *Bodies that Matter*, she writes: "it is necessary to assert political demands through recourse to identity categories"; "it remains politically necessary to lay claim to 'women,' 'queer,' 'gay,' and 'lesbian,' and to mark the differential relations of power through categories of race and ethnicity."[33] Quoting Gayatri Spivak—the selfsame author of "strategic essentialism"—she seems to have come to acknowledge that "identity" is a "necessary error."[34] Similarly, while remaining highly skeptical in regard to universalism and its function in masking the operations of hegemonic power, in her most political text, "Contingent Foundations," a text written in the wake of the Gulf War, Butler proposes a reconceived anti-foundationalist notion of the universal, as a "site of insistent contest and resignification."[35]

The result of this relentless American critique of universalism in all its many forms and meanings, coming first from so-called bourgeois feminists, then women of color, then constructivist feminists, and now queer theoreticians—and my list is far from all-inclusive—has produced the situation with which we are all familiar: on the one hand the promotion of those subjectivities whose marginalization underwrites the classic Enlightenment production of the universal, and on the other the loss of commonality, of any positive access to the universal. Now, while some would argue that this commonality never existed except as an effect of (false) universalism, I would argue that such a commonality, however tenuous, however contested, however limited in its geopolitical sphere of application, did exist in the early days of feminism and did make possible some of its greatest gains.

And yet just as some women have resisted the critique of universalism, so, too, universalism has clung to life. This refusal simply to fade away gracefully is indicated by the recent return of the universal among some of the feminists and postmodernist theorists who at other times and in other situations wholeheartedly embraced the critique of universalism. I count myself among them. I share with many other middle-aged feminists a nostalgia for the first decade of feminist critique, not because it enshrined women or the feminine, but because it allowed feminist critics to reinvent the universal: "Challenging the universality of the male autobiographical subject—the universal, but as it turned out Western, European, heterosexual, in a word, canonical "I"—seemed an all consuming task; the Female Subject was its counterpart and adversary."[36] "We're not trying to become part of the old order misnamed 'universal' which has tabooed us; we are transforming the meaning of universality."[37]

But those days are long gone, and it is generally recognized—and this, as Miller would say, is the good news—that the much battered universal must be patiently and cautiously rethought and reconfigured if it is to retain any purchase for a new generation of feminists. If Auschwitz dealt the Enlightenment ideal of universalism—a notion rejected by fascism—a death blow, what may pass for the repetition of Auschwitz, the ongoing ethnic cleansing in Bosnia-Herzegovina, has if not revived universalism then called into question the celebration of particularisms, at least in their regressive ethnic form.[38]

I would date the return of universalism within the precincts of the American academy to November 16, 1991. On that day, a day-long conference on "Identity in Question," cosponsored by *October* and the Collège International de Philosophie, was held at the CUNY Graduate Center in New York. The proceedings were then published in a special issue of *October*. In an appendix to that issue the charge sent to the future participants is printed in toto; it consists in a series of key words: the Avant-garde, Agency, Liberalism, Plurality, Nationality, Alterity, Subjectivity, Methodology, and Theory.

The question that seems to have sparked real interest and a surprising consensus on the part of nearly all the participants, however, involved none of the above but yet another keyword, Universality, which is defined as follows:

Universality: Do there exist values, principles, or objectives that tran-
scend all particular identifications, and to which all particular oppressed
or disadvantaged groups can, or must, appeal? Need such appeals postu-
late fixed rules or formal procedures derived from a foundational philosophy of humanity or reason? What relation would such appeals have
to the particularities of the 'identity' or 'culture' of the various groups?
Does or can there exist such a thing as a universal 'culture,' or only the
particular ones that secure the identities of groups? What is universality,
what is particularity, and what is the relationship between the two?
(pp. 121–22)

Judging by the frequency of reflections on the notion of universality in the
papers presented, this question captured the imagination and mobilized the
thinking of the distinguished panelists assembled there.[39] Nearly all take up
the issue, though not all would agree on its timeliness. For a number of
panelists, thus for Chantal Mouffe, universalism is radically distinct from essentialism, whereas for others, such as Stanley Aronowitz, they are so closely
allied that he even goes so far as to call for a new look at essentialism.

   To suggest that universalism is in need of rethinking at this time is to cross
at least two borders: one a sort of glass barrier that separates generations of
feminist thinkers, the other a crumbling but still standing border between
disciplines. When, in a feminist theory course I taught in spring 1993, I
proposed to a class of theoretically sophisticated graduate students that drop-
ping all conceptions of women along with the classic sexist conception of
"woman" was not necessarily a move I embraced, I met with total blankness.
What universal claim, I was asked, could one possibly make in the name of
women? Heads nodded in agreement; I felt old, out of it, mired in the seventies feminism it has become so fashionable in some quarters to bash. I had no
doubt made a false pedagogical move: instead of suggesting that universal
claims could be made in the name of women—a difficult notion to accept for
a class for whom women was a suspect category and sexual difference a
quaint relic of maternal feminism—I should have formulated my statement in
the form of a question or a series of questions: what becomes of universalism
in an era of ever more marginal subjectivities, ever more anti-universalist
gender disorders? According to what logic can particularism flourish, severed
from the universal? Or, to put the question bluntly: *is the universal worth saving?*
Or, more cautiously: *is there anything in the classic conception of the universal that is worth
saving?*

   For many feminist philosophers and political theorists this must seem an
absurd question, for the universal is an obligatory concept in their working

vocabulary.[40] For them the answer would have to be: how can one do without it? This points to the other fault line on which I sit: a rapidly disappearing disciplinary divide which separates those who "do Theory" from those who "do philosophy." Among political philosophers there is, as I understand it, a lively debate over the necessity to rethink universalism in the light of the communitarian critique, indeed to save it in order to elaborate a poststructuralist, postmodernist universal in ethics and politics. Conversely, universalism, to the extent that it figures at all in current feminist theoretical debates, is viewed, as I have attempted to demonstrate, as an unfailingly negative notion, at the very least as a totally expendable ism. Which is to say that the specificities of the universal in each disciplinary formation must be carefully attended to: there are overlaps, mutual debts, and borrowings, but there are also deep and fundamental divergences, telling disparities, a dialogue of the deaf.

Hence, even for those feminists who like myself are not trained in philosophy, but who find themselves engaged with general philosophical questions, especially such isms as essentialism, idealism, and now universalism—what Michael Walzer has referred to as "the fervent *isms*"[41]—there is an obligatory detour via philosophy. All the more so in the French context, where one cannot speak of universalism without invoking at some point the writings of Hegel. Because what Freud represents in terms of the analysis of modern subjectivity, Hegel represents in terms of the modern ethical subject. And just as one cannot talk about Hegel in early French feminism without talking about Beauvoir, one cannot talk about Hegel in second-wave French feminism without talking about Irigaray.[42]

II

Since the community only gets an existence through its interference with the happiness of the Family, and by dissolving [individual] self-consciousness into the universal, it creates for itself in what it suppresses and what is at the same time essential to it an eternal enemy—womankind in general. Womankind—the everlasting irony [in the life] of the community—changes by intrigue the universal end of government into a private end, transforms its universal activity into a work of some particular individual, and perverts the universal property of the state into a possession and ornament for the Family. Woman in this way turns to ridicule the earnest wisdom of mature age which, indifferent to purely private pleasures and enjoyments, as well as to playing an active part, only thinks and cares for the universal. In general, she maintains that it is the power of youth that really counts.—Hegel, *Phenomenology of Spirit*

Given the extraordinary influence exerted by Hegel's ideology of gender as it is expressed in *Phenomenology of Spirit* and *The Philosophy of Right*, it should come as no surprise that Luce Irigaray has carried on a long and discreet affair with this philosopher of philosophers: "For a very long time, but with greater continuity since 1981, I have been on a familiar footing with Hegel's oeuvre."[43] Indeed, ever since *Speculum*, but especially since her ethical turn (ca. 1986), Irigaray has returned obsessively to Hegel and especially to that part of his writings that deals with the dissymmetrical relationships of man and woman to the universal and the particular, the public and the private, the community and state and the family; see her *Ethique de la différence sexuelle, sexes et parentés (Sexes and Genealogies)* ("Each Sex Must Have Its Own Rights," "The Female Gender," and especially "The Universal as Mediation") and *J'aime à toi* ("La différence sexuelle comme universel").

Irigaray's Hegelianism did not go unnoticed even by her earliest critics but has been flagged for future attention by her most perceptive recent ones, notably Margaret Whitford, who writes:

> Although Irigaray's relation to Hegelian and post-Hegelian philosophy is undoubtedly one of the perspectives which would shed considerable light on her formulations of questions of desire, subjectivity, identity, and death, it is not my theme in this book. For in order to examine her from this perspective, it would be necessary to see her first as a philosopher, and this is the position that I want to establish here.[44]

Thanks to Whitford's magisterial study of Irigaray as a feminist philosopher, it is no longer necessary to defer the discussion of her relationship to Hegelian philosophy. Indeed, for Irigaray to "hang out" with Hegel is to achieve legitimation as a philosopher; it is precisely because Irigaray reads Hegel that she is credentialed as a philosopher, that is, a philosopher in the continental tradition.

Yet if what brings her to Hegel is her concern with ethics and with being taken seriously as a feminist in the house of philosophy, what keeps her there is Hegel's philosophical legitimation of the ideology of gender set into place by the French Revolution in the wake of such Enlightenment philosophies as Rousseau's.[45] There is no understanding woman's exile from civil society without rereading Hegel. Thus, if Irigaray returns to Hegel, it is to trace back to his failures woman's secondary role as a citizen, her lack of civil rights, her confinement to the private realm. In other words, what is significant about her rereading of Hegel is not only that she sees his role as crucial but that because his thinking has been so influential his omissions and oversights have cast a long shadow. But there is more: for Irigaray to be a philosopher is not only to read and reread Hegel, it is also to work on the universal, which is perhaps one and the same gesture. Let us note in passing that Irigaray's universal is not posited as immutable, eternal; if it must be constantly re-thought, it is because it is subject to history: "Philosophy's job is to work on the universal. But what is there to be done with the universal? Now and always it needs to be thought about. It changes from century to century, and the status of the universal is to be a mediation."[46]

Given what we have already said about the critique of the universal by second-wave feminists, Irigaray's basic critique of Hegel is, not surprisingly, the singularity of Hegel's notion of the universal; just as we spoke earlier of ethnocentric universalism, I would describe Hegel's as phallocentric: "The universal was conceived of as one, on the basis of one. But this one does not exist."[47] The universal is man's work: it is man who insures (assures) "the hard work of the universal."[48] There is, then, no direct access to the universal for woman; paraphrasing Milton, one might say: he for the universal only, she for the universal in him.

In fact the situation is far more complicated: paradoxically, far from being condemned to the particular, woman in Hegel, that is, the married woman who is restricted to the domestic sphere, is condemned to the universal: "In the ethical household, it is not a question of this particular husband, of this particular child, but simply of husband and children generally; the relationships of woman are based, not on feeling, but on the universal" (emphasis added). Because she has no direct access to the public universal, except through her husband, what she lacks is the ability to desire, to love, which is always particularistic. What woman lacks and man possesses is precisely access to the universal as mediation; her universalism is immediate, unmediated:[49]

> The difference between the ethical life of the woman and that of the man consists in just this, that in her vocation as an individual and in her pleasure, her interest is centered on the universal and remains alien to the particularity of desire; whereas in the husband these two sides are separated: and since he possesses as a citizen the selfconscious power of universality, he thereby acquires the right of desire, and, at the same time, preserves his freedom in regard to it.[50]

In glossing this challenging passage, Irigaray makes a decisive move, shifting from the recognition that man has preempted the enabling universal to a call for a female appropriation of the universal, thereby separating herself both from Beauvoir and from the tradition of feminist theory I am calling American. Whereas the universal that Beauvoir wants women to access is gender neutral, Irigaray's is gender specific: "For the woman the universal is reduced to practical work included in the horizon of the universal defined by the man. Deprived of the relation to the singularity of love, the woman is also deprived of the possibility of a universal of her own."[51]

In short, what is missing in Hegel is (among other things) any notion of a sexual difference that would inhabit the universal, split it in two, producing what Gayatri Spivak nicely calls a "bicameral universal,"[52] for as Spivak artfully phrases it in her sympathetic reading of Irigaray's ethics: "An ethical position must entail universalization of the singular. One can wish not to be excluded from the universal. But if there is one universal, it cannot be inclusive of difference. We must therefore take the risk of positing two universals, one radically other to the other in one crucial respect."[53] Hegel's omission is all the more deplorable, as sexual difference is in fact the royal way to the universal, precisely because it is the universal of universals. For Irigaray there is a hierarchy of universals, and this accounts for her privileging of sexual difference over the racial. If Irigaray seeks to improve upon Hegel by regendering a neutered universal, she simultaneously reveals her own blind spot, an insensitivity to the very problem of racial difference that led to the shattering of the category woman in the United States and elsewhere. In a sense, we should not be surprised by this double insensitivity, first to racism and second to heterosexism, because it is the corollary of the split between French feminist universalism and American particularism.

> Sexual difference is doubtless the most adequate content of the universal. Indeed, this content is both real and universal. Sexual difference is an immediate natural and it is a real and irreducible component of the universal. The entire human species is composed of women and men and is composed of nothing else. The racial problem is in fact a secondary problem.[54]

The conclusion to this line of argument is inevitable: for a woman, access to the universal necessarily passes through the acknowledgment of her own sexual singularity. Assuming one's difference, one's specificity, is, for a woman, a necessary stage of coming to the universal: "My belonging to the universal is to recognize that I am a woman."[55] The future of the universal lies in the direction of a taking into account of its gendering: "The culture of this universal does not exist yet. The individual has been considered as particular without a sufficient interpretation of that universal that is in it: woman or man."[56] If the work of the philosopher is constantly to rethink the universal, then the specific task of a late-twentieth-century feminist philosopher is to inscribe the mark of gender onto the alleged neutrality of the universal handed down by Enlightenment and post-Enlightenment philosophers. For

Irigaray, where Hegel fails most grievously is in his inattention to the gendered nature of language. The failure to factor in gender in formulating the universal is bound up with the failure to factor in the gendered nature of language.

Just as Irigaray's romancing of Hegel has only emerged in her most recent work, her long involvement with linguistics, which may otherwise appear naive and regrettable,[57] only takes on meaning when reinserted within this philosophical context: the necessary updating of Hegelian philosophy. Just as Lacan brings Saussure to bear on Freud, Irigaray brings semiotics and linguistics to bear on Hegel. What she faults Hegel with is not so much his participation in the traditional disqualification of woman as ethical subject but rather his failure to interrogate language's role in grounding the myth of a singular universal. To dismantle the universal one must dismantle the neutral:

> The most powerful goal of interpretation is the analysis of discourse as sexualized and not neuter. This can be demonstrated with linguistic and semiotic tools. To undertake this task is to complete the extra turn into self-consciousness that Hegel fails to make. . . . This task in no way implies the destruction of Hegel's philosophy since he points out the method. But this philosopher of the universal, of the achieved whole, of the absolute spirit, happily has his limits, as do we all. He was a male, he lived between the eighteenth and nineteenth centuries, he was mortal. I would add that he was shaped by his language and that language's way of expressing gender.[58]

What is finally most significant for Irigaray is not Hegel's failure to recognize the universality of sexual difference and hence the significance of the recognition of sexual difference as a means of access to the universal, but the role that language plays in this coming to the universal of woman. In order for women to have access to a universal of their own, language must be gendered: it is this gendered language, and not the feminized writing of the body, that is Irigaray's true *parole féminine*. And this gendered language is the product of a voluntaristic and lifelong interest in a specific category of pronouns, the third person: " . . . in the history of culture—in philosophy, theology, even linguistics—there is a great deal of talk of I and *you* and very little of he and *she*."[59]

The result of this Irigarayan reconfiguration of Hegelian social thought is perhaps most clearly articulated by one of her most acute readers, Rosi Braidotti, who writes: "In my understanding, there can be no subjectivity outside sexuation, or language, that is to say, the subject is always gendered: it is a 'she-I' or a 'he-I.' "[60] Flying in the face of much contemporary American feminist theory, and its readings of French feminist theory, and true to what I take to be the most fundamental impulses of French feminism—with the emphasis on French—Irigaray is committed to reclaiming the universal for women, or rather to feminizing it by branding it with the mark of gender. Again I quote Braidotti: "If we take as our starting point sexual difference as the positive affirmation of my facticity as a woman, that is to say, if we push to the extreme the recognition of sexual difference, *working through* the layers of complexity of the signifier 'I, woman,' we end up opening a window into *a new genderized universal*" (p. 189; emphasis added).

Based on this account of Irigaray's project of providing women with a universal of their own—however vague and abstract it remains—it would appear that no one could be more antithetical to Irigaray than Wittig in her take on the relationship between gender and the universal.

With Wittig we come full circle: for Wittig stands somewhere between Beauvoir, to whom she pays explicit homage (by titling one of her best known essays "One Is Not Born a Woman"), and Irigaray, whom she implicitly criticizes as a practitioner of *écriture féminine*.[61] And yet, as I am not the first critic to point out, Wittig is neither as close to Beauvoir as she might seem, nor, as I have just observed, is she as far from Irigaray as some might wish. What Wittig's critics too often fail to take into account in their readings is the centrality of literature in Wittig's theoretical writings on gender; what links her up with Beauvoir is not so much her constructivism as her privileging of artistic creation, her humanist aesthetics. Or rather, just as Beauvoir reads universalism through the double lens of politics and aesthetics, so, too, does Wittig. An astute critic of the false universalism of white, property-owning men, Wittig locates true universalism in the practice of great writers. Wittig, as is all too often forgotten by gender theorists—Butler is a notable exception—is first and foremost a writer, and her theoretical essays are in the service of an ambitious aesthetic project, the appropriation by homosexual writers—male and female—of the universal, which for her as for Beauvoir is the hallmark of the greatest creators. If one is to take Wittig on, it is not as an essentializing anti-essentialist (Fuss), or even as an unrepentant metaphysician (Butler), but as a producer of war machines, of avant-garde literary equivalents to the Trojan Horse: that is, a " 'simulacrum' that works to decenter the subject by adopting the appearance of the (phallic) universal":[62] "Any important literary work is like the Trojan Horse at the time it is produced. Any work with a new form operates as a war machine, because its design and goal is to pulverize the old forms and literary conventions" (pp. 68–69).

Wittig's history of modern war machines begins with Proust, because whereas at first *La Recherche* appeared as an innocuous roman à clef, with time its latent subversive power has become clear: it is the first work by a homosexual to claim for the homosexual the universal point of view preempted by straight men under the regime of heterosexuality. And in Wittig's personal pantheon the greatest writers are those who transform a particular point of view into a universal one:

> For in literature, history, I believe, intervenes at the individual and subjective level and manifests itself in the particular point of view of the writer. It is then one of the most vital and strategic parts of the writer's task to universalize this point of view. (p. 74)

> It is the attempted universalization of the point of view that turns or does not turn a literary work into a war machine. (p. 75)

What, then, prevents the mechanization of the literary work? What are the means of accessing the universal? The answer to this last question follows from the first: what makes the universal such an exclusive point of view is that it excludes all forms of particularity, notably gender, notably the feminine, which is the particular par excellence:

> Gender is the linguistic index of the political opposition between the sexes. Gender is used here in the singular because indeed there are not two genders. There is only one: the feminine, the "masculine" not being a gender. For the masculine is not the masculine but the general. The result is that there are the general and the feminine, or rather, the general and the mark of the feminine. It is what makes Nathalie Sarraute say that she cannot use the feminine gender when she wants to generalize (and not particularize) what she is writing about. (p. 60)

So far, there is no difference between Wittig and other French feminists of the universal including both Beauvoir and Irigaray. All valorize the universal, all agree that the universal is coextensive with the masculine, that woman has been the victim of a veritable universal theft: "It is part of our fight to unmask them, to say that one out of two men is a woman, that the universal belongs to us although we have been robbed and despoiled at this level as well as at the political and economic ones" (p. 55). Further, both Wittig and Irigaray (and one could add Cixous) agree that the prime vehicle for spreading gender through language is the personal pronoun. For French feminists the shifter is the empty signifier par excellence; it is in the personal pronoun that the universal is lodged: "It is without justification of any kind, without questioning, that personal pronouns somehow engineer gender all through language." (p. 78).

But it is at this point that Wittig parts ways with Irigaray: whereas Irigaray as a feminist philosopher of difference and a linguist seeks to imprint personal pronouns with the stamp of the feminine, to inscribe gender on a recalcitrant neutered language, Wittig's aim as a "minority" writer is to experiment with personal pronouns in order to free writing by women, and especially by lesbians, of the restrictive regime of gender, of the shackles of the (universal) straight mind. In the one instance, the temptation is to promote an *écriture féminine*; in the other, any form of scriptural specificity, including a homosexual one, is rejected. Hence these seemingly paradoxical remarks about Djuna Barnes:

> Djuna Barnes dreaded that the lesbians should make *her their* writer, and that by doing this they should reduce her work to one dimension. (p. 63)

> A text by a minority writer is effective only if it succeeds in making the minority point of view universal, only if it is an important literary text. . . . Barnes's oeuvre is an important literary oeuvre *even though* her major theme is lesbianism. (p. 64)

If personal pronouns are the prime elements in the grammar of gender, then Wittig's task as a writer committed to the universal is to enlist the personal pronoun in her attempt to break down the hierarchical difference between the "minority writer" and the universal one: "I said that personal pronouns engineer gender through language, and personal pronouns are, if I may say so, the subject matter of each one of my books" (p. 82). Thus each of her books experiments with a different technique for appropriating the universal for the particular. For example, commenting on the *Oppoponax*, she explains: "I wanted to restore an undivided 'I', to universalize the point of view of a group condemned to being particular, relegated in language to a subhuman category" (p. 82). Similarly, speaking of *Les Guérillères* she writes: "In *Les Guérillères*, I try to universalize the point of view of *elles*. The goal of this approach is not to feminize the world but to make the categories of sex obsolete in language" (p. 85).

Like Irigaray's, Wittig's linguistic universalism is utopian, voluntaristic. Though one seeks to feminize the universal and the other "employs the universal to deconstruct the 'feminine,' "[63] both seek to bring about transformations in the prevailing order of gender through the syntactical element of the shifter. Products of an age of avant-garde aesthetics and structuralist linguistics, both Irigaray and Wittig share a belief in the omnipotence of language in effecting social change that now seems oddly dated and plainly inadequate to the task of revisiting the universal from a feminist perspective.

III

I am not sure that feminism must renounce its designs on the universal which have usually been denied women, who are then historically in a sensitive position to criticize its illusions, since feminism assumes in fact a general anthropological and political aim.—Christine Planté, "Est-il néfaste pour qui veut lire de penser à son sexe?"

What I call the aspiration towards universality none the less remains. In the reworking of contemporary political theory and ideals, feminism cannot afford to situate itself for difference and *against* universality, for the impulse that takes us beyond our immediate and specific difference is a vital necessity in any radical transformation.—Anne Phillips, "Universal Pretensions in Political Thought"

The time has come to move toward closure, and I might begin this last section by asking: what, finally, is the meaning of my enigmatic title? Is it merely to confirm previous critical readings of French feminisms by suggesting that they are all neohumanistic, that just as for Sartre existentialism is a humanism, so, too, for Beauvoir and her French daughters is feminism? Is this statement merely a citation, an intertextual reference, or is it to be understood as an implicit condemnation or exhortation? Is it the good news or the bad news? Am I a new universalist? And what is the new universal? And what does it have to do with feminism?

In this age of difference(s), any attempt to bring back the universal is fraught with perils. However much misery identity politics may cause some, it has instilled in an entire generation of American feminists a very real fear of a premature "(re)universalization."[64] And given America's current hegemonic position in the "new world order," there is good reason for feminist theoreticians to share with other radical political analysts a deep-seated pessimism as to the viability of alternative universalities, a notion of the universal that would not serve as an alibi for an updated imperialism of the universal. Unquestionably to date, the call for a new universalism has resulted in abject failure; the setting into place of an American "imperialism of the universal" can hardly be viewed as an encouraging sign. As Edward Said remarks, more in sorrow than in anger:

We now have a situation . . . that makes it very difficult to construct *another* universality alongside this one. So completely has the power of the United States—under which in some measure we all live—invested even the vocabulary of universality that the search for "new ideological means" to challenge it has become in fact more difficult, and therefore more exactly a function mainly of a renewed sense of intellectual morality.[65]

And yet, as I have argued all along, the universal remains a preoccupying category—and not just in the sphere of French feminism. There seems to be an ever-widening recognition in some quarters that a century marked by a multidisciplinary dismantling of the Enlightenment and its legacy may presage a new century of reinventing the universal. To the extent that the old universalism, what Cornel West calls a "pseudo-universalism,"[66] bears the indelible stamp of its Enlightenment origins, it cannot simply be reactualized, but at the same time, just because the old universalism is embedded in a discredited context, universalism as an ideal need not be abandoned. In the words of philosopher Alessandro Ferrara: "More than likely, our century will go down in history as a skeptical one. Among the targets of its critical focus is the conception of rationality and validity associated with the Enlightenment. Among the tasks that it will leave for future accomplishment is the reestablishment of a credible form of universalism in philosophy and in social theory."[67]

Those calling for a new universalism run the gamut from postcolonialist critics of nationalism like Partha Chatterjee to theological democratic socialists like Cornel West to neo-Kantian feminist readers of Habermas like Seyla Benhabib, who argues for "a post-Enlightenment defense of universalism."[68]

Because, as Anne Phillips reminds us, feminism has traditionally been animated by "an aspiration or an impulse toward universality" (p. 12), it has at this turn of a century a pivotal role to play in the "resignification" (Butler) of the universal. Indeed, feminism has at least in the West a special stake in the fate of universalism. Politically the acquisition and preservation of women's rights depends on some notion of the universal; in the sociosymbolic system, women's role as cultural actors depends on their speaking from a position of the universal.

But what form shall this new universal take? How will it differ from the old? There should be no confusing the old universalism, that old-fashioned category, with the postparticularistic, differentiated universal that many seem to be groping for as we slouch toward the millennium. The impetus for this transformed universal is the necessity to rethink democracy in order to adapt it both to societies with no democratic traditions and to old democratic societies with new and increasingly militant minority constituencies. The goal is to arrive at a new universal that would include all those who wish to be included and that would above all afford them the opportunity to speak universal while not relinquishing their difference(s). Evoking in the concluding pages of *The Other Heading* the duty confronting Europe, Derrida writes: "The *same* duty also dictates welcoming foreigners in order not only to integrate them but to recognize and accept their alterity: two concepts of hospitality that today divide our European and national consciousness" (p. 77). The age of difference (say roughly the last quarter of a century) has brought to the fore differences unimagined by the authors of the Declaration of the Rights of Man and Citizen, and the recognition of these claims to difference and of others that may be forthcoming is irreversible. But the need for the universal remains, for as Derrida goes on to say: "The *same duty* dictates respecting differences, idioms, minorities, singularities, but also the universality of formal law, the desire for translation, agreement and univocity, the law of the majority, opposition to racism, nationalism, and xenophobia" (p. 78).[69]

Recent developments in feminism have demonstrated what is to be gained by diversification, but also what is to be lost by a premature renunciation of the universal, not the least of which is the cultural authority derived from speaking as a universal subject. There are many aspects of the French feminism of the past two decades that I do not endorse; the universalism of French feminism is hardly new, and, what is more worrisome, it is deeply informed by the particularity of French universalism and its ingrained inhospitability to differences.[70] But French feminism does have the merit of having kept universalism as a category alive for feminism and even, as in the case of Irigaray's Hegelian notion of the universal as mediation, of having taken the first step toward defining a new universal. Reinscribing universalism on the agenda of feminism is, *relatively speaking*, the easy part. Determining what might constitute a specifically feminist universal for our time—which would, it appears, have something to do with a certain freedom of determination by women regarding what is done to their bodies (rape, sati, clitoridectomy, enforced sterilization, and enforced reproduction are some of the dubious practices that come to mind as necessitating a feminist universal to be combatted)—presents a far more daunting challenge. We must not let our fear of the old universalism prevent us from meeting that challenge.

II.

Essentialism

Dreaming Dissymmetry: Barthes, Foucault, and Sexual Difference

. . . the risk of essence may have to be taken.
—Stephen Heath, "Difference"

On the very first page of the important preface to *Powers of Desire: The Politics of Sexuality*, a bulky 1983 anthology bringing together some of the most significant recent texts on feminism and the discourses of sexuality, the three editors pay hom(m)age—or is it femmage—to Michel Foucault, historian of sexuality. Briefly summarizing Foucault's paradoxical reading of so-called sexual liberation as in fact a further turn of the screw of repression or oppression, the editors praise Foucault for his "subtle rendering of the general argument that sex and capitalism have gone hand-in-hand too long for sex to be interpreted at face value as a radical force."[1] On the very next page, however, Foucault is summarily dismissed as just another purveyor of "the obsessive male sexual discourse that runs through the centuries from St. Augustine to Philip Roth."[2] The editors point out that if, for men who have regulated the discourse of sexuality throughout the history of Western civilization, silence is an option, for women, whose relationship to sex has traditionally been aphasic, "it is too soon . . . for silence."[3] Setting aside for the moment the question of Foucault's phallogocentrism, of the inscription of his discourse on sexuality in the order of male discursive practices, I want to make another point. The mention of Foucault at the very beginning of this lengthy preface is striking in two ways: it is the only mention of both a *French* and a *male* theoretician in this otherwise indigenous, not to say ethnocentric, overview of the burgeoning field of feminist discourse on sexuality. One could imagine a homologous anthology which would represent the French point of view, and while I will not speculate here on its table of contents, I think it is safe to

assume that though most likely equally ethnocentric, it would be less gyno-
centric, because as historians of French Feminisms have often pointed out, in
France recent feminist thought has always functioned in dialogue with the
reigning male *maîtres à penser*, notably Lacan and Derrida. One figure is almost
never mentioned in this context, and that is Roland Barthes. And yet, I will
want to argue here that it is perhaps in Barthes, who was in his own words a
sort of "echo chamber"[4] of contemporary French thought, that we can most
easily grasp the dominant male discourse of sexuality in poststructuralist
France, what I will call the *discourse of in-difference* or of *pure difference*, for they are
in fact one and the same.

    Barthes's major rhetorical strategy is seduction, and many feminists—there
are some notable exceptions[5]—have succumbed without much resistance to
his subtle persuasion. Nor is this seduction totally misguided, for there is
much in Barthes that speaks to some of the central preoccupations of French
neofeminists. Most seductive, most resonant, has been the later Barthes's
valorization of the body and its pleasures, his insistence that one must write
the body, that writing must render the very grain of the voice, that most
intimate and idiosyncratic corporeal imprint. Then there is also Barthes's
valorization of *jouissance*, the most intense form of sexual pleasure, which
French women writers and theorists have in the wake of Lacan claimed for the
feminine.[6] There is another more subtle reason why so many feminists have
felt a special sympathy for Barthes: even at his most doctrinaire, Barthes's
voice is never strident; it is a voice whose grain reveals vulnerability and not
an obsession with force and penetration. Rejecting the violence of "arro-
gance," Barthes speaks from the margin, aligning himself with the excluded
of the bourgeois social order, with all those who resist ordering.

    There are, however, a growing number of signs that in the ongoing process
of dismantling the master discourses of the past twenty years, feminists are
beginning to resist the seductions of Barthes's text and to examine the ways in
which these seductive texts participate nonetheless in a masculine discourse
on sexuality, which is not to say, of course, that women, indeed feminists, do
not also practice this discourse, for they do. In what follows I propose to
answer the question of the feminist critique of and complicity with what I
take to be one of the dominant discourses on sexuality by undertaking to read
from a feminist perspective some texts first by Barthes and then by Michel
Foucault, with particular emphasis on his more recent work, notably the
second and third volumes of his *History of Sexuality*.

    In a fragment of *Roland Barthes by Roland Barthes* titled "Pluriel, différence, conflit—
Plural, Difference, Conflict," speaking of himself in the third person, Barthes
writes:

He often resorts to a kind of philosophy vaguely labeled *pluralism*.

Who knows if this insistence on the plural is not a way of denying sexual duality? The opposition of the sexes must not be a law of Nature; therefore, the confrontations and paradigms must be dissolved, both the meanings and the sexes must be pluralized. (p. 69)

Denied sexual difference shades into sexual indifference and, following the same slippery path, into a paradoxical reinscription of the very differences the strategy was designed to denaturalize. This sequence of events is traced out in a recent review article on Barthes's *A Lover's Discourse* (*Fragments d'un discours amoureux*) by Stephen Heath, who writes: "The subject of *Fragments*, of its discourse on love, is unisex, an indifference, only a 'lover' (the scenes permutate 'he' and 'she', hetero- and homosexual love, marking as little as possible the difference of the sexes)." Heath is quick to point out the dangers inherent in this sort of erasure of the inflections of gender, what we might call the *effet pervers* or perverse effect of Barthes's sexually unmarked erotics: the return of a "certain myth of the 'feminine,' " as when Barthes writes "the man who waits and suffers from it is miraculously feminized," and, further, "the future will belong to the subjects *in whom there is something feminine*." Heath comments: "To envisage a future that will belong 'to the subjects in whom there is something feminine' might be heard on the one hand as the projection of a new order, beyond the phallic . . . , on the other as a derivation from the existing order, a repetition of its image and essentialization and alibi, its perspective of 'Woman.' "[7]

Jane Gallop, on the other hand, speculates apropos of Barthes's *The Pleasure of the Text* that "the wish to escape sexual difference might be but another mode of denying women."[8] To decide whether or not Barthes's discourse of indifferentiation ends up re-essentializing woman and/or denying her specificity altogether, I want to study in some detail a recurrent strategy Barthes deploys when confronted with the question of difference, a synecdoche for femininity, since in Western conceptual systems the feminine is always defined as a *difference* from a masculine norm. It is the recurrence of this strategy or move that interests me, for on this matter there is no gap between Barthes's prestructuralist, high structuralist, and poststructuralist discourse. Redundancy, according to Barthes, does not always ensure communication; on the contrary, as he notes in the fragment of *Roland Barthes* titled "Les idées méconnues— Misunderstood Ideas," the recurrence of an idea from one book to the other virtually guarantees its incomprehension: "it is *precisely* where I dare to encourage myself to the point of repeating myself that the reader 'drops' me" (p. 103).

I would like to begin with perhaps the most famous example of Barthes's displacement of sexual difference. It is located in S/Z, Barthes's brilliant and highly influential analysis of a bizarre tale by Balzac which tells of the ill-starred love of the sculptor Sarrasine for la Zambinella, a Roman castrato whom Sarrasine willfully persists in mistaking for a woman despite the many early warnings he receives. Barthes's choice of this formerly obscure tale by Balzac seems motivated in part by a desire to dramatize the dangers of essentialism—"Barthes," according to John Sturrock, "began . . . as an enemy of essentialism and he has remained one"[9]—and in late Western culture those dangers can best be dramatized by de-essentializing woman, woman as cultural construct, universal woman as opposed to women as historical subjects, Woman with a capital W. And no text could better serve to dramatize the dangers of essentializing woman than *Sarrasine*, for it is precisely Sarrasine's blind reliance on the conventional signs of femininity that lead to his death; essentialism in the case of Sarrasine is fatal.[10] In order to de-essentialize "woman," Barthes enlists a familiar strategy: what Heath first termed displacement, Barthes's general strategy for shaking up the "habits of intelligibility" of the doxa.[11] Noting that the female characters of the novella are split by a difference internal to femininity, Barthes writes:

> sexual classification is not the right one. Another pertinence must be found. It is Mme de Lanty who reveals the proper structure: in opposition to her (passive) daughter, Mme de Lanty is totally active: she dominates time (defying the inroads of age); she radiates (radiation is action at a distance, the highest form of power); bestowing praises, making comparisons, instituting the language in relation to which man can recognize himself, she is the primal Authority. . . . In short, the precursor of Sappho who so terrifies Sarrasine, Mme de Lanty is the castrating woman, endowed with all the hallucinatory attributes of the Father: power, fascination, instituting authority, terror, power to castrate. Thus, the symbolic field is not that of the biological sexes; it is that of castration: of *castrating / castrated, active / passive*. It is in this field, and not in that of the biological sexes, that the characters in the story are pertinently distributed.[12]

At first glance there is much here that is of use to feminist theory. What Barthes does here in exemplary fashion is to de-naturalize difference, stressing what Kaja Silverman has called the "disequivalence between sexual and symbolic differentiation in Balzac's tale,"[13] uncoupling man and activity, woman and passivity. If the characters in *Sarrasine* cannot be usefully classified according to their biological sexes it is because that classification relies on the double equation: masculine = active, feminine = passive, which has at least since Aristotle fixed woman in the inferior position in the sexual hierarchy. Feminists have long fought to break down the assignation of fixed sexual roles to biological men and women and have claimed for women, but also for men, the possibility of oscillating between activity and passivity, and to that extent Barthes's substitution of the active/passive for the male/female paradigm can be seen as beneficial. However, if one takes a closer look at what is going on in this passage we note the following: no change has really been effected in the representation of woman, since Mme de Lanty does not cease to be classified as a woman; rather she has been reclassified as that most fearsome of female monsters: the castrating woman, the phallic mother with all her terrifying attributes of super-power. What Barthes calls the women's camp has now become that of "active castration," a questionable reversal: first because it lends credence to a phantasmatic construct of maternal omnipotence, second because it is *merely* a reversal, which leaves standing what Barthes was to call some years later the "binary prison" of sexual classification.[14]

In S/Z, Barthes seeks to de-biologize difference by substituting the paradigm castrating/castrated for the paradigm male/female. This suggests that what is really at stake in S/Z is sexual difference—but a symbolic rather than an anatomical one. This presumption is quickly dispelled when one turns to an essay Barthes wrote on the same Balzac tale, titled "Masculine, Feminine, Neutral." In this early version of what was to become S/Z, Barthes suggests that the centrality of sexual difference in *Sarrasine* is in fact illusory, a lure: "Its apparent center is sexuality."[15] Because for Balzac—and, of course, for Barthes—the castrato escapes the binary sexual taxonomy into the neutral, Barthes argues that in *Sarrasine* we are in fact outside the symbolic realm of sexuality altogether:

> In reality, and linguistics attest to this fact, the neutral cannot be directly implicated in a sexual structure; in Indo-European languages, the opposition of the masculine and the feminine is less important than that of the animate and the inanimate; indeed it follows from it:
> *Animate (Masculine/Feminine)/Inanimate (Neutral).*

If this is so, the question in *Sarrasine* is not the transgression of the bar of castration that separates the masculine from the feminine—since they are located on the same side of the bar which divides the animate from the inanimate—but rather what Barthes calls a "transgression of objects." Thus the paradigm of sexual difference is canceled by the opposition of life and death.

So far, we could speak merely of displacement: the paradigm *man/woman* is displaced by two other paradigms, in the first instance *castrating / castrated*, in the other *animate / inanimate*. But as I turn to my third and final example of Barthes's strategy of indifferentiation, I want to introduce another term to characterize Barthes's move. Borrowing, however loosely, from Lucretius via Harold Bloom, I want to call Barthes's movement away from sexual difference a *clinamen* or swerve.[16] I prefer this term to the more common *displacement*, because displacement implies taking a concept or a word and transporting it over to another conceptual field, thereby creating a new and startling configuration. Whereas displacement denotes a *shift*, the clinamen as I am using it here denotes a *shift away from*; whereas in displacement the two paradigms coexist, in the Barthesian clinamen one paradigm is literally effaced by the other. But in order to demonstrate that what is at stake here is not a displacement (either single or double), but rather a clinamen (however minimal), and further than the clinamen is a swerve away not merely from sexual difference but specifically away from femininity, let us look at my third and final example, which is drawn from *The Fashion System*.

The Fashion System was originally meant to be Barthes's doctoral thesis. It was begun in 1957, completed in 1963, and first published in France in 1967. The book is intended to be "the structural analysis of women's clothing as currently described by Fashion magazines."[17] Now although *The Fashion System* is essentially an attempt to carry out Saussure's program for a general science of signs by studying the language of fashion, Barthes subsumes the signifiers of fashion to those of language and is concerned here exclusively with fashion in its textual inscription, that is, in the captions that gloss the pictures in the glossy magazines. Because, as Barthes notes in one of those parentheses where he tucks away some of his more memorable asides, Fashion is a discourse that "deals only with the Woman, for women" (p. 258), one might expect that Barthes would at some point in the book have to deal with woman or at the very least femininity. And that expectation seems to be borne out when we note that one of Barthes's subheadings is precisely "Femininity." Because *The Fashion System* is possibly Barthes's least pleasurable text to read, I skip ahead to the section on femininity. It begins on a fairly conventional note, but then comes the clinamen, the moment at which Barthes's paradigm shift becomes an erasure of the very femininity foregrounded in the section title. Fashion, according to Barthes, "understands the opposition between masculine and feminine quite well; reality itself requires that it do so" (p. 257). What distinguishes women's clothes from men's are often details, and despite the clear distinction between men's and women's fashion, some degree of crossdressing is permissible, at least for women, for whereas there is a social prohibition against the feminization of men, there is almost none against the masculinization of women: Fashion notably acknowledges the *boyish look*. *Feminine* and *masculine* each have their own rhetorical version; feminine can refer to the idea of an emphatic, quintessential woman . . . ; when noted, the *boyish* look itself has more a temporal than a sexual value: it is the complementary sign of an ideal age, which assumes increasing importance in Fashion literature: the *junior*; structurally, the *junior* is presented as the complex degree of the *feminine / masculine*: it tends toward androgyny; but what is more remarkable in this new term is that it effaces sex to the advantage of age; this is, it seems, a profound process of Fashion: it is age which is important, not sex. (pp. 257–258)

Perhaps the best word to describe Barthes's erasure of sex, now to the advantage of the neutral, now to the advantage of age, is Foucault's term "desexualization." Foucault's use of the word "desexualization" occurs, perhaps not coincidentally, in his response to an interviewer's question regarding the women's and homosexuals' liberation movements. Foucault says:

The real strength of the women's liberation movements is not that of having laid claim to the specificity of their sexuality and the rights pertaining to it, but that they have actually departed from the discourse conducted within the apparatuses of sexuality. These movements do indeed emerge in the nineteenth century as demands for sexual specificity. What has the outcome been? Ultimately, a veritable movement of desexualization, a displacement effected in relation to the sexual centering of the problem, formulating the demand for forms of culture, discourse, language, and so on, which are no longer part of that rigid assignation and pinning-down to their sex which they had initially in some sense been politically obliged to accept in order to make themselves heard.[18]

In both Barthes and Foucault the move toward desexualization takes the form of a fascination with limit-cases of difference: to Barthes's *Sarrasine* corresponds Foucault's *Herculine Barbin*. The volume whose English edition bears the mock-libertine title *Herculine Barbin: Being the Recently Discovered Memoirs of a Nineteenth-Century French Hermaphrodite* is made up of an introduction by Foucault, the memoirs of Herculine, excerpts from the medico-legal texts on the case, and finally a fictionalized version of the story by the German psychiatrist Oscar Panizza. Herculine Barbin was born in 1838 in Vendée. She was educated in

Catholic women's schools, first a convent and then a normal school, where she obtained her teaching certificate. Herculine's first post as a schoolmistress was with a widow with three daughters. During the three years Herculine spent there, she and one of the daughters became lovers. Found out by a doctor who examined her, Herculine decided to request an official change of her civil status. In 1860, when Herculine was twenty-two years old, she was officially reclassified as being of the male sex, and she changed her name to Abel. Alone, miserable, and destitute, Abel committed suicide in Paris in February 1868, leaving his memoirs and body to posterity.

For Foucault, what is of interest in this sad story is the new relationship between desire and the law that was being put into place at the very moment when Herculine's story was unfolding. Whereas in the past hermaphrodites were free to choose their sex, in the eighteenth and nineteenth centuries a new order of discourse decreed that all hermaphrodites were "pseudo-hermaphrodites"—that is, beneath the ambiguity of their anatomy lay concealed a single "true" sex, whose discovery it was the task of the medical profession to carry out. Accordingly, Foucault reads the memoirs of Herculine as utopianism masquerading as nostalgia. He contends that the memoirs reveal a longing for the "happy limbo of a non-identity."[19] Indeterminacy is bliss; if only Herculine/Abel had been able to continue indefinitely in her/his sexual in-between state, she/he might have lived happily ever after.[20] In his fragment "Active/passive," Barthes describes the utopia of indeterminacy this way: "once the alternative is rejected (once the paradigm is blurred) utopia begins: meaning and sex become the object of a free play, at the heart of which the (polysemant) forms and (sensual) practices, liberated from the binary prison, will achieve a state of infinite expansion. Thus may be born a Gongorian text and a happy sexuality."[21]

The memoirs of Herculine Barbin first appeared in 1978, when Foucault was still committed to pursuing the History of Sexuality, inaugurated in 1976, in its originally announced form. The five volumes Foucault projected writing suggested that the entire project would be ruled by the dream of escaping from what he termed the "austere" binarisms of the sexual order. However, in the course of working on his History, as he explains in the preface to the first volume of what we might call the new History of Sexuality, he found himself obliged to revise completely his original plan. He realized that in order to carry out his project it was necessary to study the genealogy of man as subject of and to desire: " . . . in order to understand how the modern individual could experience himself as a subject of a 'sexuality,' it was essential first to determine how, for centuries, Western man had been brought to recognize himself as a subject of desire."[22] To do this he would have to return to the classical foundations of Western civilization, to the ethics of sex elaborated by the philosophers of ancient Greece and Imperial Rome. The archeological move backward to the origin of Western sexual discourse on sexuality provides a much needed perspective on the discourse of sexuality. Sexuality, it will be remembered, is the term Foucault reserves for the discourse on sex elaborated by the bourgeoisie during the nineteenth century in order to codify the respective and complementary places of men and women in society.

Now precisely because sexuality is a discourse with fairly precise sociotemporal boundaries, the question becomes, what came before? In his latest books Foucault sketches out a more comprehensive periodization than that proposed in The Will to Power, where Church doctrine had constituted his historical horizon. In the West, man's relationship to his own desire has, according to Foucault's Hegelian design, passed through three phases: (1) the *aphrodisia*, which is to say the classical discourse on sexual ethics; (2) the "flesh," that is, the Christian discourse on sexuality; and, finally, (3) the very recent sexuality in its restricted Foucauldian sense. Foucault's last two books explore in depth only one of these stages, the first, but look ahead to the others. Three diverse but related aspects of Foucault's curiously restrained and limpid final works—so different in tone from the feisty polemics of The Will to Power—seem to me of particular interest to feminist analyses of sexuality: first, the scrupulous attention Foucault pays to the gender of the enunciating subject; second, the subtle way in which he decenters the "woman question"; and third and finally, the pride of place he accords to a model of heterosexual relations based on reciprocity and mutual respect.

From the outset, Foucault makes clear that the *aphrodisia* was a discourse which circulated only among men: "It was an ethics for men: an ethics thought, written and taught by men, and addressed to men—to free man, obviously" (p. 22). Given this remarkable statement it becomes difficult to maintain, as do the authors of Powers of Desire, that Foucault participates in the obsessive male discourse on sexuality. Or rather, if he does, he does so in his last works with an intense awareness of the phallocentrism of that discourse; though Foucault can never write from the place of enunciation of a woman— nor does he attempt to—he makes it very clear that he is not complicitous with the "hommosexual" (Lacan and Irigaray) communication circuit he so insistently lays bare. Because of the eminence of Foucault's position on the intellectual scene, his categorical assertion of woman's exclusion from the aphrodisia, as both sender and receiver, encoder and decoder, matters; that Greco-Roman civilization excluded woman, as well as other marginal members of society (slaves and young boys), from access to the symbolic codes will surely come as no surprise to students of classical antiquity but that it is

Michel Foucault who is insisting on this exclusion will surprise feminists. What Foucault does here is to recognize, as he never had before in his work, the centrality of gender—a question which simply does not arise in *The Will to Power*.

Woman as object of discourse and subject of history is, of course, spectacularly in evidence in *The Will to Power*, where Foucault argues that one of the key strategies deployed by the power-knowledge system to ground its tentacular investment of the human body is what he calls the "hysterization" of the female body: a three-step operation involving, first, a reduction of woman to her sex; second, a pathologization of that sex; and third, a subordination of the female body to the reproductive imperative. But the question of gender cannot be said to inform Foucault's project. In *The Will to Power* we are introduced to a History of Sexuality wherein the notion that the history of sexuality might be different if written by women is never entertained; a single, universal history is presumed to cover both sexes, as though the History and, more important, the Historian of sexuality himself had no sex.

Throughout Foucault's presentation of the *aphrodisia*, he continues to insist on their phallocentrism though, significantly, the word is conspicuously absent from the text. Thus he observes that temperance, that discipline of self-mastery which ensures the exercise of one's freedom, is a masculine virtue par excellence. This does not mean that women are not enjoined to practice this virtue, but: "where women were concerned, this virtue was always referred in some way to virility" (p. 83). In other words, temperance, like Freudian libido, is always masculine. Similarly, Foucault emphasizes the ways in which what he calls the "ejaculatory schema" of the sexual act is in the teachings of a Hippocrates simply transferred from male sexuality onto the female: in this old dream of symmetry—which survives well into the pornographic texts of a Sade or a Cleland—the two are assumed to be isomorphic. "This 'ejaculatory schema,' through which sexual activity as a whole—and in both sexes—was always perceived, shows unmistakably the near-exclusive domination of the virile model." However, even within the isomorphism of masculine and feminine sexual activity, a hierarchy is at work: "The female act was not exactly the complement of the male act; it was more in the nature of a duplicate, but in the form of a weakened version" (p. 129). Female sexuality in this schema has no specificity other than its distance from the male norm.

In Freud, the valorization of the same does not always preclude—indeed it requires—the centrality of the Other; phallocentrism revolves around the riddle of femininity. What Foucault reveals is that in Greco-Roman moral discourse—mythology tells another story—phallocentrism is not also a gynocentrism: what is problematic and intellectually challenging for classical thinkers is the pederastic relationship to boys, that is, the erotic relationship between two free men separated only by an age difference; what is problematic in the conceptual framework of the aphrodisia is not female passivity, which is viewed as so natural as to be nonproblematic, but masculine passivity, the feminization of man. The line of demarcation passes here not so much between men and women, or even between homosexuals and heterosexuals, but between active and passive men, with the result that the opposition between men and women and the concomitant obsessive focus on the enigma of femininity is decentered, even as the myth of a happy pederasty is exploded:

> Later, in European culture, girls or married women, with their behavior, their beauty, and their feelings, were to become themes of special concern; a new art of courting them, a literature that was basically romantic in form, an exacting morality that was attentive to the integrity of their bodies and the solidity of their matrimonial commitment—all this would draw curiosity and desires around them. No matter what inferior position may have been reserved for them in the family or in society, there would be an accentuation, a valorization, of the "problem" of women. Their nature, their conduct, the feelings they inspired or experienced, the permitted or forbidden relationship that one might have with them were to become themes of reflection, knowledge, analysis, and prescription. It seems clear, on the other hand, that in classical Greece the problematization was more active in regard to boys, maintaining an intense moral concern around their fragile beauty, their corporeal honor, their ethical judgment and the training it required. (pp. 213– 214)

But then again, the *aphrodisia* is not a monolithic discourse; in the course of its passage from Greece to Rome a subtle and gradual shift takes place, and eventually the fascination with boys is displaced by a preoccupation with woman. In the section of *The Care of the Self* titled "The Wife," woman assumes a new centrality in the context of a reconceptualization of marriage. "The intensification of the concern for the self goes hand in hand with a valorization of the other."[23] And with this dawning recognition of alterity, what I will call conjugal man is born. The model of conjugal relations posited by the Stoics is radically opposed to the model that prevailed in Athens; if under both regimes woman has no existence outside the marital couple, under this new ethos, the couple becomes a privileged social unit, bound together by mutual respect and obligations. Fidelity is no longer woman's natural destiny; men, too, are held to the same standard. Reciprocity replaces domination. And heterosexual married love displaces pederastic love as the valorized model of eroticism and privileged locus of problematization. This does not mean, of course, that homosexual love ceases to be practiced or permitted in Imperial Rome, but merely that the love for boys no longer is problematized. Foucault's tone throughout these two books is, as already noted, remarkably dispassionate; he exposes the interlocking discourses on pederasty and conjugality without ever suggesting the superiority of the one to the other, without ever taking a clear position in regard to them: the texts are, as it were, allowed to speak for themselves, presentation preempts representation. And yet, despite the impersonality of the voice, or perhaps because of it, a system of values is established, and a model of human sexual relations which is both heterosexual and conjugal is promoted, precisely because it recognizes the alterity of woman.

There are from a feminist perspective at least two problems with Foucault's eerily timely reconstruction of the Stoic ethics of sexuality—an ethics of sexual austerity fueled by a preoccupation with what we might call, anachronistically, physical fitness: the woman who becomes, in Foucault's words, "the other par excellence" is "the woman as spouse [la femme-épouse]" (p. 164), and, furthermore, alterity is, of course, not specificity. And therein lies the clearest and most persistent dissymmetry between men and women in feminism today: whereas many theoreticians, some of them women, have eagerly seized upon and used the tools of deconstruction to dismantle metaphysical woman, no feminist theoretician *who is not also a woman* has ever fully espoused the claims to a feminine specificity, an irreducible difference. Even the most enlightened among the male feminists condone claims to female specificity *only* as a temporary tactical necessity for pressing political claims; in the promised utopia of sexual indifferentiation and multiple singularities, they assure us, there will no longer be any place or need for sexual difference; it will simply wither away. At the risk of being a wallflower at the carnival of plural sexualities, I would ask: what is to say that the discourse of sexual indifference / pure difference is not the last or (less triumphantly) the latest ruse of phallocentrism? If one lends an ear to what some of the most sophisticated feminist theoreticians are writing these days, the resistance to the hegemony of the discourse of indifference is powerful and growing. That difference does have a future is forcefully argued by Myra Jehlen, who, taking note of the emergence of a politics of difference in recent American feminist writings, comments:

> In the evolution of feminist analysis . . . this about-face hardly signifies
> that women have, typically, changed their minds. On the contrary, it

reflects a deeper analysis. In the first place the claim of difference criticizes the content of the male universal norm. But beyond this, it represents a new understanding that if the other is to live, it will have to live as other, lest the achievement of integration be crowned with the fatal irony of disappearance through absorption.[24]

A chiasmus best figures the cross-purposes of those who currently maintain, respectively, masculine and feminine positions on difference: whereas those who adopt the masculine position press for an end to sexual difference and only grudgingly acknowledge claims for feminine specificity, those who adopt the feminine position concede the strategic efficacy of undoing sexual oppositions and positionalities, all the while pursuing the construction of difference. The most active site of the feminine resistance to the discourse of indifference is a certain insistence on doubling, which may well be the feminine mode of subverting the unitary subject: mimeticism (Irigaray and Kolodny), the double and even double identification of the female film spectator (Mulvey, Doane, de Lauretis), women's writing as palimpsest (Gilbert and Gubar), female fetishism (Kofman, Berg, Schor), the foregrounding of the "other woman" (Gallop), and the elaboration of a "doubled strategy" of deconstruction and construction (Martin) are some of the varied forms this insistence on doubling has taken and is taking.[25]

Whether they are producers or consumers of cultural artifacts and theories, the claim in all these texts is that women occupy in modern Western culture a *specific liminal cultural position* which is, through a tangled skein of mediations, somehow connected to their anatomical difference, to their femaleness. Women are bilingual, bifocal, bitextual. Now "perhaps," as Simone de Beauvoir writes in *The Second Sex*, "these differences are superficial, perhaps they are destined to disappear. What is certain is that right now they do most obviously exist."[26] Or as Hélène Cixous writes in *La jeune née*, after having imagined a utopia of multiple differences not unlike those of her male contemporaries, Barthes and Foucault: "But we are still floundering about—with certain exceptions—in the Old order."[27] Doubling holds open for now a space that has only begun to be explored: the pitch-black continent of what patriarchal culture has consistently connoted as feminine and hence depreciated. Before tearing down the cultural ghetto where the feminine has been confined and demeaned, we need to map its boundaries and excavate its foundations in order to salvage the usable relics and refuse of patriarchy, for to do so is perhaps the only chance we have to construct a postdeconstructionist society which will not simply reduplicate our own.

This Essentialism Which Is Not One: Coming to Grips with Irigaray

As Jacques Derrida pointed out several years ago, in the institutional model of the university elaborated in Germany at the beginning of the nineteenth century no provision was made, no space allocated, for the discipline of women's studies: "There was no place foreseen in the structure of the classical model of Berlin for women's studies."[1] Women's studies, a field barely twenty years old today, is a belated add-on, an afterthought to the Berlin model, which was taken over by American institutions of higher learning. For Derrida the question then becomes: what is the status of this new wing? Does it function merely as an addition, or rather as a supplement, simultaneously within and without the main building: "with women's studies, is it a question of simply filling a lack in a structure already in place, filling a gap?"[2] If the answer to this question were yes, then in the very success of women's studies would lie also its failure. "As much as women's studies has not put back into question the very principles of the structure of the former model of the university, it risks being just another cell in the University beehive."[3] The question, in other words, is: is women's studies, as it has from the outset claimed to be, in some essential manner different from the other disciplines accommodated within the traditional Germanic institutional model of the university, or is it in fact more of the same, different perhaps in its object of study, but fundamentally alike in its relationship to the institution and the social values it exists to enshrine and transmit? What difference, asks Derrida, does women's studies make in the university: "what is the difference, if there is one, between a university institution of research and teaching called 'women's studies' and any other institution of learning and teaching around it in the university or in society as a whole?"[4] Derrida goes on to suggest strongly that in the accumulation of empirical research on women, in the tenuring of feminist scholars, in the seemingly spectacular success of women's studies, the feminist critique of the institution has been scanted. In the eyes of deconstruction, women's studies is perilously close to becoming "just another cell in the academic beehive."

Derrida's account of the relationship of women's studies to the institution is perhaps not entirely fair, not sufficiently informed: women's studies—if one can generalize about such a vast and heterogeneous field—has been neither as successful nor as easily coopted as Derrida makes it out to be, no more or less so than deconstruction, with which, as he points out, it is often linked by their common enemies. My concern, however, lies elsewhere: what I continue to find perplexing about Derrida's remarks, remarks that were made at a seminar given at Brown University's Pembroke Center for Teaching and Research on Women, is his failure to articulate the grounds on which women's studies would found its difference. My perplexity grows when I read in the published transcription of the seminar, which I both attended and participated in, the following:

> This is a question of the Law: are those involved in women's studies—teachers, students, researchers—the guardians of the Law, or not? You will remember that in the parable of the Law of Kafka, between the guardian of the Law and the man from the country there is no *essential difference*, they are in oppositional but symmetric positions. We are all, as members of a university, guardians of the Law. . . . Does that situation repeat itself for women's studies or not? Is there in the abstract or even topical idea of women's studies, something which potentially has the force, if it is possible, to deconstruct the fundamental institutional structure of the university, of the Law of the university?[5]

Is what Derrida is calling for, then, that potentially deconstructive *something*, on the order of an essential difference? Is what he is calling for a women's studies that would be *essentially different* from its brother and sister disciplines? How, given the anti-essentialism of deconstruction (about which more in a moment), should an essential difference between feminine and masculine guardians of the law be founded? How can women's studies be essentially different from other disciplines in a philosophical system that constantly works to subvert all essential differences, all essentializing of differences?

These questions are of special concern to me because the conflict *within* the faculty of women's studies has from its inception been to a large extent a conflict—and a very violent one—over essentialism, and it is to this conflict that I want to turn in what follows. I will first consider the critiques of essentialism that have been advanced in recent years, then compare briefly Simone de Beauvoir and Luce Irigaray, the two major French feminist theoreticians who are generally held to exemplify, respectively, anti-essentialist and essentialist positions. Finally, in the space I hope to have opened up for a new look at Irigaray, I will examine her troping of essentialism.

This Essentialism Which Is Not One

What revisionism, not to say essentialism, was to Marxism-Leninism, essentialism is to feminism: the prime idiom of intellectual terrorism and the privileged instrument of political orthodoxy. Borrowed from the time-honored vocabulary of philosophy, the word essentialism has been endowed within the context of feminism with the power to reduce to silence, to excommunicate, to consign to oblivion. Essentialism in modern-day feminism is anathema. There are, however, signs, encouraging signs, in the form of projected books, ongoing dissertations, and private conversations, not so much of a return of or to essentialism as of a recognition of the excesses perpetrated in the name of anti-essentialism, of the urgency of rethinking the very terms of a conflict which all parties would agree has ceased to be productive.[6]

What, then, is meant by essentialism in the context of feminism, and what are the chief arguments marshaled against it by its critics? According to a standard definition drawn from the Dictionary of Philosophy and Religion, essentialism is "the belief that things have essences." What, then, is an essence? Again from the same dictionary: "that which makes a thing what it is," and further, "that which is necessary and unchanging about a concept or a thing."[7] Essentialism in the specific context of feminism consists in the belief that woman has an essence, that woman can be specified by one or a number of inborn attributes that define across cultures and throughout history her unchanging being and in the absence of which she ceases to be categorized as a woman. In less abstract, more practical terms, an essentialist in the context of feminism is one who, instead of carefully holding apart the poles of sex and gender, maps the feminine onto femaleness, one for whom the body, the female body that is, remains, in however complex and problematic a way, the rock of feminism. But, by defining essentialism as I just have, have I not in turn essentialized it, since definitions are by definition, as it were, essentialist? Anti-essentialism operates precisely in this manner, that is, by essentializing essentialism, by proceeding as though there were one essentialism, an essence of essentialism. If we are to move beyond the increasingly sterile conflict over essentialism, we must begin by de-essentializing essentialism, for, no more than deconstruction, essentialism is not one.[8] The multiplicity of essentialisms—one might, for example, want to distinguish French essentialism from the native variety, naive essentialism from strategic essentialism, hetero-sexual from homosexual—is revealed by the multiplicity of its critiques. Now, most often these critiques are imbricated, so tightly interwoven in the space of an article or a book that they appear to form one internally consistent argument directed against one immutable monolithic position. And yet if one takes the trouble, for purely heuristic purposes, to disentangle the various strands of these critiques—I will distinguish four such critiques—it becomes apparent that they serve diverse, even conflicting interests and draw on dis-tinct, often incompatible, conceptual frameworks. However much in practice these critiques may overlap and intersect, when separated out they turn out to correspond to some of the major trends in feminist theory from Beauvoir to the present.

1. *The Liberationist Critique.* This is the critique of essentialism first articulated by Beauvoir and closely identified with the radical feminist journal, *Questions féministes*, which she helped found. "One is not born, but rather becomes a woman," Beauvoir famously declared in *The Second Sex.*[9] This is the guiding maxim of the culturalist or constructionist critique of essentialism, which holds that femininity is a cultural construct in the service of the oppres-sive powers of patriarchy. By promoting an essential difference of woman grounded in the body, the argument runs, essentialism plays straight into the hands of the patriarchal order, which has traditionally invoked anatomical and physiological differences to legitimate the sociopolitical disempower-ment of women. If women are to achieve equality, to become fully enfran-chised persons, the manifold forms of exploitation and oppression to which they are subject, be they economic or political, must be carefully analyzed and tirelessly interrogated. Essentialist arguments which fail to take into ac-count the role of the socius in producing women are brakes on the wheel of progress.

2. *The Linguistic Critique.* This is the critique derived from the writings and seminars of Lacan and promoted with particular force by Anglo-American film critics and theoreticians, writing in such journals as *Screen*, *m/f*, and *Camera Obscura*. What the socius is to Beauvoir and her followers, language is to Lacan and Lacanians. The essentialist, in this perspective, is a naive realist who refuses to recognize that the loss of the referent is the condition of man's entry into language. Within the symbolic order centered on the phallus there can be no immediate access to the body: the fine mesh of language screens off the body from any apprehension that is not already enculturated. Essentialism is, then, in Lacanian terms, an effect of the imaginary, and it is no accident that some of the most powerfully seductive evocations of the feminine, notably those of Irigaray and Cixous, resonate with the presence and plenitude of the

prediscursive pre-Oedipal. In the symbolic order ruled by the phallus, "there is no such thing as The Woman," as Lacan gnomically remarks.[10] What we have instead are subjects whose sexual inscription is determined solely by the positions they occupy in regard to the phallus, and these positions are at least in theory subject to change. The proper task of feminist theory is not, however, to contribute to changing the status of women in society—for the Law of the symbolic is posited as eternal—but rather to expose and denaturalize the mechanisms whereby females are positioned as women.

3. *The Philosophical Critique*. The reference here is to the critique elaborated by Derrida and disseminated by feminist Derrideans ranging from Irigaray and Cixous to some of the major transatlantic feminist critics and theoreticians. Essentialism, in this view, is complicitous with Western metaphysics. To subscribe to the binary opposition man/woman is to remain a prisoner of the metaphysical with its illusions of presence, Being, and stable meanings and identities. The essentialist in this scheme of things is not, as for Lacan, one who refuses to accept the phallocentric ordering of the symbolic, but rather one who fails to acknowledge the play of difference in language and the difference it makes. Beyond the prison house of the binary, multiple differences play indifferently across degendered bodies. As a strategic position adopted to achieve specific political goals, feminist essentialism does, however, have its place in deconstruction.

4. *The Feminist Critique*. I have deliberately reserved this rubric for the only critique of essentialism to have emerged from within the women's movement. No proper name, masculine or feminine, can be attached to this critique as its legitimating source; it arises from the plurivocal discourses of black, Chicana, lesbian, and first and third world feminist thinkers and activists. The recent work of Teresa de Lauretis, *Alice Doesn't*, and the edited volume of conference proceedings, *Feminist Studies/Critical Studies*, might, however, be cited as exemplifying this trend.[11] Essentialism, according to this critique, is a form of "false universalism" that threatens the vitality of the newly born women of feminism. By its majestic singularity, Woman conspires in the denial of the very real lived differences—sexual, ethnic, racial, national, cultural, economic, generational—that divide women from each other and from themselves. Feminist anti-essentialism shares with deconstruction the conviction that essentialism inheres in binary opposition, hence its displacement of woman-as-different-from-man by the notion of internally differentiated and historically instantiated women.[12]

Unlike deconstruction and all the other critiques of essentialism that I have reviewed all too briefly here, the feminist is uniquely committed to constructing specifically female subjectivities, and it is for this reason that I find this critique the most compelling. It is precisely around the issues of the *differences* among as well as within women that the impasse between essentialism and anti-essentialism is at last beginning to yield: for just as the pressing issues of race and ethnicity are forcing certain anti-essentialists to suspend their critiques in the name of political realities, they are forcing certain essentialists to question their assertion of a female essence that is widely perceived and rightly denounced by minority women as exclusionary.[13]

Beauvoir and Irigaray: Two Exemplary Positions

Quelle femme n'a pas lu *Le deuxième sexe?*
—Irigaray, *Je, tu, nous*[14]

The access of women to subjectivity is the central concern of the two major French feminist theoreticians of the twentieth century: Simone de Beauvoir and Luce Irigaray. Indeed, despite their dramatically opposed positions, both share a fundamental grounding conviction: under the social arrangement known as patriarchy, the subject is exclusively male: masculinity and subjectivity are coextensive notions. Consider these two celebrated assertions, the first drawn from Beauvoir's *The Second Sex,* the second from Irigaray's *Speculum:* "He is the subject, he is the Absolute;"[15] "any theory of the 'subject' has always been appropriated by the 'masculine.'"[16] Almost immediately the suspicion arises that though both are centrally concerned with the appropriation of subjectivity by men, Beauvoir and Irigaray are not in fact speaking about the same subject. Subjectivity, like essentialism, like deconstruction, is not one. There is a world of difference between Beauvoir's subject, with its impressive capitalized S, reinforced by the capitalization of *Absolute*, its homologue, and Irigaray's *subject,* with its lower case *s* and the relativizing quotation marks that enclose both subject and masculine. Beauvoir's subject is the familiar Hegelian subject of existentialist ethics, a heroic figure locked in a life-and-death struggle with the not-self, chiefly the environment and the Other:

> Every subject plays his part as such specifically through exploits or projects that serve as a mode of transcendence; he achieves liberty only through a continual reaching out toward other liberties. There is no justification for present existence other than its expansion into an indefinitely open future. Every time transcendence falls back into immanence, stagnation, there is a degradation of existence onto the "en-soi"—the brutish life of subjection to given conditions—and of liberty into con-

straint and contingence. This downfall represents a moral fault if the subject consents to it; if it is inflicted upon him, it spells frustration and oppression. In both cases it is an absolute evil.[17]

Subjectivity for Beauvoir is activity, a restless projection into the future, a glorious surpassing of the iterativity of everyday life. The dreadful fall from transcendence into immanence is woman's estate. Consigned by the masterful male subject to passivity and repetition, woman in patriarchy is a prisoner of immanence. Beauvoir's theory of subjectivity, thus, as has often been observed, dismally reinscribes the most traditional alignments of Western metaphysics: positivity lines up with activity, while passivity and with it femininity are slotted as negative. At the same time, however, Beauvoir's exemplary anti-essentialism works to break the alignment of the transcendent and the male; by leaving behind the unredeemed and unredeemable domestic sphere of contingency for the public sphere of economic activity, women, too, can achieve transcendence. Liberation for women in Beauvoir's liberationist macronarrative consists in emerging from the dark cave of immanence "into the light of transcendence."[18]

Deeply implicated in the radical reconceptualization of the (male) subject that characterizes post-Sartrean French thought, Irigaray's subject is a diminished subject that bears little resemblance to the sovereign and purposeful subject of existentialist philosophy. For Irigaray—and this displacement is crucial—the main attribute of the subject is not activity but language. The *homo faber* that serves as Beauvoir's model gives way to *homo parlans*. Thus Irigaray's subject is for all practical purposes a speaking subject, a pronoun, the first-person-singular I. And that pronoun has, under current social arrangements, been preempted by men: "The I thus remains predominant among men."[19] The much-touted death of the subject—which can only be the male subject[20]—leaves Irigaray singularly unmoved: "And the fact that you no longer assert yourself as absolute subject does not change a thing. The breath that animates you, the law or the duty that lead you, are they not the quintessence of your subjectivity? You no longer cling to [*ne tiens pas à*] your 'I'? But your 'I' clings to you [*te tient*]."[21]

For women to accede to subjectivity clearly means becoming speaking subjects in their own right. It is precisely at this juncture that the major difference between Beauvoir and Irigaray begins to assert itself, and once again I take them as representative of what Anthony Appiah has called the "classic dialectic": whereas for Beauvoir the goal is for women to share fully in the privileges of the transcendent subject, for Irigaray the goal is for women to achieve subjectivity without merging tracelessly into the putative indifference of the shifter. What is at stake in these two equally powerful and problematic feminist discourses is not the status of difference, but rather that of the universal, and universalism may well be one of the most divisive and least discussed issues in feminism today. When Irigaray projects women as speaking a sexually marked language, a "parler femme," she is, I believe, ultimately less concerned with theorizing feminine specificity than with debunking the oppressive fiction of a universal subject. To speak woman is above all *not* to "speak 'universal' ";[22] "No more subject which is indifferent, substitutable, universal";[23] "I have no desire to take their speech as they have taken ours, nor to speak 'universal.' "[24] For Beauvoir, on the other hand, it is precisely because women have been prevented from speaking universal—indeed, because they have "no sense of the universal"—that they have made so few significant contributions to the great humanist tradition. Mediocrity is the lot of those creators who do not feel "responsible for the universe."[25]

My task here is not to adjudicate between these two exemplary positions I am outlining but to try to understand how, starting from the same assumptions about women's exile from subjectivity, Beauvoir and Irigaray arrive at such radically different conclusions, and further to show that Irigaray's work cannot be understood without situating it in relation to Beauvoir's. In order for this to be done, Beauvoir's and Irigaray's theories of subjectivity must be reinserted in the framework of their broader enterprises. Beauvoir's project throughout *The Second Sex* is to lay bare the mechanisms of what we might call, borrowing the term from Mary Louise Pratt, "othering":[26] the means by which patriarchy fixed women in the place of the absolute Other, projecting onto women a femininity constituted of the refuse of masculine transcendence. Otherness in Beauvoir's scheme of things is utter negativity; it is the realm of what Kristeva has called the abject. Irigaray's project is diametrically opposed to Beauvoir's but must be viewed as its necessary corollary. Just as Beauvoir lays bare the mechanisms of othering, Irigaray exposes those of what we might call, by analogy, "saming." If othering involves attributing to the objectified other a difference that serves to legitimate her oppression, saming denies the objectified other the right to her difference, submitting the other to the laws of phallic specularity. If othering assumes that the other is knowable, saming precludes any knowledge of the other in her otherness. If exposing the logic of othering—whether it be of women, Jews, or any other victims of demeaning stereotyping—is a necessary step in achieving equality, exposing the logic of saming is a necessary step in toppling the universal from his/(her) pedestal.

Since othering and saming conspire in the oppression of women, the workings of both processes need to be exposed. And yet, to date, the articulation of these two projects has proved an elusive, indeed insuperable, task for feminist theoreticians, for just as Beauvoir's analysis precludes theorizing difference, or rather—and the distinction is crucial—difference as positivity, Irigaray's proves incapable of not theorizing difference, that is, difference as positivity. One of the more awkward moments in Beauvoir comes in the closing pages of *The Second Sex* when she seeks to persuade the reader that women's liberation will not signify a total loss of difference between men and women, for the entire weight of what precedes militates against theorizing a positive difference, indeed against grounding difference, since both the body and the social have both been disqualified as sites of any meaningful sexual difference. Beauvoir gives herself away in these final pages when speaking of women's failure to achieve greatness in the world of intellect: "She can become an excellent theoretician, can acquire real competence, but she will be forced to repudiate whatever she has in her that is 'different.' "[27] Similarly, by relentlessly exposing the mechanisms of saming, the economy of what she calls the "echonomy" of patriarchy, Irigaray exposes herself to adopting a logic of othering, precisely what has been called—her protestations notwithstanding—her essentialism.[28]

What I am suggesting here is that each position has its own inescapable logic, and that that inescapability is the law of the same / other. If all difference is attributed to othering, then one risks saming, and conversely: if all denial of difference is viewed as resulting in saming, then one risks othering. In other words, it is as disingenuous to reproach Beauvoir for promoting the loss of difference between men and women as it is to criticize Irigaray for promoting, indeed theorizing, that difference. And yet the logic I am trying to draw out of these two exemplary feminist discourses seems to have escaped Irigaray's most incisive critics, who have repeatedly sought to sever her brilliant exposure of the specular logic of phallocentrism from her theorization of a specifically feminine difference. Toril Moi's formulation is in this regard typical: " . . . having shown that so far femininity has been produced exclusively in relation to the logic of the same, she falls for the temptation to produce her own positive theory of femininity. But, as we have seen, to define 'woman' is necessarily to essentialize her."[29]

My argument is *a contrario*: that Irigaray's production of a positive theory of femininity is not an aberration, a sin (to extend the theological metaphor), but rather the logical extension of her deconstruction of the specular logic of saming. What is problematic about Irigaray's theorization of the feminine— which, it should be pointed out, is in fact only one aspect or moment of her work—is indicated by Moi's use of the word "positive." For, finally, the question posed by Irigaray's attempts to theorize feminine specificity—which is not to be confused with "defining" woman, a task, she writes, that is better left to men—is the question of the difference *within* difference. Irigaray's wager is that difference can be reinvented, that the bogus difference of misogyny can be reclaimed to become a radical new difference that would present the first serious historical threat to the hegemony of the male sex. Irigaray's wager is that there is a (*la / une femme*) woman *in* femininity: "Beneath all those/her appearances, beneath all those/her borrowed finery, that female other still sub-sists. Beyond all those/her forms of life and death, still she is living."[30] *Mimesis* is the term Irigaray appropriates from the vocabulary of philosophy to describe her strategy, transforming woman's masquerade, her so-called femininity, into a means of reappropriating the feminine:

> One must assume the feminine role deliberately. Which means already to convert a form of subordination into an affirmation, and thus to begin to thwart it. . . . To play with mimesis is thus, for a woman, to try to recover the place of her exploitation by discourse, without allowing herself to be simply reduced to it. It means to resubmit herself—inasmuch as she is on the side of the "perceptible," of "matter"—to "ideas," in particular to ideas about herself that are elaborated in/by a masculine logic, but so as to make "visible," by an effect of playful repetition, what was supposed to remain invisible: the cover-up of a possible operation of the feminine in language. It also means to "unveil" the fact that, if women are such good mimics, it is because they are not simply resorbed in this function. *They also remain elsewhere.*[31]

Mimesis (*mimétisme*) in Irigaray has been widely and correctly interpreted as describing a parodic mode of discourse designed to deconstruct the discourse of misogyny through effects of amplification and rearticulation that work, in Mary Ann Doane's words, to "enact a defamiliarized version of femininity."[32] But there is yet another aspect of mimesis—a notoriously polysemic term[33]—which has been largely misread, and even repressed, because it involves a far more controversial and riskier operation, a transvaluation rather than a repudiation of the discourse of misogyny, an effort to hold on to the baby while draining out the bathwater. For example, in *Le corps-à-corps avec la mère*, Irigaray writes: "We are historically the guardians of the corporeal, we must not abandon this charge but identify it as ours, by inviting men not to make of us their body, a guarantee of their body."[34]

Irigaray's use of the word *mimesis* mimes her strategy, bodies forth her wager, which might be described as an instance of what Derrida has termed paleonymy: "the occasional maintenance of an *old name* in order to launch a new concept."[35] In the specific context of feminism, the old mimesis, sometimes referred to as *masquerade*, names women's alleged talents at parroting the master's discourse, including the discourse of misogyny. At a second level, parroting becomes parody, and mimesis signifies not a deluded masquerade, but a canny mimicry. And, finally, in the third meaning of mimesis that I am attempting to tease out of Irigaray's writings, mimesis comes to signify difference as positivity, a joyful reappropriation of the attributes of the other that is not in any way to be confused with a mere reversal of the existing phallocentric distribution of power. For Irigaray, as for other new French antifeminists, reversal—the coming into power of women which they view as the ultimate goal of American-style feminists—leaves the specular economy she would shatter in place. The mimesis that lies beyond masquerade and mimicry—a more essential mimesis, as it were, a mimesis that recalls the original Platonic mimesis—does not signify a reversal of misogyny but an emergence of the feminine, and the feminine can only emerge from within or beneath—to extend Irigaray's archeological metaphor—femininity, within which it lies buried. The difference within mimesis *is* the difference within difference.

Coming to Grips with Irigaray

Est-ce qu'il n'y a pas une fluidité,
quelque déluge, qui pourrait ébranler
cet ordre social? —Irigaray, *Le
Corps - à - corps avec la mère*

Où sont, au présent, les fluides?
—Irigaray, *L'oubli de l'air*

Few claims Irigaray has made for feminine specificity have aroused more virulent accusations of essentialism than her "outrageous" claim that woman enjoys a special relationship with the fluid. One of the earliest such assertions occurs in *This Sex Which Is Not One*, where in the heyday of "écriture féminine" Irigaray characterizes both women's writing and speech as fluid: "And yet that woman-thing speaks. But not 'like,' not 'the *same*,' not 'identical with itself' nor to any x, etc. . . . . It speaks 'fluid.' "[36]

So uncomfortable has this assertion made certain feminist theoreticians that they have rushed to ascribe it to Irigarayan mimicry as ironic distancing, rather than to the positive form of mimesis I have delineated above: "Her association of femininity with what she refers to as the 'real properties of fluids'—internal frictions, pressures, movement, a specific dynamics which makes a fluid nonidentical to itself—is, of course, merely an extension and a mimicking of a patriarchal construction of femininity."[37] And yet, as Irigaray's linking up of feminine fluidity with flux, nonidentity, proximity, and so forth indicates, the fluid is highly valorized in her elemental philosophy: "Why is setting oneself up as a solid more worthwhile than flowing as a liquid from between the two [lips]?";[38] "My life is nothing but the mobile flexibility, tenderness, uncertainty of the fluid."[39]

Where, then, does this notion of the fluidity of the feminine, when not the femininity of the fluid, come from? Undeniably it is appropriated from the repertory of misogyny: "Historically the properties of fluids have been abandoned to the feminine."[40] What is worse for the anti-essentialists, it appears to emanate from an unproblematized reading out of the female body in its hormonal instantiation. It is, indeed, triply determined by female physiology:

> The anal stage is already given over to the pleasure of the 'solid.' Yet it seems to me that the pleasure of the fluid subsists, in women, far beyond the so-called oral stage: the pleasure of 'what's flowing' within her, outside of her, and indeed among women.[41]

> The marine element is thus both the amniotic waters . . . and it is also, it seems to me, something which figures quite well feminine jouissance.[42]

The ontological primacy of women and the fluid are for her one of the represseds of patriarchal metaphysics; the forgetting of fluids participates in the matricide that, according to Irigaray's myth of origins, founds Western culture: "He begins to be in and thanks to fluids."[43]

Unquestionably, then, Irigaray's linking up of the fluid and the feminine rests on a reference to the female body.[44] The anti-essentialist would stop here, dismiss Irigaray's claims as misguided, and turn away—and few of Irigaray's sharpest critics have bothered with the work published after 1977, which is to say the bulk of her writing.[45] In so doing they miss another and equally troublesome, but ultimately more interesting, aspect of her work. And that is her reliance on the universe of science, notably physics (but also chemistry to the extent that the borders between them cannot always be clearly drawn), which enjoys a strange and largely unexamined privilege in Irigaray's conceptual universe.[46] Indeed, in her writings on the repressed feminine element of water, the referential reality that Irigaray most ardently invokes to ground her assertions is not so much physiological as physical; it is on the rock of materialism and not of essentialism that Irigaray seeks to establish the truth of her claim. Thus, in an essay titled "The Language of Man," she writes: "But still today this woma(e)n's language [*langage de(s) femme(s)*] is censured, repressed, ignored . . . even as the science of the dynamic of fluids already provides a partial interpretation of it."[47] The real in Irigaray is neither impossible, nor unknowable: it is the fluid. Thus, further in the same essay, Irigaray insistently associates the fluid and the real, speaking of "the real of the dynamic of fluids" and "an economy of *real fluids*."[48]

Two remarks are in order here: first, given all that I have said before, this new criticism of Irigaray may appear curious. But my desire in this essay is neither to "defend" Irigaray nor promote essentialism, but rather to de-hystericize the debate, to show how the obsessive focus on what is so loosely termed the *biological* has worked to impoverish the reading of as challenging and ambitious a thinker as Irigaray. Second: there is, on the other hand, nothing particularly surprising from the perspective of anti-essentialism about the complicity of essentialism and scientism, in that both imply at least at some level a fundamental materialism. But because of the red flag (when it is not a red herring) of essentialism, the question of Irigaray's materialism is never really addressed. It is as though certain feminists were more comfortable evacuating the body from the precincts of high theory—thereby, of course, reinforcing the very hierarchies they would dismantle—than carefully separating out what belongs to the body and what to the world of matter.

To say that science enjoys a special status in Irigaray's writings is not to say that science, the master discourse of our age, has escaped Irigaray's feminist critique. It has not. Laughter and anger are Irigaray's reactions to the supposed neutrality of scientific language, a form of writing which, like all writing, is inflected by gender but which, more so than any other, disclaims subjectivity. Science's failure to acknowledge the gendering of language results in its failures adequately to theorize that which it aligns with the feminine, notably the elements, notably the liquid. Thus, in "The 'Mechanics' of Fluids," Irigaray takes "science" to task for its failure to elaborate a "theory of fluids." And yet, in some of her more recent writings, while remaining highly critical of the ideology of science, she constantly invokes scientific theories as models, analogons for female sexuality. For example: rejecting as more adequate to male than to female sexuality the thermodynamic principles that underlie Freud's theory of libido, Irigaray writes:

> Feminine sexuality could perhaps better be brought into harmony if *one must evoke a scientific model*—with what Prigogine calls "dissipating" structures that operate via the exchange with the external world, structures that proceed through levels of energy. The organizational principle of these structures has nothing to do with the search for equilibrium but rather with the crossing of thresholds. This would correspond to a surpassing of disorder or entropy without discharge.[49]

Similarly, later in the same essay, Irigaray suggests that recent work in physics, as well as in linguistics, might shed light on the specificities of women's relationship to enunciation: "Some recent studies in discourse theory, but in *physics as well*, seem to shed light upon the locus from which one could or could not situate oneself as a subject of language production."[50] Whatever her questions to the scientists, and some of them—as in "Is the Subject of Science Sexed?"—are impertinent, Irigaray repeatedly attempts to anchor the truth of her theories in the latest scientific knowledge. She knows that scientific discourse is not neutral, but nevertheless she looks to it as the ultimate source of legitimation. Science is Irigaray's fetish.

Why, then, is science and especially physics privileged in Irigaray's writings? The answer emerges from a consideration of the pivotal role of Descartes in Irigaray's writings. As Moi has noted, the Descartes chapter in *Speculum* is located at the "exact center of the 'Speculum' section (and of the whole book). . . . Descartes sinks into the innermost cavity of the book."[51] This chapter is, as Moi further remarks, traditional at least in its presentation of the subject of the Cogito: the "I" of the Cogito is self-engendered, constituted through a radical denial both of the other and of man's corporeal origins: "The 'I' thinks, therefore this thing, this body that is also nature, that is still the *mother*, becomes an extension of the 'I' 's disposal for analytical investigations, scientific projections, the regulated exercise of the imaginary, the utilitarian practice of technique."[52]

What is at stake here is the constitution of an ontology that excludes all considerations having to do with the physical world: "The same thing applies to the discussions of woman and women. Gynecology, dioptrics, are no longer by right a part of metaphysics—that *supposedly unsexed anthropos-logos whose actual sex is admitted only by its omission and exclusion from consciousness*, and by what is said in its margins."[53] How surprising, then, to discover in *Ethique de la différence sexuelle* another Descartes, a Descartes whose treatise on the passions of the soul contains the concept of admiration, which fully realizes Irigaray's most cherished desire, the (re)connection of the body and the soul, the physical and the metaphysical: "One must reread Descartes a bit and recall or learn how it is with movement in passions. One must meditate also on the fact that all philosophers—except for the most recent ones? Why?—have always been physicists, have always rested their metaphysical research on or accompanied it with the cosmological. . . . This cleavage between the physical sciences and thought doubtless represents that which threatens thought itself."[54]

It is, then, in Descartes's treatise that Irigaray finds the alliance of the physical and the metaphysical, the material and the transcendental, which represents for her the philosophical ideal. Little matter that in elaborating his notion of admiration Descartes does not have sexual difference in mind: "Sexual difference could be situated here. But Descartes doesn't think of it. He simply asserts that what is different attracts";[55] "He does not differentiate the passions according to sexual difference. . . . On the other hand, he places admiration first among the passions. Passion forgotten by Freud? Passion which holds open a path between physics and metaphysics, corporeal impressions and movements toward an object, be it empirical or transcendental."[56] Thus, in Irigaray, Descartes functions both as the philosopher who irrevocably sunders body from soul and the one who most brilliantly reunites them. Physics is here placed in service of Irigaray's radical materialism, her desire to return to a pre-Socratic (but also post-Nietzschean and post-Bachelardian) apprehension of the four generic elements as foundational, which is—I repeat—not the same thing as essentialism.

But there is more: Irigaray's ultimate goal is not, so to speak, to put the physics back into metaphysics, but rather the ruining of the metaphysics of being through the substitution of a physics of the liquid for a physics of the solid. Heidegger names that moment in the history of philosophy when a possible questioning of the primacy of the solid remains earthbound, grounded in the very soil of metaphysics. The ruining of metaphysics is bound up with an anamnesis, a remembering of the forgotten elements:

> Metaphysics always supposes, somehow, a solid earth-crust, from which a construction may be raised. Thus a physics which privileges or at least has constituted the solid plane. . . . So long as Heidegger does not leave the earth, he does not leave metaphysics. Metaphysics does not inscribe itself either on/in water, on/in air, on/in fire. . . . And its abysses, both above and below, doubtless find their interpretation in the forgetting of the elements which don't have the same density. The end of metaphysics would be prescribed by their reinvention in contemporary physics?[57]

Finally, calling into question Irigaray's relationship to science returns us to the question of the institution, for what emerges from a reading of *Parler n'est jamais neutre* is that her interventions cannot be read without taking into account their institutional context. It is altogether striking in this regard to consider the difference between two of the most powerful essays in the volume, "The Misery of Psychoanalysis" and "Is the Subject of Science Sexed?" In the first of these essays, where Irigaray's addressees are the male guardians of the (Lacanian) psychoanalytic institution, her tone is from the outset self-assured, truculent, outraged. How different is the tone of her speech to the scientists. Addressing the members of the "Seminar on the history and sociology of scientific ideas and facts" of the University of Provence, Marseilles, Irigaray confesses to a rare attack of stage fright: "For a long time I have not experienced such difficulties with the notion of speaking in public,"[58] she tells her audience. The problem is a problem of address: whereas the text to the analysts begins with a peremptory "Messieurs les analystes," the speech to the scientists begins by interrogating the very act of address: "How does one talk to scientists?"[59]

Standing before the scientists, Irigaray stands like a woman from the country before the law: "Anxiety in the face of an absolute power floating in the air, of an authoritative judgment: everywhere, yet imperceptible, of a tribunal, which in its extreme case has neither judge, nor prosecutor, nor accused. But the judicial system is in place. There is a truth there to which one must submit without appeal, against which one can commit violations . . . unwillingly or unknowingly. The supreme instance which is exercised against your will."[60] According to Derrida's reading of Kafka's parable, there is no essential difference between the man from the country and the guardians of the law. Their positions in regard to the law are opposite but symmetrical: "The two protagonists are both attendant to the law but opposing one another," writes Derrida.[61] But what if the man from the country is replaced by a woman? Is there no essential difference between the woman from the country, here the feminist philosopher Luce Irigaray, and the guardians of the law, in this instance the scientists whose faculty is to a very large extent hegemonic in our universities today?[62] If the man from the country is replaced by a woman, can one so easily speak of positions that are opposite and *symmetrical* without risking relapsing into a logic of saming, precisely what Irigaray has called an "old dream of symmetry"?

There can be no easy answers to these questions, which are immensely complicated by the very powerful interpretation Derrida has advanced of the law in Kafka's parable. If, however, Irigaray can be taken here as exemplifying the feminist intervention in the institution, then one can, however tentatively, discern the difference that women's studies can make: for instead of simply addressing the guardians of the law—if indeed any address is ever simple— Irigaray transforms the very conditions of the law's production and enforcement. In raising the question of the gender of the producers of knowledge, women's studies always involves a radical questioning of the conditions of the production and dissemination of knowledge, of the constitution of the disciplines, of the hierarchical ordering of the faculties within the institution. Further, by allying herself with the most radical elements in science, Irigaray points the way to what, paraphrasing Prigogine—who borrows the phrase from Jacques Monod—we might call a "new alliance" between women's studies and the law, one which would go beyond mere opposition. In other words, it is finally by insisting on the *dissymmetry* of the positions occupied by the guardians and the woman from the country in regard to the law, that women's studies, at least in its "utopian horizon," can never be "just another cell in the academic beehive."

III.

Professionalism

Thème et Version

In his *Dictionnaire des idées reçues,* Flaubert writes under the rubric "Thème": "In school demonstrates diligence, just as 'version' demonstrates intelligence. But in the world one is expected to laugh at those who excel at 'thème.' "[1] Amazingly, more than a hundred years after Charles Bovary bumbled into that classroom in Rouen, foreign languages both dead and alive are still taught in France and in French schools worldwide through the classical means of "thème," or the translation of a text from one's native language into a foreign one, and "version," or the rendering into one's native language of a text in a foreign tongue. Despite the apparent symmetry of the two forms of translation, in actual practice the texts assigned for version are much longer than those assigned for thème, at least on the secondary-school level. At the more advanced level, say for students getting a higher degree in a modern foreign language, the emphasis shifts away from version to thème, which serves as a critical measure of one's mastery of foreign syntax and vocabulary. What I want to discuss here is why, during my school years at the Lycée Français de New York, I was such a mediocre practitioner of both these pedagogical exercises and what the consequences of my singular lack of both "application" and "intelligence" have been for my career as a professor of French in the United States.

When I speak of my inept efforts at thème and version I shall, of course, restrict myself to the living languages of French and English, since my concern here is with modern languages, and the question of Latin-French or Latin-English bilingualism does not really arise. And it is the question of bilingualism that I particularly want to address. Since most job descriptions in the area of the foreign languages call for near-native competence—on the assumption, of course, that the applicants are not, as they often are, 100 percent native speakers of whatever the language happens to be with a near-native command of English—the ideal candidate would presumably be bilingual, a whiz at both thème and version. But is being bilingual always a desirable professional qualification for a professor of foreign languages and literatures? And what do we mean when we say bilingual?

Any discussion of bilingualism immediately entails a consideration of what exactly it means to be a native speaker, since the layman's assumption is that bilingualism signifies native competence in two languages. Now it is a cliché of the extensive literature on the subject that so-called native competence is a very shaky notion, indeed that the singular native speaker is an ideal construct that covers a wide and heterogeneous range of individual linguistic competencies. Once one is disabused of the notion that there exists any stable definition of native competence, it becomes almost impossible to say with any certainty what constitutes bilingualism. And most of the experts in the field seem to opt for a very flexible and open definition of the term. Far from signifying, as the layperson generally imagines, an identical or monolingual competence in both languages, most specialists espouse the notion of bilingualism as a "fluency continuum."[2] Or, as another writer notes: "The concept of bilingualism is a relative one; it constitutes a continuum rather than an absolute phenomenon."[3] But even when one abandons the notion of an ideal speaker with native or near-native competence in two languages, the supposition lingers—and not just in the layperson's mind—that the bilingual speaker enjoys unique advantages in performing translations, and this hypothesis has been repeatedly subjected to scientific testing with inconclusive results. Based on my unscientific sample of one, though I would situate myself at the higher end of the fluency continuum in both French and English since early childhood, I enjoy no advantage in performing acts of translation, and would instead go so far as to confess to or claim a certain handicap in this area. What I want to do, then, is to explore the ways in which bilingualism can in certain cases actually disqualify one as a translator both in the narrow sense of actual renderings of texts from one language into another and, more especially, in the broader sense of the word of serving as a mediating agent between two cultures.

But first a brief linguistic autobiography. Born to Polish Jewish parents who had settled in France shortly before the Second World War but who somehow managed to make it to the United States in 1941, I grew up in a complex linguistic environment. Between themselves my parents spoke Yiddish and Polish, and to me they spoke first Polish, then French, and then in time

English—and not the King's. Social events in our home tended to be Balkanized affairs, heavy on the Slavic languages, with a smattering of romance languages thrown in. Because our most intimate circle was composed of French speakers, my first words were in French, and it is still unclear to me just when, where, or from whom I picked up English, although family lore includes an anecdote about a well-meaning aunt who had presumably learned English in the kitchen of the restaurant she ran in Brooklyn, earnestly instructing me to say "oily" instead of "early." Despite the handicaps common to first-generation children of immigrants, I did manage to learn English while remaining fluent in French. As for my knowledge of Polish and Yiddish, it remained forever limited, alas, to a passive, impoverished, but ardent aural comprehension. To complicate matters further, when I was midway through first grade at my local Public School and on my way to achieving some degree of linguistic and cultural assimilation, my parents decided to switch me to the Lycée Français de New York, where I remained throughout my school career. As previously noted, my scholarly successes there did not include either the thème or version exercises, though I was rather better at thème since my English was nearer native than that of most of my schoolmates and even some of my teachers. Indeed, English and American literature were not only among my best but also my favorite subjects, and so when I entered Barnard College I decided to major in English. Nevertheless, when it came time to apply to graduate school, despite my love of English and especially American literature, I decided to go into French. Having been a "petite Américaine" in a French school and a somewhat exotic English major in an American college had led me to conclude quite cynically and appropriately that my strength, my unique edge lay in being a French scholar in an American University.

Unquestionably my early bilingualism and Lycée training have stood me in good stead throughout my professional life, except, of course, on those not infrequent occasions when I have had to translate, but then I could always rely on the native kindness and competence of friends. And yet in one significant way my bilingualism, which is of course also a biculturalism, has proved a disability: it has made me dysfunctional as a transmitter of theories between national entities. In what follows I should like to consider the work of two colleagues who have played a crucial part as interpreters of recent French feminist and poststructuralist theory in the United States in order to see how their projects involve a highly self-conscious strategic positioning in relation to those national entities, France and the United States, a positioning grounded in their early monolinguism.

From the very first paragraph of *The Daughter's Seduction*, Jane Gallop clearly situates herself as a non-French reader of French texts, characterizing her study this way:

> while working to produce an acquaintance with psychoanalytic and feminist thinking current in France, it is continually posing questions that are not specific to the *exotic* space of France, but which are equally nagging at any Anglophone site of this text: the site of its writing as well as of reading it.[4]

The operative word in this passage is the italicized adjective "exotic," which is used to modify France. It functions as a marker indicating that the critic's project will take the form of a sort of critical ethnography, will be an attempt to make familiar what appears at first to be a strictly foreign set of concerns that on closer inspection turn out to be uncannily domestic. But the word "exotic" does not merely signify foreignness, it also signifies a fascinating and romantic otherness. To say that France occupies an exotic space is to call up a massive cliché of our culture: namely that France is sexy. The trope of France's exotic sexiness is a recurrent one in Gallop's writings, for as she remarks in "Beyond the *Jouissance* Principle": "in Anglo-Saxon countries the French probably benefit from a long-standing reputation for superior savoir-faire, as we say, in things erotic: a tradition it would be quite interesting to investigate, so as to uncover what sorts of ideological baggage, massive projections, and repressions it carries. As well, perhaps, to understand why some of us became professors of French."[5] Or, elsewhere: "In English, perhaps the most immediate association to the locution *la différence* is the French expression *Vive la différence*, by which we understand that The Difference, for the French, is sexual difference, and by which we imagine that the French have a peculiarly affirmative and sexy relation to that difference" (p. 162). Gallop's enlistment of the trope of French sexiness is nothing if not canny: always careful to distance herself from the "naive" (p. 165) American point of view which mistakes ideology for reality, she nevertheless capitalizes on the supposed sexiness of "those French" (p. 162) by enlisting things French in her larger project of thinking through and speaking of the body in its raunchiest instantiations. By constantly playing on the alleged supersexiness of the French she makes herself into a professor of desire, eroticizing her writing and turning on her readers.

But what interests me most about Gallop's careful positioning of herself in relation to France is the virtually astronomic distance that she sets between herself and all that is connoted as French; in relation to France she adopts the stance of an eternal American graduate student, writing: "An American becoming a professor of French, I was in search of high culture, *necessarily not my* own. Yet I was seeking to understand myself and my world. The split between high and popular culture was, for me, mapped onto the difference between France and America: high culture mispronounced as *haute couture*" (p. 88). The unattainability of the exclusive worlds of the French fashion system and high culture is embodied by the barriers constituted by unpronounceable vowels and strange signifiers. Commenting on her misuse of the word "mauve," Gallop writes:

> I guess, for me, "mauve" simply meant fancy pink, a "fanciness" exemplified by its French name. My "mauve" points to high feminine culture at the same time that its incorrect use marks me as outside that realm. I belong as little to the world of "high sewing" as I do to the world of masculine high culture. My fantasy geography clearly locates both in Paris. No wonder I went into French.[6]

However strategic these moves, however much they serve to create a reassuring bond with the presumably equally unchic, unFrench ideal reader in need of a fashion makeover, they draw on a profound sense of the foreignness of French culture and language, as well as of the difficulties inherent in negotiating between the exotic space of France and the Anglophone sites of the inscription and reception of Gallop's texts. But, as Gallop continues to position herself, in the introduction to *The Daughter's Seduction*, she goes on to claim for her excentric, non-Francophone location, "these English-speaking shores," the status of a privileged standpoint: "Both French feminism and French psychoanalysis are fields of stubborn polemic between various exclusive little circles. The advantage of writing from here is the possibility of creating exchanges between the discourses of people who do not speak to each other" (p. xi). Writing from an unspecified "here," far from the polemic-torn cliques of the Left Bank, turns out to be a positive advantage, positioning the commentator as an intermediary not only between some unlocatable Anglophone space and France, but also between French and French.

Writing from a very different place of enunciation, Alice Jardine harbors no such fantasies about serving as a mediator or go-between between warring French theoretical tribes, noting that cross-cultural texts do not travel well: "Reading and writing across cultural boundaries very often produces a strange brand of text which rings totally false in the culture it is 'translating.' Inevitably? Perhaps."[7] Jardine's guarded pessimism about intervening on the French scene corresponds to the specifities of her location. Whereas the scene of Gallop's writing is here, Jardine's is very much over there; whereas Gallop stayed home to write *The Daughter's Seduction*, Jardine went to Paris to write *Gynesis*: "Most of this book," she tells us on the opening page, "was written in

France to be read in the United States" (p. 13). Not only has the scene of inscription shifted, but the scene of intended reception has been narrowed from some vague Anglophone readership to a very specific American feminist. But what emerges most clearly from the comparison of the position statements made by both Gallop and Jardine is that whereas for Gallop the question is ultimately not a troubling one, for Jardine it is. Thus Jardine's lengthy "Preliminaries" section is given over to a complex problematization of her position as a speaking subject. For her the "case of the American critic observing, reading, and writing another culture" is fraught, and never more so than when that critic also happens to be a feminist.

Gone is Gallop's polymorphously perverse reveling in the supposed sexiness and stylishness of French culture. Viewed from within the beast's belly, Jardine paints a dramatic picture of a Paris in the grip of a major "intellectual crisis." Despite haute couture and le French sexy, when the fantasy becomes a reality, it turns out that being an American feminist in Paris is no fun, because seen at close range those French are neither particularly sexy nor, one might add, particularly stylish. What appears as the stubborn polemics of inbred Left Bank cliques when viewed from the security of English-speaking shores takes on, for the worker in the field, a more ominous aspect of "struggles of epic proportions." But then again, viewed from Paris, the American scene is revealed to be torn by similarly violent dissension. In fact, perhaps the most striking difference between Gallop's and Jardine's points of view is that whereas Gallop provides us only with a perspective on France, Jardine, a self-described "transatlantic" feminist, affords us an unfamiliar stereoscopic view, confronting the familiar American critiques of French feminism with its unfamiliar and unsettling mirror opposite:

> The specific intellectual and political stakes of the importation and exportation of feminist theory have come into sharp focus over the past few years with reference to France and the United States. American feminists have, on occasion, accused French women theorists of reverting to "essentialist" definitions of woman, of being hopelessly enamored of "male theoretical structures" . . . , natural definitions of woman, and so on. French women in turn often argue that American academic feminists are blind to the ways that capitalist, patriarchal ideology governs their thinking; that they are more worried about tenure for their work on women than they are about working with women to change symbolic structures. (p. 16)

The question that immediately arises is: where does the transatlantic feminist stand in relation to these two warring factions—with the exemplary modernist French feminist and male theorists or with the politically and intellectually naive Americans? Jardine is the first to recognize the untenability of an unsituated position: "in attempting this trans-position, I am neither 'above it all' nor somewhere in the middle of the Atlantic. But then neither is my reader, no matter how I might have initially idealized her or him" (p. 18). In speaking of and to Americans she is careful to use the pronoun "we." However exemplary their intellectual and political savoir faire, however intimate her contacts with them, the French remain for Jardine "they," other, not-me. Jardine in the end comes home, bearing the word.

Where does all this leave or take me? What is my position in relation to American and French feminism, and how has it been inflected by the circumstances of my coming into language and culture? In sampling the literature on bilingualism, what I discovered was this: of the many types of bilingualism—and linguistics remains the paradise of binarisms—two are frequently opposed in the literature, though their fortunes seem to rise and fall: the compound and the coordinative. What characterizes the coordinative bilingual is that for her the two languages constitute, at least at the outset, two distinct, separate fields. Traute Teaschner describes the situation this way:

> The child who lives from birth in an environment where he hears two languages does not acquire equivalents in this manner [that is, as an adult who learns through translation], but rather in two fundamentally different ones. The child learns the word *Baum* in one context and "tree" in another. In other words, the child has two pragmatic-semantic fields at first, and only later, in a process of generalization . . . , is he able to make the connection between the two fields and understand that "tree" and *Baum* are equivalent. (p. 23)

When I discovered this paradigm I felt I had found the key to understanding, or at least a reassuring scientific explanation to legitimate what I had long experienced as a bizarre and annoying personal idiosyncrasy. Brought up in French and schooled in the French educational system, there is for me nothing exotic about the French, though in fact, like many a good colonial subject, I did not actually set foot in the metropolis whose every geographical detail I had memorized and mapped, whose glorious history I had been taught to venerate, whose sentence structure I had learned to parse in excruciating detail until I was fifteen. French is for me not primarily associated with sex or style—though I do love both French men and French clothes and have been known to marry the first and wear the latter—but rather with the most archaic affects and appetites. When I read in French, I am, at least linguistically and culturally, French; I espouse the very life of the language; I am, as it were, one with it. When I speak French, I am secure that except in some very special cases I will get my genders right. But again like the colonial subject that I am, at least in cultural terms, I am acutely aware of the gulf that divides me from the French, and I have never tried to pass, nor have I ever seriously considered settling in France, though I do have fairly serious fantasies about retiring to Paris.

My life has been one of alternation, rather than conjunction: first attending the Lycée, then Barnard; first writing in French, then in English. The kind of split subjectivity I am describing is of course on a continuum with the sort of schizophrenia we all experience as professional bilinguals and biculturals. The difference is perhaps only one of degree, but it is significant. As a coordinative early-childhood bilingual and bicultural, I am singularly ill fitted to act as a cultural go-between: when I am here I am here, and when I am there I forget about here. Coordinative bilingualism-biculturalism is, then, closer to aphasia than it is to a psychotic splitting or fragmenting of the psyche, because it involves an inability to be equally and simultaneously in metaphor and metonymy. Or, to pursue this analogy further, my form of coordinative bilingualism takes the form of an excess of metonymy over metaphor, since metaphor equals transportation and implies the ability to move with ease between two semantic poles, however far apart, whereas metonymy is under the sway of contiguity and a sort of radical being there.

My conclusion has at least the virtue of not being self-serving. It is this: though it is perfectly legitimate to expect professors of French and other foreign languages to possess a very high level of competence in all language skills, in our hiring practices we members of departments of foreign languages need to recognize that the ability to translate into the terms of one's own culture the products of another—which is one of our main cultural missions—requires a deep understanding of one's own culture and a higher competence in the target symbolic system than in the source. We need to make room in our departments for those scholars with a special gift for translation at the highest level or risk a slow and debilitating brain drain to departments of comparative literature and even (horrors) English. Perhaps we should think of rewriting some of our job ads to read, "Assistant professor of French, tenure track. Near-native reading knowledge desirable."

The Righting of French Studies: Homosociality and the Killing of "La pensée 68"

Que les femmes dont la vie a été tourmentée par de grandes infortunes fassent parler leurs douleurs; qu'elles exposent les malheurs qu'elles ont éprouvés par suite de la position que les lois leur ont faite et des préjugés dont elles sont enchaînées; *mais surtout qu'elles nomment*. . . . Que tout individu enfin, qui a vu et souffert, qui a eu à lutter avec les personnes et les choses, se fasse un devoir de raconter dans toute leur vérité les événements dans lesquels il a été acteur ou témoin, et *nomme* ceux dont il a à se plaindre ou à faire l'éloge; car je le répète, la réforme ne peut s'opérer, et il n'y aura de probité et de franchise dans les relations sociales que par l'effet de semblables révélations.—Flora Tristan, *Les Pérégrinations d'une paria*

While the airwaves and the columns of the newspapers and professional journals have been filled with increasingly violent diatribes against the decadence of American universities, many of which target foreign, chiefly French, theoreticians as the perpetrators of the decline of standards, a little-noticed series of disturbing developments have been going on in those very departments, viewed by some as the staging areas for foreign incursions—notably departments of French and Comparative Literature at several of the nation's most prestigious universities. I associate these developments with a number of professors who have in recent years mounted a campaign to reclaim French studies in America back from all those who for some twenty years or so have made French departments synonymous with a set of radical theories—first structuralism, then those theories loosely classified as post-structuralist, including in particular deconstruction and feminism. This campaign is a two pronged effort, which involves: (1) returning to the canon as it was before 1970 and as it still exists in French universities today, and (2) displacing the theories of Lacan, Derrida, Foucault, Irigaray, Kristeva, et al. either by a set of theories more congenial to a conservative political agenda or, quite simply (and implausibly), no theory at all—in other words, what we might call business as usual.

What is most disturbing to me is that this effort is bound up with an increasingly transparent desire to diminish the power of those whom these scholars view as having usurped control over French studies, namely American born and/or educated professors of French and especially "transatlantic" feminists—a control traditionally held in this country by a small coterie of French men (often, though not always, products of the prestigious Ecole Normale Supérieure).[1] In short, what we have here is a Restoration, a bid for a return to power by leading members of the Ancien Régime, and, like all such reactionary moves, it takes no account of the fact that because the very nature and exercise of power is transformed by a revolution, the power one seeks to reclaim is not the power one has lost. Much of the force and impact of both feminism and deconstruction are derived from their questioning of institutional power, their perhaps utopian longing for a different university, a university of differences.

What does some little quarrel in French studies have to do with the current challenge of the competing claims of the general and the particular in a period concerned with diversity? Who, outside the people in the field, cares about what goes on in French departments? Or to put the question another way: is there any significant difference in the debate over so-called political correctness between the field of French and other fields? Why invoke yet another ignored constituency when the elaboration of a new discourse of commonality is being called for? If we wish to figure out whether it is possible, indeed desirable, to bridge the multiple rifts that have fractured our profession, dividing us into increasingly fragmented, isolated epistemic or identitarian communities, surely speaking from the standpoint of a national literature is not the way to go.

Talking in terms of gender poses a similar problem: the need to choose between what Monique Wittig called, in her 1983 essay on "The Point of View," the "Universal or [the] Particular" strikes at the very heart of the feminist project, with its roots in universalist enlightenment philosophies and its contemporary embrace of ever more particularistic modes of thought and practices. The competing claims of the universal and the particular is one of the great unaddressed questions in contemporary feminist theory. Indeed, the still ongoing debates within feminist and gender studies over essentialism—widely held to be the extreme or false form of feminist universalism—could be viewed as in fact a covert debate over universalism, although at least in Beauvoir—who speaks for universalism while critiquing essentialism—the two are hardly coextensive. How the two notions have come to be conflated, and thus how the condemnation of essentialism has silently and effectively destroyed any claims to universality that might be made on behalf of Woman is a story that must be told.

And yet, perversely and for reasons which have to do with my sense that the current emphasis on diversity has left the hegemony of English departments basically in place, I write not simply as a feminist, but more specifically as a feminist in French. When I write from the perspective of a so-called national literature, I feel relegated to a ghetto, cut off from the discourse of the general, condemned to particularism no matter what the general theoretical issues I am addressing. The particularities of various feminisms can be transcended; fragile bridges or alliances can be built between its diverse constituencies, and general theoretical works about gender can still be written if only to call the very category into question, but the particularities of the national literatures and their texts remain stubbornly resistant to any form of generalization. The British novel is still referred to by most of its critics as simply the Novel. One has only to go to the book exhibit at the MLA to know that, with exceptions, British realism is Realism, as though French or Russian realism had never existed. In the United States the discipline of English—at least in relation to its European counterparts—still takes itself as the measure of the universal. The following declaration by Gerald Graff in the opening pages of *Professing Literature* is a case in point:

> Though I refer generically to 'academic literary studies' and 'the litera-ture department,' most of my evidence is drawn from research-oriented departments of English at major universities, and I make only occasional attempts to distinguish patterns in English from those in other modern language departments or departments of comparative literature. Perhaps I ought to have subtitled the book "A History of English Studies," but I decided that essential traits have been similar enough to warrant the broader label.[2]

Graff's gesture is by no means an isolated or egregious one; rather, by its very self-awareness it is exemplary of a heuristic move we all make in the interest of expediency, of what we might call *provisional* when it is not *premature* generalization. I could easily adduce other instances of this generalizing move and even include in it some examples drawn from my own writing, but there is no need to accumulate examples to demonstrate how in our critical practice generalization has at least up to now entailed making assumptions about what constitutes the model, the rule, the standard, and what constitutes the trivial exception; and that model has almost always been provided by the dominant group, whether it be men, Anglo-American feminists, or elite English departments.

My justification for going public here with an account of what I would describe as "the backlash in the backwater," the Franco-American culture wars, is double: first, what happens in the backwater of the national literature departments matters precisely because, as has repeatedly been the case at least since the postwar period, it is via these now scorned departments, often treated as mere service departments kept on to provide a cultural gloss for the future business and government elites of the internationalized or multina-tionalized world, that some of the most productive and unsettling critical theories have made their way into mainstream American thought.[3]

But there is another reason to pay close attention to these developments: what is being restored by these obscure forces of reaction is precisely univer-salist humanist thinking. Now, of course, the same is true of the champions of the canon and enemies of radical theory in the United States, but rather than subsume the debate over political correctness in French studies to that in English—which would certainly facilitate generalization—I want to ask whether and how taking account of locational differences, indeed the local particularities of this debate, might alter the account of the debates and the issues derived solely from the American scene. The issue here is not *defending* political correctness—no one has ever accused me of being politically cor-rect!—or even accepting the term except as a convenient shorthand but un-settling the ethnocentric definition of the debate. Finally, because French departments in the United States may be threatened by a brain drain—in the last few years several distinguished professors of French have officially moved out of departments of French or Romance studies into English or other departments—it is, I think, important to denounce what I see as unfriendly takeover bids designed to secure this institutional backwater for a group of foreign-born scholars with a generally hostile, not to say contemptuous, attitude toward their American colleagues.[4] The fact that this group is both male and foreign indicates perhaps the culture shock that European men, recently arrived in this country, experience when they become aware of the presence of feminism in the university.

An anecdote: two year ago I invited a visiting professor of French literature to dinner. While in my home he picked up the recently published *New History of French Literature*, which was sitting on my coffee table. After quickly rifling through its pages he said: "Well, this may be of interest to Americans, but Americans have nothing to teach the French about French literature." Admit-tedly this particular colleague is something of a boor, given to making pro-vocative statements, and this breathtakingly rude remark was of a piece with his general lack of social graces. Nevertheless his remark deserves to be taken as seriously as any other anecdotal material, because it had the unquestioned virtue of making explicit what many French scholars believe in their heart of hearts to be true but would never dare say; just as some feminists would claim that one needs to be a woman to do feminist work, some French scholars are convinced that one needs to be French to work on French literature; French-ness is to French studies what femaleness is to feminism; the enemies of political correctness in French studies are male essentialists, otherwise known as nationalists. It is of more than passing interest that it is the *New History* that provoked this *cri du cœur*, because its basic premise—American critics of French do have something to teach (even) the French about French literature (the book has been translated into French)—directly challenges the presumption of nationalist privilege. The fact that the editor of *New History* is himself an eminent French expatriate scholar, Denis Hollier (currently chair of the Yale Department of French), provides a crucial illustration of the fact that there is division even within the community I have identified as problematic.

As symptomatic as this debate over the *New History* is, it would be of less concern if it did not go hand in hand with a particular animus against the scholars of French who have arguably offered the greatest challenge in recent years to French male hegemony over the literary patrimony of France: I speak of American feminists writing in the wake of French Feminism. The anti-feminist (when it is not anti-Marxist, anti-deconstructionist) rhetoric of these scholars—and I shall name them in a moment—is far stronger than their anti-Americanism and far more cause for concern, at least for feminists. Consider the case of the *Stanford French Review*.

In recent years, under the executive editorship of Jean-Marie Apostolidès, until recently the chair of the Stanford French Department, this publication has become the chief organ of the homosocial network I focus on here, and it includes Apostolidès, Antoine Compagnon of Columbia University, and Thomas G. Pavel of Princeton. Before looking in some detail at specific articles by the latter two, I want to provide a context for my remarks by recalling a forgotten polemic that took place in the pages of *Critical Inquiry* a couple of years ago. Following the publication of Jacques Derrida's "Paul de Man's War," there was a flurry of responses. That of Apostolidès, titled "On Paul de Man's War," is a short text which says simply that at least five years before the scandal broke, in the course of doing research on Hergé (the Belgian creator of Tintin), he had discovered Paul de Man's wartime writings but had been unable to arouse any interest in this discovery in his Boston-area colleagues, including the unnamed but clearly designated Simon Wiesenthal of literary criticism, Jeffrey Mehlman. In a sentence that might have gone unnoticed were it not for Jacques Derrida's talents as a close reader, Apostolidès notes: "That is to say that, as far as I know, several people at Harvard and in the Boston area (*where deconstruction and feminism were and continue to be a recurrent theme*) were aware of de Man's former affiliation with rightist circles."[5]

Considering the six responses arrayed before him, Derrida singles out this inconspicuous parenthesis, this textual detail, as most likely to have the longest life—let us recall that Derrida's piece is titled "Biodegradables." I wish I could reproduce in its entirety the quite manic fantasy Derrida elaborates, imagining some eager Tintin-like explorer-researcher "in centuries to come"[6] coming upon this nonbiodegradable piece of textual detritus on a beach on Cape Cod and trying to make sense of Apostolidès' bizarre logic. But since Derrida actually devotes five pages to this flight of fantasy, I will limit myself to a single quote destined to show how Apostolidès' obsession with feminism[7] could lead one to the wrong conclusion:

> From the first sentence of the paragraph, he believes he may conclude that between, on the one hand, this thing which is holding sway with such "recurrence" in "the Boston area," that is, deconstruction (which the author oddly calls a "theme") and, on the other hand, a certain de Man, there must have been a relation, to be sure, but also that this de Man must have been a feminist. Whether he knew it or not! Otherwise, what would this allusion to feminism, this other "theme," be doing here? (p. 833)

The point, of course, is that it is here because it lies at the heart of Apostolidès' own quarrel with the American university, and in this quarrel he is not alone. In a recent special issue of the *Stanford French Review* on the topic "France-Amérique: Dialogue and Misreadings," edited by Thomas G. Pavel, there appears an article by Antoine Compagnon, "The Diminishing Canon of French Literature," that may stand as an official declaration of war in the Franco-American Battle of the Books I am discussing here. Written in the form of a personal letter to the editor, Compagnon responds to Pavel's invitation to "contribute an article on 'aspects of French literary research that should be called to the attention of our American colleagues' " (p. 203). I will not comment in detail here on the condescension implied in that invitation, but suffice it to say that Compagnon rises to the occasion, provocatively arguing that "our American colleagues" are woefully ignorant of French literary criticism, especially that produced by the admittedly mediocre (Compagnon's word) French university, and that moreover they "are also unfamiliar with French literature" (p. 104). As proof he lists the shocking omissions of the *New History*—to which both he and I contributed—and finally goes on to lay the blame for the "shrinking of the canon"[8] squarely at the feet of American feminists, since, as he concludes, "it is not excessive to conclude that feminism presently has a near monopoly on modern French studies" (p. 113). Contrary to feminism's claim to have broadened the canon, feminism has, in collaboration with a modernist belief in progress and following Marxism, done little but reshape the canon in service of its ideology, and, writes Compagnon:

> Without negating the utility of ideology, nor the legitimacy of feminist politics, I am not in favor of the confusion of criticism and militancy. Still, it is feminism that defines French literature in America today. It is true that it has given rise to reading texts heretofore neglected, that it has increased the books, but like all ideology, it is threatened by buzzwords. (p. 114)

Compagnon's rhetorical moves in the passage cited above are oddly contorted: a recognition of the impact of feminist literary criticism on the *expansion* of the French canon is sandwiched between two conventional condemnations of ideology, an invocation of a supposedly ideology-free, old-time erudition. For all its bold and provocative assertions, upon closer inspection Compagnon's article is given to variations on this hesitant two-step: thus, on one page he asserts that there is no volume on Flaubert in the Chelsea series of critical essays edited by Harold Bloom—an assertion I immediately knew to be false, as an essay of mine is included in the allegedly nonexistent volume—then, on the very next page, Compagnon corrects himself in the present of enunciation, as though more up-to-date and accurate information did not cancel out a patent error: "But I am consulting a more recent volume of the collection, the one on Malraux, and I see that a series of French writers have been added to the avant-garde" (p. 106). There is a Flaubert volume after all; the scandal of its absence is a trumped up scandal, a fiction of his imagination. Why, then, leave the initial misreading in place?

The most disturbing instance of this ambiguous form of argumentation is one of Compagnon's final remarks regarding the exclusions of the shrunken canon. What Compagnon most regrets having been eliminated from the revised canon is the unsavory underside of modernity, which he describes in the following ambivalent terms, hovering precariously between condemnation and nostalgia: "Of course, everyone would readily agree that the rest is detestable: it is the quintessential France—provincial, petit bourgeois, Catholic, reactionary, anti-Semitic [he might add misogynist]—that no longer exists in America, that one prefers to omit, and with it, the essential ambivalence of modernity" (p. 114).

Let us now turn to the last member of the trio, the editor of the special issue of *Stanford French Review* and the addressee of Compagnon's letter, Thomas G. Pavel. In a little-noticed but important, even prescient, article of his that appeared in *Diacritics* in Spring 1989, Pavel, whom I would call the thinker in this neoconservative configuration, provides the context for understanding this movement, this French version of the attack on the "politically correct." The article, titled "The Present Debate: News from France," is a review of a special issue of *Le débat*, on French Intellectual History from 1953 to 1987. As Pavel recounts it, *Le débat*'s history is informed by an axis of progress (to borrow a term of opprobrium from Compagnon) which leads from the night of Marxism-Leninism to the daylight of liberalism. In the new French cultural consensus forged on the grave of imperialism, both right and left,

> The new model thinkers are moderate humanists and supporters of democracy: Raymond Aron in the twentieth century, Benjamin Constant, François Guizot, and Alexis de Tocqueville in the previous. The disappearance of historical ideology leads to a renewed interest in the role of individual human agents and their conscious intentions. The renaissance of liberalism and individualism goes hand in hand with a new sense of the uniqueness of European culture. (p. 22)

Now there is much that is intelligent and illuminating in Pavel's account of the new French cultural consensus—and it is not entirely uncritical of the trends it purports simply to present[9]—but there is also much that is disturbing, especially Pavel's closing prediction that despite the unpromising look of things in 1989, it is only a matter of time until these developments hit our shores:

> There is little evidence yet that a massive comeback of national liberalism is about to occur in the humanities. In the long range, however, relentless criticism of rationality is self-defeating. Illuminating as they are, the indigenous attempts to reduce literature to self-contradiction, history to discourse, and anthropology to fiction, will sooner or later be replaced by more positive trends. (pp. 31–32)

A Janus-like figure, Pavel has now claimed for himself or been accorded the role of go-between, bringing the news of the new French cultural consensus to the attention of his American colleagues (as in his *Diacritics* piece), providing information about the new American (academic) cultural consensus to his French, indeed European, interlocutors (as in his recent article in *Le Messager européen*). This unusually thoughtful and relatively well-informed—though

Pavel, like Graff, takes his own particular research-oriented university (Princeton) as the privileged exemplum of trends in American higher education—account of the culture wars in the United States ends on a note whose pessimism mirrors or echoes the conclusion of the *Diacritics* piece:

> By virtue of their traditional autonomy, American universities have the courage to innovate, a courage they sometimes push to the point of temerity. Nevertheless nothing guarantees that the rejection of the classics, if it triumphs, will do much good for the institutions that encourage it. In the modern world everyone is free to doubt God's existence; it is no less true that the churches preaching atheism will be the first to empty out.[10]

According to Pavel, then, American academics should wake up to two related realities: both their romance with progressive irrationalisms and their rejection of the canon are suicidal forms of behavior. If there are grounds for hope, it lies in what seems to fascinate Pavel most about the organization of the American academy: its decentralization, which contrasts sharply not only with the structure of totalitarian states—Pavel is Romanian—but also the structure of French society and its institutions of learning and government.

What conclusions might we draw from this look at the backlash in the backwater? Do the site and context of the debate over Eurocentrism affect the debate? Are Apostolidès, Compagnon, and Pavel just Bate-Bloom-Bennett wannabes, spokesmen for a cultural trend that is merely derivative, or are they the prophets of a distinctively European jeremiad? Does taking developments in French studies into account enable, indeed force, us to revise the general account of these developments or at any rate to gain a better understanding of what is going on in America, developments being read as eagerly as tea leaves in the traditionally rightist and recently leftist salons of Paris?

The year 1991–1992, part of which I spent in Paris, saw the multiplication in France of articles and colloquia attempting or rather purporting to report on the current American PC debates. Most of these presentations have been marked by a dismaying lack of seriousness; French intellectuals have taken over hostile American journalistic accounts without bothering to check their facts—and sympathy. What was once a loose leftist alliance of American and French intellectuals has now been broken, just as on the national level Franco-American intellectual relations are at a (cyclical?) all-time low. Many examples of these articles—which have appeared in such reputable journals as *L'Esprit, Le Débat, La Recherche,* and *Critique*—could be cited here. But one example should suffice; it is drawn from a review published in *Le Monde* of a book on literary trials in nineteenth-century France. The author of the review is Philippe Sollers, who should know better. According to him the literary censorship of the second Empire is alive and well today in the United States and Iran! "*Madame Bovary* and *Les Fleurs du mal*, for example, no longer sully campuses; the PC movement—'*politically correct*'—rejects them lock, stock, and barrel."

Why, then, this split between the cultures, one I experience as wrenching, given my own divided loyalties (bilingual since early childhood, educated in French, raised in the United States, "in" French, and a feminist)? Many reasons could be brought forward, but if there is one difference between the two cultures that holds maximum explanatory power in this context it is the significance in France of the notion of the universal, and of France and its language as its measure, the French nation as its embodiment, the French revolution as its praxis. There is a difference between the ideology of imperialism and the legacies of postcolonialism, between the ideal of a melting pot, even of pluralism (much maligned by multiculturalists), and that of assimilation. The plea for an old, unexamined French universalism as a defense against the threat of multiculturalism coming from the United States is often couched in the seductive terms of a new democracy, as in this symptomatic intervention at a recent conference on the "politiquement correct":

> "It's not PC itself that is a threat, but it shows us what results from a disastrous social policy and breakdown in democracy." Ms. Gaillard said that the best way to avoid the mistakes and the resulting social ills of the United States was to practice *what she called "universalism"—the integration of different cultures into the system through efficient social policies and education.*[11]

As I was in the process of revising this article, a lengthy petition appeared in *Le Monde* regarding the imperiled future of the French language. It contained another definition of the universal, one which points up what is problematic about the assimilationist model proposed by the new democrats. It is by Sartre, a figure not much cited these days: "We are for the universal, an authentic universal, that is, as Sartre used to say, one that is 'singular and concrete,' 'embodied in peoples made of men of flesh and blood,' grasped in 'their situation, their culture, their language and not as empty concepts.' "[12]

If the general returns, it must be different, a general that does not simply extrapolate from a particular and partial instance, a general that accommodates instead of brackets multiple differences, while not lapsing into the generic. Indeed, this is a paradoxical moment, when, despite the proliferation of differences, subjectivities, ethnicities, and sexualities, the theoretical discourse on these very notions has in the United States become monolithic, repetitious, almost entirely predictable. Hence the notion of PC. But this is also an extraordinary moment, a moment of intense ferment when American concerns with diversity and particularity converge and clash with European concerns about a new post-Marxist world order, a new democracy and a new universal. These debates have just begun.

I n the mid-1920s it became known that the Gustave Lanson library was for sale. Lanson's only son Michel had been killed in the First World War and presumably Lanson needed the money. Several American universities where Lanson had taught or lectured, notably Harvard, Columbia, and Princeton, expressed an interest in purchasing parts of the collection, but only Duke University, which had been founded in 1924 and was in urgent need of building, virtually from scratch, a library commensurate with its ambitions, was willing to buy the entire collection, and Lanson wanted to sell it in its entirety. Duke thus became the first American university to make a bid on this important collection. And in 1927 the deal was done: through Lanson's agent in Paris, one Auguste Picard, and the then chairman of the Duke Department of Romance Languages, one A. M. Webb, a deal was negotiated according to whose terms Duke agreed to purchase, for the then sizable asking sum of twelve thousand dollars, Gustave Lanson's library, which included, along with documents and personal manuscripts, some eleven thousand volumes, many of them gifts sent and personally dedicated to the master by their authors. For the most part these dedications are brief and conventional, indicating affection and admiration bordering on veneration. Occasionally one can make out the spidery annotations Lanson penciled in on the flyleaf. Perhaps the most moving of these autographs is the simple dedication Lanson inscribed on the flyleaf of his 1930 *Essai sur Montaigne*: "Offert à la bibliothèque de Duke University." In the end, between 1927 and 1934, the year of Lanson's death, some fifteen thousand volumes constituting Lanson's library were sent to and placed on the shelves by Duke University. Wandering through the stacks one can easily spot the books from the Lanson collection with their distinctive fleuron embossed on the spine; an ineffable sadness emanates from these crumbling volumes, especially from the literary texts by a pleiad of obscure, long forgotten authors.

For anyone who knows the primordial role Gustave Lanson played in determining the canon of French literature for the twentieth century on the one hand and the role Duke University has played or been said to play in the recent debates over the canon on the other, there is an irresistible irony in this anecdote. If entire libraries and especially Lanson's can be purchased, crated up, and shipped like some ruined castle—lock, stock, and barrel—to provide instant pedigree to a newly rich American South—the coin of the realm was tobacco—then we must acknowledge that once a national literature leaves home there is no saying where it will end up. I offer this piece of local history as a parable for addressing the question before us: "à quoi s'*expose* la littérature française en se laissant enseigner à l'extérieur de son système d'éducation nationale?" or, in its English rendition, what happens to French literature when it is "*estranged* from its national habitat, taught in foreign institutions?" Of course there is no single answer to this question that holds true across time: the risks or painful alienation to which a French literature in exile is said to be prey are not set once and for all; the institutional setting in which Lanson's library was originally housed is not the same as the one in which it currently resides; what was initially a relatively harmonious transplantation has emerged in the late twentieth century as the site of a debate where what is at stake are deep cultural differences and momentous social changes. How did things come to this?

Such is the hold of universalism over French culture that one can never sufficiently emphasize the significance of the universal in French culture, nor by the same token should one salute too quickly its demise. For despite a recent willingness to pay at least lip service to its own particularism, to acknowledge the naiveté of its earlier claims to the universal, French thought remains saturated with the universal. As the final sentence of Pierre Nora's epoch-making seven-volume *Lieux de mémoire* makes clear, the aspiration to the universal remains alive and well in French discourse on the French nation. Nora writes: "The imperial, messianic, and warrior nation is behind us. Today, the opening out of the nation onto the outside world entails (passer . . . par) the complete mastery of one's legacy. Its international future, its secure relationship to the nation's past. And access to the universal, what we have attempted here: an exact measure of the particular."[1]

From the outset, French nationhood and French claims to represent the universal are imbricated, mutually reinforcing notions, and this, according to Ernst Robert Curtius's 1932 *Essai sur l'identité de la France* is what opposes it to Germany and constitutes its specificity among European nations: "If we compare the developments of France and Germany we see that in Germany the idea of nationality and the idea of the universal are constantly opposed to each other whereas in France they are constantly united."[2] Not only does France take itself for the measure of the universal, and French as the universal language, but it seeks through its political and cultural institutions to extend its hold on the universal and thus secure its preeminent place among nations. In placing the universal in the service of the nation, according to a widely accepted genealogy, France takes on the mantle of Rome and its Catholic, that is, universal church (katholikos)—and universalism would seem to have a particular purchase in Christian, not to say catholic, nations.[3] Again Curtius:

> All the claims for universalism were transferred to the national idea, and it is in serving its national idea that France claims to achieve a universal value. In the course of its historical formation we see it engender a new universalism whose ambitions are pitted against those of other powers. In annexing the ideas of universality potentially contained in the Roman heritage, the French nation annexed the Roman idea itself; and in so doing it carried over in its own name the totality of the claims of Rome.[4]

It follows that in the educational system legislated by Napoleon and which extends despite myriad reforms well into the twentieth century, the canon of literary works to be taught should move seamlessly from the protection of the Church to that of the Nation. Thus, writing of the canon of French literature, Daniel Milo observes: "For a canon to crystallize, then to become universal, it must enjoy an institutional promotion. The ancient canon, which was a-national, had the universal Church as authority; the modern canon, which is national, needed the State."[5] The pedagogy of the universal, according to Milo's authoritative account, relies on a strong central authority, on centralization itself.

The more the system is centralized, the more it becomes stable and universal.[6] In short, the centralization of the French educational system goes hand in hand with the claims of its literature to universal significance; centralization—all would agree—is the linchpin of the French national educational system, just as it is of the French administrative structure. The very notion of a French educational *system* institutes a form of untranslatability: "in the nineteenth century everything sets French schools apart from the Anglo-Saxon. The first belong to a centralized system, where everything depends on the State, budgets as well as programs. The second, on the other hand, are part of a decentralized system: indeed, can one even speak of this lightly structured world as a 'system'?"[7]

One of the consequences or corollaries of the mutual implication of universalism and centralization is that the farther away one moves from the controlling center, the less firm the hold of the universal. It is centralization that produces the illusion of universality; hence, as the fate of the Lanson library illustrates, French universalism, like certain fine wines, cannot travel. The phenomenon I am describing is already true of the teaching of foreign literatures in France. Because they are less implicated in the ideological function of the classics of French literature, when foreign literatures are studied in France the strictures of canonicity are loosened, the imperatives of the national agenda relaxed. They enjoy what Milo calls "irresponsibility."[8] But how much truer still this is of the teaching of French literature in America, and especially in recent years, when the reign of the universal has come under withering and far-reaching attack from all those who know that the supposedly universal Declaration of the Rights of Man was not written with them in mind—even though, as they also know, it did operate historically as the lever for their obtaining those rights. I am referring to the constituency of the multicultural: women, people of color, women of color, members of sexual and ethnic minorities, and so forth—in short, the main proponents of so-called identity politics.

Two qualifications are immediately in order: first, not all multiculturalisms can be subsumed to identitarian politics, for there are at least as many feminists, to cite only them, who contest identity politics as there are those who uphold it. It would be difficult, I think, to imagine a more penetrating and influential critique of identity than that recently produced by Judith Butler, who in *Gender Trouble* contests the very existence of a prediscursive female identity that would ground a feminist politics. And to question the foundational role of identity in feminism is by the same token to question the "presumed universality and unity of the subject of feminism,"[9] that is, woman. And this leads me to the second of my two qualifications: universalism is not the exclusive property of the French. As what many regard as a Christian nation, founded on Enlightenment principles, America, too, has a very significant legacy of universalist thought. If there is a difference between these two universalisms it may well lie in what they excluded in principle or in reality and the burdensome legacy these exclusions from universal brotherhood have left behind. Thus, according to Marc Shell, what racism is to America, misogyny is to France, and I hasten to add that this is not to say that France is above racism or America free of misogyny.

calling black men and women less than human or treating them as such was a factor in America's political foundation—even in its sexual history—which distinguished it from the foundation of modern France.

[I]n revolutionary France, the Platonic ideal of sexual and propertal communalism—of *égalité*—was obscured, as women were excluded conceptually and politically from the human species and that *alma mater* "Lady Liberty" was won, if at all, only at the expense of a Rousseauist sororal oppression.[10]

The complexities of comparing and contrasting universalisms—for all universalisms are not identical; the French and the American are not merely mirror images of each other—are daunting and certainly beyond the scope of this text, but this much can be affirmed: the recent encounter of a French national literature traditionally dedicated to the universal with an American critical scene currently riven by particularism has been fractious, and has led to much mutual recrimination and misunderstanding. Thus, for reasons we are perhaps now in a better position to understand, the feminism practiced by American students of French literature has been singled out as somehow destructive of the French canon.

In the ensuing melée a key point has been overlooked: feminist criticism, at least as it manifested itself in American departments of French literature in the seventies and eighties, remained closely allied to the literary text and deeply committed to the French canon, which it sought to question both by revisioning classics such as La Fayette's *La Princesse de Clèves* or Flaubert's *Madame Bovary* and by exhuming forgotten works such as Duras's *Ourika*. In view of more recent developments (about which more in a moment) and with the wisdom of hindsight, one may now see that to the extent that feminism, or the black studies on which feminism builds, is an identity politics, identity politics is one of the closest allies there is of the national literature model of teaching literature. This is not particularly surprising, since nationalism is today the most lethal form of identity politics, indeed the very model of it, as is evident from this recent characterization: "Identity politics commonly evokes notions of community and always entails the quest for self-presentation." It upholds "unequivocal identities grounded in naturalized histories that hark back to the uniqueness of climate, territory, or biology, or, more commonly mythical images of a glorious and heroic origin."[11] Pressing this complicity to its logical extreme, one might go so far as to view the feminist criticism that I among others enthusiastically practiced and promoted in the seventies and eighties as serving, however unwittingly, to prop up both a national literature and a certain concept of literature at the very moment when the nation-state was showing severe signs of stress and Literature with a capital L was being displaced by visual media. In this sense, I would say that those who derogate the impact of feminism on French studies in America and claim that American women are distorting the history of French literature are barking up the wrong tree. The problem here is not feminism and its relationship to a national literature, but rather the fact that feminism is a strong, overwhelmingly American form of literary criticism and as such contests the hermeneutic privilege of the native French reader.

As great and salutary is the challenge posed by feminist criticism to French studies in America, it is not the major challenge confronting those of us in French today. If today we find ourselves anxiously questioning the nature of our object of inquiry and the future of our discipline, it is because of the impact on French studies of a form of cultural studies oriented toward so-called world literature and increasingly absorbed by mass culture.[12] While French literary critics seem to be caught up in reinforcing the national literary canon by attempting to derive a new form of criticism, known as genetic criticism, from painstaking critical editions of the manuscripts of some of France's major authors, or in transforming the excitement of structural poetics into a formulaic new form of *bachotage*, or writing yet another literary history, American literary studies are caught up in a wave of interest in mass culture that is transforming the study of literature and forcing us to confront some of our basic assumptions about our professional activities. Miming their colleagues in English, tenured American scholars in French departments are now in the grip of the crossover book: medievalists are writing about Buffalo Bill, 17ièmistes about Bill Clinton, 18ièmistes about soap operas.

A few bored, middle-aged scholars do not, of course, make a revolution. But their malaise is symptomatic of a major epistemic shift. In short, postmodernism has caught up with French studies because, as Fredric Jameson, my colleague at Duke, has remarked: "one fundamental feature of all the postmodernisms" is "the effacement in them of the older (essentially high-modernist) frontier between high culture and so-called mass or commercial culture."[13] And that mass culture is one of the prime productions and exports of the United States; it is the American universal. What high culture and literary studies are in theory to French universalism, mass culture and cultural studies are in fact to the American universal. From the outset, the emergence of a distinctively American national literature as an autonomous field of study was marked by a recognition that what set American literature apart from its British model was its inclusion of mass cultural texts alongside high literary texts. According to Gerald Graff:

> American patriotism, then, was the force that initially reawakened the old concern with nationality as an organizing category of literary study, but as American literature studies became professionalized the reasser-

tion of nationality had less to do with exclusionary piety about the national spirit than with transcending positivist specialization, embracing diversity as part of the whole, and even bridging the gap between high and popular American culture.[14]

The notion of a canon of exclusively high literature can only be a European import; like the neo-Gothic architecture of the Duke campus—Duke is familiarly referred to by its undergraduates as the Gothic wonderland—the canon enshrined in the Lanson library has no organic relationship to its surroundings; it is a simulacrum, or, in the words of my colleague Alice Kaplan, a kind of "theme park." Originally the Duke brothers wanted to purchase not just a collection, but a university. But Princeton objected to being renamed Duke.

Once one fully grasps the workings of postmodernism and one understands that one is postmodernist whether one likes it or not, whether one uses that word or not, then the very notion of the canon, not to say French literature, is in crisis. What I am identifying as the postmodernisation of French studies in America might not seem so new or radical a development to some, nor perhaps even a particularly alarming one—"il faut être de son temps"—but however one assesses such a change, it signals a new chapter in the peregrinations of the national literature, especially the literature of a nation which assigns to literature a privileged role in defining its cultural identity, for, commenting on "the extraordinary civic implication of cultural facts in the national tradition," Pierre Nora asks: "In what other country could one have described 'the consecration [sacre] of the writer'?"[15] The issue is no longer to arrive at an accurate account of the history of French literature, of literature in French, but the future of the traditional concept of literature itself. In an elegant but melancholic attempt to turn the "death" of the French language to account, Denis Hollier writes: "There is only literature of a dead language."[16] After the death of the author, the death of national languages. The stage on which this drama is played out is by now strewn with corpses. However elegant Hollier's formulation, it nevertheless strikes me as a somewhat desperate holding operation to preserve and even enhance the classical status of French literature in the face of the English juggernaut and, I would add, the move toward a transnational, global, or world literature. For what if a certain concept of literature, which is, after all, as Raymond Williams has most persuasively reminded us,[17] a historical notion, were already dead? Can French studies survive this death? Are there French studies after the death of a certain concept of literature—a death which has, of course, been repeatedly and prematurely announced?

French literature and culture have not, I believe, said their last word; what are needed at this critical juncture are, on the one hand, new paradigms, new protocols of reading, and, on the other, new ways of thinking about French and other European national literatures that would help make the move into the twenty-first century less traumatic, less conflictual, and more receptive to the generalized hybridization that characterizes contemporary world culture. In my own home department, which is a department of Romance studies, some of my Latin Americanist colleagues are now spearheading a move toward the inclusion of Native American languages and a renaming of the department to reflect this new orientation: Quechua, they argue correctly, is not a Romance language, nor, one might add, a Latin one. Departments, we know, make strange bedfellows, and I have my reservations about this proposal, but it does have the merit of showing those of us in French in North America yet another challenge we face in the coming years. Only time will tell what the French canon of the twenty-first century will look like, if indeed these words still mean anything at all in that distant fin de siècle.

IV.

Fetishism

Female Fetishism: The Case of George Sand

I n this age of feminism and poststructuralism I shall surprise no one by asserting that theory has a body and that that body, like all bodies, is sexed. The widespread use of the epithet "phallocentric" to qualify conceptual systems which place the phallus and the values it represents in a hegemonic position implicitly recognizes that sexual morphology informs the most apparently disembodied theories. In the past few years I have begun to explore the ways in which feminist modes of reading might be grounded in representations of the female body. My concern is not to counter phallocentrism by gynocentrism, but rather to speculate on the modes of reading that might be derived from representations of the female body, a sexual body whose polycenteredness has been repeatedly emphasized by feminist theoreticians.[1] Specifically, I have been concerned with the appropriation of psychoanalytic concepts[2] to ends for which they were not originally intended. In what follows I move from a striking representation of the female body in works by George Sand to the elaboration of a textual strategy specifically geared to taking this seemingly aberrant representation into account. Thus the writer's fetishism becomes the critic's—fetishism on fetishism, we might say.

In George Sand's early novel, *Valentine*, there occurs a scene which bodies forth in lapidary fashion, the challenge posed by Sand to psychoanalytic, and perhaps to all feminist, critics. I am referring to an episode in one of the final chapters, where the constantly deferred consummation of the adulterous passion of the low-born Benedict and the aristocratic Valentine is about to take place. Benedict has surprised Valentine in her oratory at the very moment when she is renewing her vow to the Madonna not to succumb to her illicit desires. In deference to Valentine's pleas, Benedict respects her vow, but at great cost: his diminished physical resources strained to the breaking point by this final heroic effort at sublimation, he swoons into a death-like trance. Distraught by Benedict's cadaverous appearance, Valentine drags him into her bedroom, that *sanctus sanctorum* into which Benedict had smuggled himself on Valentine's wedding night. There Valentine proceeds to brew him some tea. Thus, in the space of less than a page, the sublime heroine is metamorphosed into a bustling nineteenth-century angel of the hearth, ministering to the needs of an exhausted Byronic hero: "At that moment, the kind-hearted and gentle Valentine became the active, efficient housewife, whose life was devoted to the welfare of others. The panic terror of a passionately loving woman gave place to the solicitude of devoted affection."[3] It is at this critical juncture, when what is being emphasized is Valentine's sudden dwindling into domesticity, that the passage I want to comment on is located:

> When she brought him the calming beverage which she had prepared for him he rose abruptly and glared at her with such a strange, wild expression that she dropped the cup and stepped back in alarm.
>
> Benedict threw his arms about her and prevented her running away.
>
> "Let me go," she cried, "the tea has burned me horribly."
>
> She did, in fact, limp as she walked away. He threw himself on his knees and kissed her tiny foot, which was slightly reddened, through the transparent stocking; then almost swooned again; and Valentine, vanquished by pity, by love, and, above all, by fear, did not again tear herself from his arms when he returned to life. (p. 304 / p. 306).

What, we cannot fail to ask, is the significance of this unusual foreplay, this precoital wounding followed by the eroticization of the injured limb? Freud's essay on fetishism seems to provide the elements of an answer: what we have here is a classical instance of fetishistic eroticism, on the order of Chinese footbinding. The adoration of the previously mutilated foot typifies the fetishist's double attitude to "the question of the castration of women"; whereas the mutilation of the foot corresponds to the recognition, indeed the reinscription, of woman's castration, its adoration signals a persistent denial of the same fact.

Now if the masculine signature of the author were backed up by a certifiable male identity—if George Sand were really a man—the enlisting of the fetishistic model in our decoding of this episode would be relatively unproblematic, except, of course, for those readers who reject the psychoanalytic approach to literature altogether. But George Sand was, as we well know and cannot ignore, a woman. And that fact, I will argue here, complicates the task of the feminist psychoanalytic critic, for it is an article of faith with Freud and

Freudians that *fetishism is the male perversion par excellence*. The traditional psycho-analytic literature on the subject states over and over again that there are no female fetishists; female fetishism is, in the rhetoric of psychoanalysis, an oxymoron.[4] If such is the case, the question becomes: what are we to make of an episode imagined by a woman author which so clearly, so prophetically, rehearses the gestures of what has come to be known as fetishism? I insist on the word *prophetically*, for my argument hinges on the fact that Sand is pre-Freudian. The inscription of a scene of fetishism in a novel by a post-Freudian woman author would have a very different resonance.

Before going on to review Freud's arguments in favor of the exclusive masculinity of fetishism, I would like to bring into play a passage drawn from another novel by Sand. The benefit to be derived from this superimposition of the scene from *Valentine* on its homologue in *Mauprat* is threefold: first, it lends to our inquiry the urgency inherent in a recurrent scenario; second, it serves to make manifest the mobility of the fetish, its aptitude to press into service any wound inflicted on the female body (the fact that the female fetish par excellence in Sand should be a wound is not insignificant, for wounds per se are not generally fetishized by men); third, it eliminates any doubt as to the agent of the injury—for in the scene from *Valentine*, the spilling of the tea is not clearly assumed by either of the participants. In *Mauprat*, the wounding takes place in the course of a long conversation between Edmée and Bernard, throughout which they are separated—*more* Pyramus and Thisbe—by the wall of Edmée's chapel. Once again we find the female protagonist sheltered from the intrusion of male desire by the protective walls of her religious sanctuary. If, as Nancy K. Miller has shown, the pavilion in *Valentine*—but also in *La Princesse de Clèves*, perhaps the paradigmatic novel of female fetishism—is the utopic locus of "ideality and sublimation,"[5] the oratory—a female space within the patriarchal château walls—figures a liminal space where the struggle between male desire and female sublimation is played out. In this instance the inside/outside barrier is breached by the female character, as Edmée reaches her hand through the barred window of her chapel to touch the unsuspecting Bernard, who stands sobbing against the wall. At one point in their interminable dialogue, Bernard reverts back to his earlier wild-child behavior and tries to force Edmée to kiss him:

" . . . Edmée, I order you to kiss me."

"Let go, Bernard!" she cried, "you are breaking my arm. Look, you have scraped it against the bars."

"Why have you intrenched yourself against me?" I said, putting my lips to the little scratch I had made on her arm.[6]

Lest we imagine that Bernard is simply kissing the scratch to make it well, further on in the novel the erotic charge of the wound, here bound up by a small piece of cloth, which assumes the function of fetish by metonymy— metonymy on metonymy—is made quite clear.

> At that period it was the fashion for women to have arms half bare at all times. On one of Edmée's I noticed a little strip of court-plaster that made my heart beat. It was the slight scratch I had caused against the bars of the chapel window. I gently lifted the lace which fell over her elbow, and emboldened by her drowsiness, pressed my lips to the darling wound. (p. 36/p. 154)

If, as I noted above, the author of this scene were male, we could satisfy ourselves with the assumption that the male character somehow embodies male fantasies of wounding and reparation, male recognition and denial of woman's castration, and ultimately the male horror of female genitalia. The "darling wound" would then appear as the "*stigma indelebile*," in Freud's words, of the "aversion, which is never absent in any fetishist, to the real female genitalia."[7] In short, if the author of *Valentine* and *Mauprat* were a man, that is, so classified in the symbolic order, we would describe him as a textbook case of fetishism, before the letter.

How does Freud go about masculinizing fetishism? To begin with, as Freud states in the opening sentence of "Fetishism," his analysis is based exclusively on the case histories of *male* patients: "In the last few years I have had an opportunity of studying analytically a number of men whose object-choice was dominated by a fetish" (p. 152). One might justifiably remark that this statement does not preclude the existence of women whose object-choice would be similarly ordained. When, however, Freud goes on to explain the meaning and the significance of the fetish—it is a "penis-substitute"—the masculinity of this perverse object-choice becomes explicit: "To put it more plainly: the fetish is a substitute for the woman's (the mother's) penis the little boy once believed in and—for reasons familiar to us—does not want to give up" (pp. 152–153). It is finally in these "familiar reasons" for the little boy's unshakable belief in the maternal phallus that the masculinity of the fetish is grounded, as Freud's reconstruction of the primal scene of fetishism shows: "What happened, therefore, was that the boy refused to take cognizance of the fact of his having perceived that a woman does not possess a penis. No, that could not be true: for, if a woman had been castrated, then his own possession of a penis was in danger; and against that there rose in rebellion the portion of his narcissism which nature has, as a precaution, attached to that particular organ" (p. 153). The implied threat to his bodily integrity represented by the woman's lack of a penis powerfully motivates the little boy to deny his perception. It is the fact that he has, so to speak, something to lose that makes the little boy so vulnerable to the fear of castration.

Now what of the little girl, she who is, in Freudian terms, always already castrated, and thus impervious to all threats of castration? How does she respond to the evidence of sexual difference, which entails or presupposes her inferiority? A careful reading of Freud's writings on female sexual development strongly suggests that many little and big girls are engaged in a rebellion against the "fact" of castration every bit as energetically as the fetishist's. Indeed, if one takes as one of the hallmarks of fetishism the split in the ego (Ichspaltung) to which the fetish bears testimony, then it becomes possible to speak, as does Sarah Kofman in L'Enigme de la femme, of female fetishism, for the little girl's ego can be split along the very same fault lines as the little boy's.[8] Denial is not a male prerogative, as is proven by the behavior of those women who suffer from what Freud calls a "masculinity complex":

> Or again, a process may set in which might be described as a "denial," a process which in the mental life of children seems neither uncommon nor very dangerous but which in an adult would mean the beginning of a psychosis. Thus a girl may refuse to accept the fact of being castrated, may harden herself in the conviction that she *does* possess a penis and may subsequently be compelled to behave as though she were a man.[9]

Sand's Lélia might provide an apt literary instance of such a viriloid woman, not so much because she appears at the ball in male travesty, but because she has adopted the costume of the dandy, and the female dandy is an oxymoron on the same order as the female fetishist. In Baudelaire's words: "Woman is the opposite of the dandy."[10] Encased in the dandy's hard protective shell of impassivity, as cold and as chiseled as a classical marble statue, Lélia is an eminently phallic figure. Thus is should come as no surprise that in the remarkably complex scene by the side of the stream in which Lélia and her sister Pulchérie are precipitated from sameness into the alterity of sexual difference, Lélia is cast as a man, and, further, her masculine sexual attributes promoted as representing an aesthetic ideal:

> "I even remember something you said, which I couldn't explain to myself," replied Lélia. "You made me lean over the water, and you said, 'Look at yourself. See how beautiful you are.' I replied that I was less so than you. 'Oh, but you are much more beautiful,' you said. 'You look like a man.'"[11]

But there is more to fetishism than the splitting of the ego, more to female fetishism than the masculinity complex, more to Sand than the male impersonation which has garnered such a disproportionate share of high critical and popular attention. Sarah Kofman, who is the leading—not to say the only—theoretician of female fetishism, has persuasively argued that what is pertinent to women in fetishism is the paradigm of undecidability that it offers. By appropriating the fetishist's oscillation between denial and recognition of castration, women can effectively counter any move to reduce their bisexuality to a single one of its poles. In Kofman's Derridean reading of Freud,[12] female fetishism is not so much, if at all, a perversion as it is a *strategy* designed to turn the so-called "riddle of femininity" to women's account.

Feminists have been quick to seize on the *political* benefits to be derived from this strategy; in a review article published in the 1982 feminist issue of *Diacritics*, Elizabeth L. Berg writes: "In *L'Enigme de la femme* Kofman gives us a theoretical framework for reconciling two tendencies of feminism which have tended to remain in apparently irremediable contradiction: the claim for equal rights and the claim for acknowledgement of sexual difference."[13] But the feminization of fetishism has important implications for *textual strategies* as well. Indeed, if the recent special feminist issues of both *Diacritics* and *Critical Inquiry* can be taken as symptomatic of the current discursive moment, then fetishism can be said to pervade the critical debate of both Franco-American and Anglo-American feminists of the early eighties. Refusing to opt for either of the exemplary positions argued in the *Diacritics* issue by Peggy Kamuf and Nancy K. Miller,[14] the "transatlantic"[15] feminist literary critic finds herself saying something on the order of Octave Mannoni's legendary fetishist: "Je sais bien, mais quand même." Anglo-American critical fetishism, on the other hand, is coded in Gestalt-like terms. As Elaine Showalter writes: "woman's fiction can be read as a double-voiced discourse, containing a 'dominant' and a 'muted' story, what Gilbert and Gubar call a 'palimpsest.' I have described it elsewhere as an object/field problem in which we must keep two oscillating texts simultaneously in view."[16] In short, to borrow E. H. Gombrich's celebrated example of perceptual aporia, the female fetishist critic somehow accommodates her vision so as to see both the rabbit and the duck at the same time.

To read Sand's recurrent scenes of fetishistic eroticism in the perspective of female fetishism is to give full play to what I will call, for lack of a less awkward term, her insistent and troubling *bisexuality*. The wounds inflicted on the female protagonist's body as a prelude to her sexual initiation are the stigmata neither of a turning away from femininity nor of a feminist protest against woman's condition under patriarchy, but rather of a refusal firmly to anchor woman—but also man—on either side of the axis of castration. In Sand's texts this perverse oscillation takes the form of a breakdown of characterization, which is quite possibly Sand's most radical gesture as a writer. Just as her episodic adoption of male dress threatened the structuring difference of bourgeois society, her occasional rejection of firm boundaries between characters subverts the fiction of individuation that is the bedrock of conventional realism. Nowhere is Sand's bisextuality more prominent than in Lélia, where, as Eileen Boyd Sivert has noted, there is a remarkable "slippage of personality"[17] between the characters, whose identities are so unstable as to be in constant danger of an uncanny coalescence. Lélia is, of course, an experimental work situated at the outermost limits of nineteenth-century French fiction, yet the breakdown of individuation which it performs is at work to some degree in much of Sand's major fiction, notably in her manipulation of doubles. Indeed, I would suggest that ultimately female travesty, in the sense of women dressing up as or impersonating other women, constitutes by far the most disruptive form of bisexuality: for, whereas there is a long, venerable tradition of naturalized intersexual travesty in fiction, drama, and opera, the exchange of female identities, the blurring of difference within difference, remains a largely marginal and unfamiliar phenomenon.

Now, what we might call the first generation of feminist Sand critics argued that female doubling in Sand corresponds to her failure to imagine female desiring subjects: what we have instead, the argument goes, is a traditional masculinist split representation of woman, yet another mother/whore figure who can only be synthesized in the eyes of a desiring male beholder, such as Raymon in Indiana.[18] While generally in agreement with this feminist critique of Sand's representation of woman, I would argue that the striking commutativity of Sand's female doubles—Noun and Indiana, Lélia and Pulchérie, but also Louise and Valentine—causes male desire to misfire at the same time it perpetuates the myth of the exclusive masculinity of libido. When, in a hallucinatory scene in Indiana, a drunken Raymon imagines that through the servant Noun travestied as her mistress he is making love to the inaccessible Indiana, he experiences bliss, but when, in an uncanny repetition of that scene after Noun's suicide, Indiana entices Raymon with a luxuriant mass of hair shorn from the drowned woman's scalp, Raymon's love for Indiana precipitously and definitively dies, and he exclaims: "You have inflicted a horrible wound on me."[19]

In closing, I must give voice to a persistent doubt that nags me as I attempt to think through the notion of female fetishism. What if the appropriation of fetishism—a sort of "perversion-theft," if you will—were in fact only the latest and most subtle form of "penis-envy"? At the very least, a certain unease resulting from the continued use of the term fetishism, with its constellation of misogynistic connotations, must be acknowledged. What we have here is an instance of "paleonymy," the use of an old word for a new concept. To forge a new word adequate to the notion of female fetishism, what we need now is what Barthes called a "logothete,"[20] an inventor of a new language.

Fetishism and Its Ironies

The fetishization of irony runs unchallenged through both high modernism and postmodernism; even in the face of the major cultural mutation of the second half of the twentieth century, irony remains the indelible marker of the elite, whether it be in literature, theory, or the arts. On the other side of irony stand pathos, literalism, and immediacy, none of which have been either identified with or promoted by postmodernism, an aesthetic marked rather by what Fredric Jameson has called the "waning of affect" and the triumph of pastiche.[1] Thus it is that Flaubert, the totem figure of modern ironists, has been effortlessly recycled by many (including myself) as the patron saint of postmodernism. Commenting on Barthes's celebrated characterization of Flaubert's irony in S/Z as "impregnated with uncertainty," Jonathan Culler writes: "It is as if Barthes were saying: with Flaubert 'the code of postmodernism had been written."[2] At the same time, fetishism, the perversion par excellence of the age of mechanical reproduction and late capitalist commodification, has not escaped ironization. When, for example, in the celebrated penultimate chapter of L'éducation sentimentale, Frédéric Moreau says to his beloved Mme Arnoux, "the sight of your foot disturbs me,"[3] that expression of fetishistic eroticism comes under the sway of the corrosive irony of that belated love scene. But to speak as loosely as I have just done of the fetishization of irony and the ironization of fetishism does not begin to exhaust the intricacies of their mutual interrelationship. In what follows, I want to consider a quite different modality of the imbrication of irony and fetishism as they are emblematically inscribed in Flaubert, and, further, as they intersect with feminism. Taking as my starting point a detailed reading of Flaubert's first novel, Mémoires d'un fou, I want to speculate briefly on the implications for late twentieth-century feminism of the fetishism-irony linkage bequeathed us by the nineteenth century, notably via Flaubert.

In her brilliant reading of the text, Shoshana Felman writes: "The Memoirs of a Madman is then perhaps the madness of memories, or of memory itself."[4] She then goes on to speak exclusively of the madness in and of the text, leaving tantalizingly unexplored the other part of the title and the text, precisely the one that pertains to memory. And yet memory and its operations are arguably as central to this curious case history as is madness, for the progression of the narrative is explicitly determined by the logic of memory, and that progression is famously chaotic, maddeningly fitful, a perfect mimesis of the narrator's unstable mental state. Indeed, as Michal Peled Ginsburg has shown, Flaubert's chronic difficulty in both generating and "sustaining a narrative"[5] begins with Mémoires d'un fou. According to Ginsburg, the narrative breakdowns that constantly threaten to stall the forward movement of Flaubert's plots result here and throughout his oeuvre from the disabling tension between the imperatives of representation and those of narcissism; in Mémoires, I contend, the fitful starts and stops of the autobiographical narrative are overdetermined by the play of memory, the interplay of the plural memories inscribed in the title.

From the outset, the narrator informs us that the organizing principle of his memoirs will be antilinear, and thus, by the same token, antiliterary: "This is neither a novel nor a play with a fixed outline, nor a single premeditated idea with pickets to make thought wend down perfectly straight paths."[6] Rather than follow a preestablished plan, a constraining outline, the narrator will obey another narrative logic, the errant logic of free association: "I am going to put down on paper everything that will come into my head, my ideas along with my memories, my impressions, my dreams, my whims, everything that goes through my head and soul."[7] The narrative rule of Mémoires is, then, the cardinal rule of psychoanalysis, which commands the analysand to verbalize all her thoughts, no matter how trivial or embarrassing they may seem. Designed to circumvent the workings of censorship, the analytic contract produces as a side effect a narrative contract ruled by the unconscious.

After various preliminaries, which all have the effect of delaying the beginning of the promised memoirs, in the section numbered 3 the narrator at last seems ready to get on with his narrative: "I am therefore going to write the story of my life" ("Je vais donc écrire l'histoire de ma vie" (MF, p. 230]). The reluctance one detects in this opening statement is immediately amplified in the following, which works to arrest the narrative at the very moment when it seems at last to be on its way: "What a life! But have I lived?" ("Quelle vie!

Mais ai-je vécu?"). The existential, if not ontological, doubt of the narrator is resolved when he determines that he has lived, though it has not been a life rich in events; his is a life of the mind. The memoirs of a madman will then recount not the usual stuff of memoirs—significant lives played out on the world-historical stage—but rather the personal "impressions" of a thinker. From that point on, the narration gets under way with a rambling account of the narrator's days at boarding school and his failed initiation into society. The forward progression of the plot line, such as it is, is anything but smooth. Ellipses punctuate the text, and twice the diegesis is broken off: first (and we shall return to this in a moment) when, after a three-week interruption, the enunciation resumes with the words: "Here is where my story *truly* begins" ("Ici commence *vraiment* mon histoire"),[8] and once again, when in the midst of recounting his youthful loves, the narrator interpolates a fragment whose writing is said to predate that of the memoirs.

What, then, separates the false beginning from the "real" one? A memory, of course. A bizarre, inexplicable memory whose content is insistently dismissed as insignificant and yet whose effect is emphatically described as indelible: "There are insignificant things that have struck me deeply and whose impression I will bear forever like the mark of a branding iron, though they are banal and inane."[9] What we have, then, is a particular type of memory, what Freud terms a screen memory, distinguished from an ordinary memory precisely by the trivial, seemingly insignificant, nature of its content.[10] Accurate in every detail, screen memories paradoxically conserve apparently indifferent events, while contemporaneous events of great importance in the subject's life go seemingly unremembered, unrecorded. And yet, as Freud demonstrates, there is a relationship between the hyperclear screen memory, with its insignificant content, and the screened-off traumatic memory, whose content is anything but insignificant. And that relationship is often metonymic, involving the spatial contiguity of the screen and the screened off, the representable and the unrepresentable. Let us now turn to the madman's screen memory in order to see what, if any, other memory it might be serving to screen off from the reader's as well as the narrator's scrutiny.

The memory involves a neighboring château the narrator used to visit in his youth with his family, a melancholy place where nothing has changed since the eighteenth century, including its sole occupant, an aged noblewoman. On the face of it the description of the château and its surrounding park does indeed seem insignificant, banal. And yet the memory of his childhood visits to this fairy-tale castle is branded red hot on the narrator's mind. The recounting of this memory is subject to a double cut, an internal ellipsis that breaks up the account of the memory and an external ellipsis followed by a heading in capital letters marking a three-week interruption in the narration. It is only after these twin ellipses and this temporal disjunction that the story is said to *really* begin. What, then, is being screened off by this elaborate staging? What is the nature of the unrepresentable traumatic memory? What is the relationship between the screened-off memory and the recollected events that are said to constitute the real beginning of the madman's story? This, then, is the screen memory:

> Often we extended our visits until quite late in the evening, gathered around the old mistress, in a great room paved with white flagstones, in front of a large marble fireplace. I can still see her golden snuff-box filled with the best Spanish tobacco, her white long-haired pug, and her dainty little foot encased in a pretty high-heeled shoe adorned with a black rose.[11]

It is, then, the recollected sight of a dainty foot shod in a high-heeled shoe decorated with a single black rose that causes the text to break off, to blink as it were. For an elegiac postscript follows the first ellipsis: "It's all so long ago! The mistress is dead, her pugs too, her snuff-box is in the notary's pocket; the castle is a factory and the poor little shoe has been thrown into the river."[12]

The screen memory hides a primal, perhaps even *the* primal, scriptural scene of fetishism in Flaubert, a scene that will be repeated with variations throughout his oeuvre. The fetish might indeed be viewed as a permanent screen object destined both to screen off and to gesture toward the unrepresentable memory of the actual sighting of the mother's genitals. The black rose—rather than the shoe—is the node in this scene of fetishism, for it is the metaphor for the female sexual organ which will be disseminated throughout Flaubert's writings. What I will call Flaubert's fetish issues directly from this ornament. And that fetish is a shawl. Indeed, in the memory ushered in by this screen memory, the sacred memory of the narrator's encounter with the reassuringly maternal and phallic Maria—her downy upper lip and her great, milk-swollen breasts are among her most eroticized features—on the beaches of Flanders, a curiously striped shawl is featured. It is as though the decorated shoe, which had been cast away into the river, had washed up on the shore and the concentric black rose had been reconfigured in the vertical: "That day a charming red pelisse with black stripes had remained on the shore. The tide was rising, the shore was festooned with foam; already a more powerful wave had wet the silk fringes on this mantle. I removed it to a higher place; the material was soft and light, it was a woman's mantle."[13] Some thirty years later, Maria's striped, fringed shawl reappears, when on the boat carrying Frédéric Moreau home, he meets Maria's final avatar, Marie Arnoux: "There was a long stole with purple stripes hanging over the brass rail behind her. How many times, out at sea, on damp evenings, she must have wrapped it around her body, covered her feet with it, or slept in it! Now the fringe was pulling it down, and it was on the point of falling into the water when Frédéric leapt forward and caught it."[14]

Fetishism defines the limits of realist description, for the fetishist cannot describe that which he would deny: woman's genitals and the threat they represent. Under the linguistic regime of fetishism, the dreaded female genitals can be represented only figuratively, in the guise of a singularly apt metaphor, a black rose. For as Susan Suleiman has shown in her reading of George Bataille's pornographic *Histoire de l'oeil*, pink and black recur in periphrases for woman's genitals.[15] Fetishism necessarily speaks in tropes, but if it does, irony and not metaphor is the trope of fetishism. We return here to the question of the relationship of fetishism and irony, but this time it is necessary to define our terms as carefully as possible. There are, of course, as many definitions of irony as there are rhetoricians and philosophers writing on the subject. As the author of one guide to irony notes, quoting Nietzsche: "Only that which has no history can be defined," and irony, like fetishism, I argue, does have a history.[16] I take as my guiding definition the very apt one provided by Rainer Warning in his suggestive analysis of Flaubertian irony: "Our thesis will be that this 'order' of ironic discourse consists essentially in the citation of reference discourses and that this act of citation is to be understood in light of an ambivalent relationship of deceptive illusion and repetition, of critique and redemption, of deceptive illusion and aesthetic resemblance."[17] The cited discourse, in this instance the clichéd discourse of Romanticism, which is so often ironized in Flaubert, is then both rejected and introjected, negated and preserved, through the use of irony.

Irony in Flaubert functions as a strategy for sublation, enabling Flaubert to distance himself from Romanticism, "reactualizing" it all the while. The homology between irony and fetishism should then be quite clear: just as the fetish enables the fetishist simultaneously to recognize and to deny woman's castration, irony allows the ironist both to reject and to reappropriate the discourse of reference, Romanticism in the case of Flaubert. Surely it is of more than passing interest that the discourse of Romanticism occupies in this homology the same position as woman's castration. The discreditation of Romanticism is shown to be bound up in its association with the feminine, while femininity appears to inspire dread because of its association with a discourse of imaginary immediacy and plenitude. Flaubert's irony and Flaubert's fetishism are two aspects of the same phenomenon. In Flaubert, rhetorical undecidability is aligned with the sexual; the oscillations of the fetishist are figured by the uncertainties of the ironist. The uses of uncertainty in Flaubert are, to paraphrase Barthes, to keep the reader from ever being able to answer the question: is woman castrated?

If the connection between fetishism and irony has been made—and I am not aware that it has been, inasmuch as rhetoricians and psychoanalytic critics rarely speak the same language—then the consequences of this connection have yet to be drawn, notably as they affect women, that is, precisely those whose otherness the fetish is enlisted to block off, deny. If irony is the trope of fetishism and if female fetishism is a rare, if not nonexistent, perversion, then it would seem to follow that irony is a trope absent from women's writing. And indeed it is generally acknowledged that with the spectacular exception of Jane Austen, irony does not feature prominently in the history of women's fiction. The ironist in Western discourse has until recently almost always been male.

Some years ago in a piece titled "Female Fetishism" I called for the strategic appropriation of the undecidability of fetishism by women.[18] I now want to revise or update that formulation. For it appears to me now that what I was obscurely groping toward in that piece, though I didn't know it at the time, was in fact irony. What needs to be appropriated by women is irony, but an irony peeled off from fetishism, a feminist irony that would divorce the uncertainty of the ironist from the oscillations of the fetishist, an irony that would stand, in short, at the antipodes of the "irresponsible" (Barthes) model of Flaubertian irony.[19] In calling for a feminist appropriation of irony I am echoing, among others, Donna Haraway, whose widely read "Manifesto for Cyborgs" is a call for "an ironic political myth faithful to feminism, socialism, and materialism." "Irony," writes Haraway in the opening paragraph of her text, "is . . . about the tension of holding incompatible things together because both or all are necessary and true. . . . It is also a rhetorical strategy and political method, one I would like to see more honored within socialist feminism."[20] While I share Haraway's and other feminists' sense that, in Nancy K. Miller's words, "it may be worth the risk of trying out this kind of duplicity on the road,"[21] I fear that until irony is divorced from fetishism, the risk of irony must be taken with extreme care lest the feminist ironist find herself playing straight into the hands of the male fetishist from whose perverse images of women she sets to distance herself.

The appropriation by feminism of an irony that does not turn on castration entails the historicization of both irony and fetishism. Breaking with high structuralism's insistence on the timelessness of tropes, Warning insists on the historicity of Flaubertian irony: "Irony has its historical position in times of transition between the old that has already passed on and the new that cannot yet be made out."[22] If for Warning irony is the trope of choice in transitional historical periods, D. C. Muecke notes the "almost cancerous growth of the concept of irony since the 1790s."[23] Similar arguments could and have been made (by Stephen Heath) regarding the rise of fetishism as a widespread perversion in the age of commodification and the sexual fix. Hence the remarkable coalescence of irony and fetishism in Flaubert's fiction is neither an accident nor an idiopathic fluke; rather, it is the product of the convergence of a number of factors, among them the heightened interest in irony brought about by German Romanticism, the passage from one socioeconomic order to another, the invention of sexuality, and the pinning down of sexual difference. Today, in the age of the simulacrum, which has also been described with tremendous overoptimism as postfeminist, the conditions for the undoing of the mid-nineteenth-century concatenation of irony and fetishism are at hand. The withering away of ironic fetishism and fetishistic irony may well be a utopian scenario, rather like the one Luce Irigaray evokes in *This Sex Which Is Not One*, where she speculates on what it would be like if the "goods got together" and refused to go to market, if women refused to participate in the homosexual system of exchange. On the other hand, we cannot hope to liquidate modernism in its earliest and latest manifestations without unhooking the venerable trope of irony from the exclusively male perversion that is fetishism. We shall continue, of course, to read Flaubert but otherwise: less as an ironist and more for the pathos that is perhaps the mode of post-postmodernism.

V.

Criticism

The Portrait of a Gentleman: Representing Men in (French) Women's Writing

I want to know
your true opinion
which one you prefer, and what's
the mirror where you stare

For the mirror with no image so disrupts
my rhyme that it almost interrupts it
but then when I remember what my name records,
all my thoughts unite in one accord
—Lombarda

In 1980 an exhibition was held in London that, according to its organizers, "aroused enormous controversy and attracted record attendances."[1] The theme of the exhibit was "Women's Images of Men." Not surprisingly, male critics responded with particular outrage to this attempt on the part of women to "look back," to reverse the centuries-old model-artist relationship, just as some hundred or so years earlier the impudent gaze of Manet's *Olympia* had aroused the ire of a primarily male bourgeois spectatorship.

What made the London exhibit so shocking was not merely its display of images of men produced by women, for after all women artists have been producing male imagoes for centuries. Nor was it the fact that these images, informed by the feminist revolution of the second half of the twentieth century, were overtly political. What created the scandal and drew the crowds was that the women artists who displayed their work in various media at the Institute of Contemporary Arts, in a manner unimaginable to women artists of earlier times—who were, as we know, barred from the figure-drawing classes of the Academy—dared to depict the male nude, indeed the penis in every state from the limp to the erect. Now the transgression of the secular taboo on women representing the male sexual organ is, as Sarah Kent reminds us, a very recent phenomenon: "With a few notable exceptions like Suzanne Valadon and Alice Neel, the male nude is a subject that women have turned to only during the last twenty years—a minute length of time when compared to the illustrious history of its female counterpart."[2] To subject the penis to representation is to strip the phallus of its empowering veil, for—and much of what follows turns on this aporia—while the phallus can be said to draw its symbolic power from the visibility of the penis, phallic power derives precisely from the phallus's inaccessibility to representation. Again in the words of Sarah Kent: "This points to a fundamental problem in depicting the penis. For as a symbol of masculine power, authority, and potency within the patriarchy the phallus has to carry an enormous burden of significance. That bulge in the trousers on which the hero's sexual identity depends and on which pop stars, like Elvis, focused their fans' attention to such good effect, cannot withstand exposure to view."[3]

Clearly it is a far cry from the risqué visual representations of male sexual organs by late-twentieth-century women artists to the non—sexually explicit textual representations of male characters by such women writers as Mme de La Fayette, Mme de Staël, and George Sand, but I will want to argue here that at least in France—and the question of national difference will have to be considered—the representation of men by women writers has been every bit as subversive of phallic hegemony over the symbolic as the unveiled penises on view in the "Women's Images of Men" exhibit. But, because of the constraints of a representational system coterminous with patriarchy, the women writers I have in mind were obliged to resort to complex strategies to lay bare the source of both male power and female powerlessness. My argument is based on the close analysis of a recurrent scene, a female topos, that links up Mme de Lafayette's *The Princesse de Clèves*, Mme de Staël's *Corinne*, and George Sand's *Indiana*. Briefly stated: the scene stages the violation by the male gaze of the female protagonist's private space and the protagonist's discovery therein of a portrait, his own and/or that of another masculine figure.

But, as a preliminary to the detailed examination of this recurrent "portrait of a gentleman" scene, I want to raise the larger theoretical issue at stake here, that is, the representation of men in women's writing, a question neglected by feminist critics (myself included) more concerned with the urgent question of the representation of women first by male writers and, more recently, by women writers.[4] Though the field has hardly been exhausted, it seems opportune now to turn to the question of the representation of the Other's other, and some of the questions before us, then, are: what strategies do women writers enlist to represent men? Are they different from those at work in men's writings about women? Do they cut across national boundaries and constitute a specificity of women's fiction?

That the representation of men is problematic for the female novelist is stated very clearly by George Sand in the preface to one of her early woman-centered novellas. Responding to the criticism that in her writings she systematically foregrounds and favors her female characters, Sand writes:

> It is very difficult for a woman to successfully define and depict a fully worthy man and above all to *employ* him as the active protagonist in a novel. For a woman writer to know well the causes and the play of man's moral forces, she must with time, observation, and some studies unjustly reputed useless to her sex and estate become not man himself, for that would be impossible, but somewhat less of the child she was left by her early education. She will then be able to understand certain intellectual preoccupations foreign to her and not restrict the masculine role to his relationship to love or the family.

Lest these remarks appear to suggest that male writers experience no difficulty in representing women, Sand goes on to say:

> To be fair, let us say that men writers also experience great difficulties when it comes to entering with delicacy and impartiality into woman's heart and mind. In general they make her too ugly or too beautiful, too weak or too strong, and those who have met the rugged challenge of the work of divination know that it is no small thing.

Yet, for all her attempts at evenhandedness, Sand goes on to conclude: "Thanks to his more complete education and more practiced reasoning, man can more easily depict woman than woman can depict man."[5]

Sand's problematization of gender-bound representations is itself characteristically problematic in that it stops well short of contesting the system of values that accords less prestige to depictions of the domestic and erotic spheres inhabited by women than to the supposedly wider spheres in which men traditionally deploy their activities: commerce, the professions, war. No lover of the homely details of everyday life, Sand does not valorize the world of home and family. And yet, despite Sand's implicit endorsement here (and elsewhere) of the ideology that attaches more value to representations of public than private spaces, despite her explicit privileging of men's writing, her remarks install a significant and potentially subversive disymmetry between gentlemen and lady novelists. For whereas women writers are pre-

vented from creating well-rounded protagonists by their infantilizing education, men writers fail in their depictions of women for reasons less amenable
to remediation: lack of tact and fairness. Their representations are distorted by
a seemingly congenital blindness; theirs is a failure not of education but of
vision. Thus, while recognizing the advantages enjoyed by her male contemporaries in representing the Other, Sand implies that in the long run, when
women are given equal access to higher education, it is the men who will be
at a disadvantage. It will require a complete overhaul of the curriculum—
the introduction of women's studies, perhaps?—to enable men to represent
women without indulging in the twin excesses that are the hallmarks of male
misogyny: idealization and demonization.

Male critics who have recently raised the specter of misandry, a sort of
woman writers' revenge, would, I am well aware, want to take issue with the
scenario I have teased out of Sand's text. They would argue, as does K. K.
Ruthven, that it is only for lack of opportunity that women have not produced
a volume of misandrous representations to rival the proliferation of misogynous representations produced by men:

> If men appear to have spent more time abusing women than women
> men (which is what the textual evidence suggests), this is not because
> misandry is a more rare phenomenon than misogyny, but because for
> several centuries most printed books were written by men. "If wommen
> hadde writen stories," Chaucer's wife of Bath points out, "They wolde
> han writen of men moore wikkednesse / Then al the mark of Adam may
> redresse"—to which one can only add that feminist writing published
> during the last fifteen years or so has been doing what it can to ensure
> that misandry will eventually be as well represented in print as misogyny
> now is.[6]

That there have been excesses committed in recent women's writings about
men is open to debate, providing, of course, that specific examples of offend-
ing texts are cited in place of such unverifiable references as "feminist writing
published during the last fifteen years or so." But the unquestioned assumption that misandry simply mirrors misogyny is, arguably, only another avatar of
phallocentrism's "old dream of symmetry," to quote Luce Irigaray, and as such
is highly suspect. The important question, however, lies elsewhere and it is:
can men, who have for centuries enjoyed a virtually undisputed monopoly on
the means of representation—the pen, the brush, and the chisel—so surely
distinguish between misandry and women's talking, looking, and writing
back? The discourse of misogyny, let us recall, has throughout the centuries
singled out for unique scorn women who, refusing to be mere signs to be

exchanged among men, have sought instead to become producers and cir-
culators of signs in their own right: the *précieuse* in seventeenth-century France,
the bluestocking in nineteenth-century France and England.[7] To put the question another way: can men who have for centuries, as Virginia Woolf so
memorably phrases it in *A Room of One's Own*, consigned women to the role of
magnifying mirrors so surely distinguish between life-size representations
and caricatures? In her unendingly prescient book, Woolf suggests that when
women do write, they provide their male readers with a view of "the spot the
size of a shilling at the back of the head [which one can never see for
oneself]."[8] Finally, the question is: can men stand the sight of their blind spot,
or, having caught a glimpse of it, will they hastily turn their gaze back on
Woolf's reassuring "female looking glasses," which possess "the delicious
power of reflecting the figure of man at twice its natural size"?[9] It is with these
questions in mind that I would like to turn now to my reading of *The Princesse de
Clèves*, *Corinne*, and *Indiana*.

That *The Princesse de Clèves* is the inaugural text of the French psychological novel
is a matter of historical record, and Mme de La Fayette's place in the French
canon—unlike those of Mme de Staël and George Sand—is secure. And yet it
is only now, in the wake of pioneering feminist studies of the novel by such
critics as Nancy K. Miller, Peggy Kamuf, Marianne Hirsch, and Joan deJean
that the role of *The Princesse de Clèves* as the matrix of French women's fiction can
begin to be fully grasped and assessed.[10] French women novelists well into
the nineteenth century appear to have inscribed themselves into a specifically
female literary tradition by endlessly rewriting and refashioning the story of
the beautiful young princess who loves a man who is not her husband,
implausibly confesses her illicit love to her husband, and still more implausibly refuses to marry the object of her passion when her husband dies of grief,
leaving her free to wed whomever she pleases. My concern in what follows,
however, is with *The Princesse* as a model not for fictions of avowal and renunciation but for representations of men in a manner that calls into question
what Nancy K. Miller has described as the "subject in power['s] . . . fascination" with "his own representation."[11] What the discovery of the intertextual
relationship linking *The Princesse de Clèves*, *Corinne*, and *Indiana* demonstrates is the
persistence in French women's writings of representations of men that work
to unsettle man's secure relationship to his own image and the representational system it underwrites.

After both her husband and her would-be lover, M. de Nemours, depart
from the court at the King's bidding, the Princesse de Clèves decides to go to
Coulommiers, her country estate. In retreating to her private space, the prin-

cess does not leave Nemours altogether behind because her baggage includes some paintings of historical scenes in which the duke figures prominently.

> She went to Coulommiers, taking with her two big pictures which had been copied for her from originals painted for Madame de Valentinois's beautiful house at Anet and which represented all the outstanding events of the King's reign. Among others there was the siege of Metz, with portraits of all those who had distinguished themselves there; M. de Nemours was one of these and *perhaps* that may have been the reason why Madame de Clèves was so anxious to own these paintings.[12]

The use of the word *perhaps* here is distinctly at odds with the omniscient stance of the "knowing narrator"[13] throughout the story and thus serves to draw the reader's attention to these paintings and to the princess's interest in them well before they are foregrounded in the narrative. Indeed it is only several pages later that the doubt cast by the narrator on the princess's motives for transporting these bulky works of art—a doubt that does not so much diminish the narrator's omniscience as underscore the princess's lack of awareness of her own feelings—is lifted. Alone at night in the pavilion, where she is at least able to give free reign to her erotic fantasies, the princess contemplates the portrait of Nemours with rapt adoration: "She took a candlestick and went up to a big table which stood before the picture of the siege of Metz in which was a portrait of M. de Nemours. She sat down and gazed at this portrait with a far-away look that only love can give" (p. 168).

There is in *Pride and Prejudice* an analogous scene, where on a visit to Darcy's estate Elizabeth stands similarly transfixed before a portrait of her suitor. However, as one critic has remarked: "Elizabeth can accept the hand of the man who steps out of the frame: the princess cannot."[14] Whereas Elizabeth's intense study of Darcy's portrait causes her to view him in a new and more favorable light and eventually to marry him, the princess's dreamy contemplation of Nemours's portrait presages her final refusal to marry him and her retreat into a new and inviolable space of erotic reverie: the convent. This difference in outcome depends on another difference between the two scenes: whereas Elizabeth looks at Darcy's portrait in his absence, at the very moment when the princess gazes rapturously at the portrait of the duke, the portrait's model is gazing equally rapturously at her. For the second time in the novel— the first is when he overhears the princess's avowal to her husband—the duke has sneaked onto secluded property to spy on the princess. As he, unbeknownst to her, watches here from his hiding place in the garden, he experiences something verging on that supreme form of sexual pleasure known in French and now also in English as *jouissance*.

How to express the feelings of M. de Nemours at this moment? What lover can ever have seen, at night, in the most perfect spot imaginable, the person he adored, have seen her without her knowing it and have seen that she was only occupied with things which had to do with himself and the love she kept hidden from him? Such things had never been enjoyed or imagined by any other lover. The Prince was beside himself, so much so that he forgot the precious minutes were ticking away as he stood there looking at Madame de Clèves. (p. 168)

What makes this voyeur's pleasure so uniquely, so hyperbolically gratifying is not only that he holds the object of his desire prisoner of his gaze, not only that his gaze violates her most intimate secret, but rather and above all that what he beholds is his own likeness as viewed through the eyes of an adoring woman. *Jouissance* for Nemours is being the spectator of his own desirability. When but moments later he comes to his senses, the duke arrives at the sobering realization that his image and the fantasies it enables are his most powerful rivals for the princess's affections. But the portrait scene unfolds outside the relentless flow of narrative time, for the moment of narcissistic contemplation suspends temporality; it is a moment of eternity. I want, then, to stay with this timeless scene for just a little while longer, to scrutinize it at leisure, for in it Mme de La Fayette offers us conjointly a representation of a male protagonist and *en abîme* a commentary on man's relationship to his own representation. By training, as it were, her spotlight on the spectacle of the duke's ecstatic vision of the princess's no less ecstatic vision of his image, Mme de La Fayette places the reader in a position to discover the voyeur's secret, a secret far less innocent than the princess's. Lest we doubt that what we have here under the cunning guise of a supremely romantic episode is a devastating exposure of the male subject's fascination with the evidence of phallic power, we must now turn away from this captivating scene to the scene that immediately precedes it and from which it cannot be separated except for heuristic purposes. Moments before the princess takes up her candle to go over to the duke's portrait, she is engaged in an activity whose fetishistic significance was first pointed out some years ago by Michel Butor:[15]

She lay on a daybed and on a table beside her there were several baskets of ribbons. She was picking over these ribbons and choosing out certain ones, and M. de Nemours saw that these were the very colours he had carried at the tournament, and then he saw that she was making knots and bows to go on the unusual malacca cane which, having used it for some time, he had given to his sister. Madame de Clèves had taken it from her without seeming to recognize it as having once been his. She worked away with a grace and a look of pure goodness which reflected the state of her soul. (pp. 167–68)

The duke's blissful vision of the princess's occupation with "things that had to do with himself" both confirms and exploits the metonymic and metaphoric links between the portrait and the cane. The double scene that the duke beholds stages the generally hidden, should I say veiled, relationship between the phallus and representation in a society ruled by men. In other words, what the diegetic contiguity of these two objects lays bare is *the phallicity of the representation* and *the iconicity of the phallus*. In a scopic economy, the idolater worships indifferently at the altar of the image and the phallus, for there is at least in the "rhetoric of iconoclasm," recently studied by W.J.T. Mitchell, a pervasive symbolic equation between these two icons of the visible.[16]

If we now replace the portrait scene in the narrative, it becomes clear that the princess's ultimate enigmatic refusal is motivated not only by her fear of falling victim to the "poetics of abandonment," not only by her privileging of desire over satisfaction, but by her unwillingness to support a representational system so intimately bound up with male narcissism. The portrait scene, as already noted, repeats an earlier scene that unfolds in the same spot in the hidden presence of the same trespasser: I allude to the princess's celebrated avowal to her husband of her love for another man, a man the eavesdropping duke recognizes to be himself. Unable to keep this story so flattering to his person to himself, the duke proceeds to communicate it to his friend and traveling companion, the Vidame de Chartres. In recounting this episode the narrator is at her perfidious best, first by minimizing the seriousness of the duke's indiscretion, second by parrying the widespread assumption that women's writing is indistinguishable from autobiography. For Nemours's narrative, his sole attempt at fiction, is a flimsily distinguished autobiographical fragment that fools no one:

M. de Nemours, obsessed with his passion and the surprise of what he had overheard, now fell into a not unusual indiscretion, that of talking in general terms of one's own experience, and narrating one's own adventures with fictitious names. During the journey he brought the conversation round to the subject of love, emphasizing the pleasure of loving a person really worthy of it. He spoke of the curious manifestations it sometimes produces and finally, unable to bottle up his amazement at what Madame de Clèves had done, he told the Vidame the whole thing, without mentioning any names or saying that it had anything to do with him. However, the Vidame guessed this at once. (p. 135)

Given the laws that govern the circulation of fictions of female desire in this novel, dispossessing women, as Joan deJean has shown, of the exclusive rights to their own stories, the Vidame cannot resist repeating the duke's secret to his mistress, Mme de Martigues, who tells it to the queen-dauphine in the presence of the princess. After initially accusing her husband of having put the story into circulation, the princess comes to the inescapable conclusion that the indiscretion was Nemours's, and that realization is devastating to her love for him:

> How mistaken I was when I thought there existed a man capable of hiding anything which flattered his vanity [ce qui flatte sa gloire]. And it is for the sake of this man, who seemed to me so different, that I find myself on a level with other women, I, who used to be so different indeed. (p. 151)

The only man worthy of the love of a princess deeply marked by a maternal discourse that enjoins her to be different from other women is a man who would be similarly distinct from the other members of his sex. There is, however, a notable difference between male and female difference: to be unique among her sex a woman must practice an exemplary virtue and thus avoid, in Mme de Chartres's dying words, "descending to the level of other women" (tomber commes les autres femmes, which is more accurately translated as "falling like other women"; p. 70), whereas to rise above his peers a man must refrain from advertising his conquests.

In short, vanity and the indiscretion it provokes are to masculinity what easy virtue and the fall it entails are to femininity. In refusing to accept the duke's proposal of marriage and by placing herself beyond the reach of the irremediably specular male gaze—retired behind the walls of the convent and her country estate, the princess becomes in the end literally and quite spectacularly invisible—the princess engages, as has been pointed out by Dalia Judovitz, in the elaboration of a "new concept of ethical and aesthetic representation."[17] Judovitz locates the novelty of the princess's representation in its affirmation of the power of fiction over the real; for her, the princess's aesthetics is an "aesthetics of implausibility." For me, on the other hand, the princess's aesthetics is one of discretion, an extreme rarefaction of representation.

Discretion is hardly a virtue one would think of associating with Corinne, perhaps the most exhibitionistic female protagonist in the history of women's writing. Actress, improvisationalist, conversationalist, Corinne is constantly engaged in spectacularizing her life. From her first appearance in the novel, being crowned poet laureate on the steps of the Roman Capitol, to her last, staging her swan song, Corinne plays out her story on the public stage. Coming from England, which functions in this novel as the evil empire of patriarchy, Lord Oswald Nelvil, Corinne's lover, is both attracted to and repelled by her very public success. The attraction poses no challenge to our understanding or expectations. Nineteenth-century French fiction is full of male protagonists whose desire is mediated by the desiring gaze of other men—hence the erotic prestige enjoyed by the actress or indeed any beautiful woman who ventures into the polyfocal space of the theater. Less common in the French tradition is the reversal of this scenario, where instead of swelling male desire, the spectacle of female success irritates the lover's jealousy, arouses his desire for the exclusive possession of the admirable love object. Oswald's typically ambivalent oscillation between these two contradictory desires is given full play in chapter 3 of book 7, when he watches Corinne act the part of Juliet in a production of *Romeo and Juliet*. Before the play begins, Oswald looks forward to the event with mixed emotions:

> Oswald looked forward to this new success with a mixture of uneasiness and pleasure. For while he enjoyed the thought of it, he was also jealous, not of any man in particular, but of the public that was to witness the talents of the woman he loved. He would have liked Corinne to show an Englishwoman's diffident reserve, saving her eloquence and genius for him alone.[18]

As the play unfolds, however, Oswald's regressive fantasies of exclusive possession are for one brief moment replaced by the sense of omnipotence that comes from being loved by a star: "Tender feeling had bowed his head, but he raised it now, strong in the sense that he was monarch of the world since he reigned over a heart filled with all of life's treasures" (p. 128). The triumphant moment coincides with Oswald capturing Corinne's gaze at the very instant when she is declaring her love to Romeo. For Corinne, on the other hand, the supreme pleasure she experiences in performing the role of Juliet in front of Oswald would not be enhanced by having Oswald step onto the stage and play Romeo to her Juliet. If for her (and for the narrator) the event constitutes the high point of her doomed love affair with Lord Nelvil, it is because it constitutes a unique synchronization of their analogous but disparate desires: his to occupy Corinne's gaze exclusively and hers to have her success witnessed by Oswald. Hers can only be a reflected glory. Both Corinne and Oswald seek, then, in different ways visible proofs of the effect they produce on others: he on her and she on the crowd. He can experience power over Corinne only by capturing her gaze and she can measure her success only by seeing it reflected in Oswald's eyes. Theirs is a battle of the gaze, and, one might add, though Corinne wins many of the skirmishes, she does lose the war: in a dysphoric reversal of the *Romeo and Juliet* sequence, going to the theater in London she becomes a spectator to her own loss of effect as she watches how Lord Nelvil's gaze, once fixed on her, is transferred onto a rising star, her own half-sister Lucile, whom Lord Nelvil eventually marries:

> Suddenly, in the box facing hers, she caught sight of Lord Nelvil, whose gaze was fixed on Lucile. What a moment for Corinne! For the first time since she had left Venice, she saw again the features that had so absorbed her thought; she saw the face she constantly sought in her memory, even though it was never erased: and he was absorbed in Lucile alone. (p. 341)

Corinne differs strikingly, then, from *The Princesse* in that it lays bare the specularity of both male and female desires. How, then, does the portrait scene function in this very different context? Though not foregrounded as it is in both *The Princesse* and *Indiana*, the portrait scene in *Corinne* serves as what Michael Riffaterre, borrowing from C. S. Peirce, has called an "interpretant," an intertext that stands literally between two other texts and mediates their relationship.[19] The portrait scene in *Corinne* rewrites the one in *The Princesse* even as it anticipates the one in *Indiana*.

Corinne has gone off to a convent for her annual pre-Easter retreat. Although forewarned of her absence, Oswald is shocked to discover her departure and is overcome by a feeling of abandonment that revives his grief for his father, whose recent death hangs like a pall over him and the entire novel. To comfort him, Thérésine, Corinne's faithful maidservant, says:

> "My Lord, I'd like to comfort you by betraying a secret. I hope my mistress will forgive me. Come into her bedroom. You'll see your portrait."
>
> "My portrait!"
>
> "She did it from memory," went on Corinne's maid, Teresina, "She got up at five o'clock in the morning every day for the last week to get it done before she went off to her convent."
>
> Oswald saw the portrait which was a good likeness and painted with perfect grace: evidence of his effect on Corinne which filled him with the sweetest emotion. (p. 168)

Two related innovations serve to differentiate this scene from its homologue in *The Princesse*: Corinne is absent from the encounter between Oswald and his faithful likeness, and Corinne is herself the author of the portrait. In fact, one difference acts to cancel out the other, for the time and pains lavished by Corinne on the execution of the mimesis of her lover compensate for her absence. And yet, Corinne's absence and the noncoincidence it determines between the scene of the painting and the scene of self-contemplation introduce a time lag into the portrait scene that works to mute the emphasis on male narcissism. Indeed, though deeply touched by this "proof" of Corinne's love for him, Oswald is far less excessive in his response to the sight of his representation as produced by his lover than Nemours is to the sight of his as viewed by his beloved. And yet it is of the essence that Oswald is shown looking at the portrait signed by Corinne.

Here again, a brief comparison with an analogous scene in a work by an English woman writer serves to underscore the specificity of the insistently specular French tradition. While away from Thornfield on a visit to her Aunt Reed's, Jane Eyre draws a likeness of Rochester from memory.

> One morning I fell to sketching a face: what sort of face it was to be, I did not care to know. I took a soft black pencil, gave it a broad point, and worked away. Soon I had traced on the paper a broad and prominent forehead, and a square lower outline of visage: that contour gave me pleasure; my fingers proceeded actively to fill it with features. . . .
>
> "Is that the portrait of some one you know?" asked Eliza, who had approached me unnoticed. I responded that it was merely a fancy head, and hurried it beneath other sheets. Of course, I lied: it was, in fact, a very faithful representation of Mr. Rochester. But what was that to her, or to any one but myself?[20]

Not only is Jane's portrait of Rochester a far more spontaneous creation—it is done quickly and as though her hand were being guided by a force independent of her will—but its significance is purely personal: Rochester never sees it.

But the major difference between the portrait scenes in *The Princesse* and *Corinne* lies elsewhere: in penetrating illicitly into Corinne's bedchamber, Oswald discovers an unexpected secret: the bedchamber is in fact a miniature gallery, containing other images, notably the portrait of another man. The scene is worth quoting in full:

> His gaze wandered ardently over this bedroom he had entered for the first time. At Corinne's bedside, he saw the portrait of an old man whose face had no characteristics of the Italian countenance. Two bracelets were fastened near the portrait. One was made of black and white hair,

the other of beautiful blond: by what seemed a strange coincidence to Nelvil, it was exactly like Lucile Edgermond's hair, which had caught and held his attention three years earlier because of its rare beauty. Oswald wondered about the bracelets but said nothing, for to question Teresina about her mistress was unworthy of him. Thinking she guessed what concerned Oswald, and wanting to ward off any shadow of jealousy, Teresina hastened to tell him that in the eleven years she had been with Corinne, she had always seen her wear the bracelets, and that she knew they were made of hair from her father, mother, and sister. (p. 168)

At first glance there is something odd about Oswald's response to his latest discovery: rather than focusing on the portrait of the mysterious old man, he is seemingly fascinated by the sight of the two hair bracelets contiguous with the painting. It is the sight of these bracelets and not of the other man's portrait that awakens the jealousy Thérésine seeks to forestall; given the custom of lovers exchanging locks of hair, the presence of the bracelets suggests sexual intimacies that Oswald can only guess at. If, however, we superimpose this scene on the like scene in The Princesse, the logic at work in the displacement of Oswald's attention becomes apparent: the tressed bracelets stand in the same relationship to the portrait of the old man as the beribboned cane stands to that of the Duke of Nemours.

There is in these novels—and Indiana will only serve to confirm this observation—a persistent association between the representation of the representation of men and fetishism, the perversion, that is, that enshrines the centrality of the phallus. What is troubling to Oswald is the uncanny doubling of the fetish, for this multiplication works to undermine the uniqueness of the phallus and to underline its infinite substitutability. The doubled hair bracelet is in fact symptomatic of what Mme de Staël sets out to do in Corinne, namely to ruin the foundation of man's relationship to his own image by a strategy of proliferating images. Indeed often classified as a guidebook, Corinne has bewildered, not to say dismayed, many readers by its seemingly aberrant generalization of description. Leaving aside the masterworks on view in the churches, monuments, and galleries (both private and public) that Corinne visits with Oswald, the novel features a small collection of portraits: in addition to the portraits of Oswald and Corinne's father, there are two portraits of Corinne, during and after her relationship with Oswald. Significantly, on her deathbed Corinne asks the attending priest to remove Oswald's portrait and to replace it with the image of Christ, as though only what René Girard once termed "transcendental mediation" offered a way out of this universe marked by a deliberate and spectacular *excess* of representation.[21]

Texts published anonymously or under a pseudonym constitute a supreme test for theories of sexual specificity in writing: a test that critics of French literature have famously failed to meet in the celebrated cases of The Letters of a Portuguese Nun and The Story of O. Indiana, the first major novel George Sand published under her new masculine pseudonym, briefly obliged critics—for the biological sex of the suddenly famous author quickly became known—to articulate their assumptions about what it meant to write like a woman or a man. Most of these critics resorted to conventional ideas about gender to make their case, arguing, for example, that men write better of sensual love, and women, of refined feeling—hence, this love story, both sensuous and delicate, must be a collaborative effort, on the model of George Sand and her lover Jules Sandeau's Rose et Blanche.[22] Sainte-Beuve, however, goes beyond the predictable clichés and locates the femininity of the writing of Indiana precisely in the unsparing representation of one of its male protagonists, the vile seducer Raymon. According to Sainte-Beuve, "This disappointing character, exposed and unveiled [dévoilé] in detail in his miserable egotism, as never a man, were he a Raymon, could have realized it and would have dared to say it,"[23] is the surest giveaway of the author's sex.

Writing like a woman for Sainte-Beuve is in this instance bound up with a literal unveiling of the full horror of male egotism, the pre-Freudian term for narcissism. Now this gesture of unveiling is figured *en abîme*, as it were, in the portrait scene in Indiana. Raymon de Ramière, a dashing young aristocrat whose country home borders on that of Indiana and her husband, M. Delmare, has (unbeknownst to Indiana) become the lover of Noun, Indiana's maidservant and foster-sister. In a pathetic attempt to revive Raymon's flagging desire for her, Noun hits upon the idea of making love with him in Indiana's bedroom, while the Delmares are away in Paris. This arrangement suits Raymon fine for two reasons: first, it enables him to imagine that in making love to the sensual Noun he is possessing the unattainable Indiana, to whom (unbeknownst to Noun) he is attracted; second and perhaps more important, it allows him to penetrate into the private space of Indiana's curiously shaped bedroom. When, on the morning after their lovemaking, Noun hides Raymon in the bedroom, he continues to explore his surroundings with a mixture of reverence and ill-concealed curiosity:

> When Noun left him to go and find something for breakfast, he set about examining by daylight all those dumb witnesses of Indiana's solitude. He

opened her books, turned the leaves of her albums, then closed them
precipitately; for he still shrank from committing a profanation and
violating some feminine mystery. At last he began to pace the room and
noticed, on the wooden panel opposite Madame Delmare's bed, a large
picture, richly framed and covered with a double thickness of gauze.

Perhaps it was Indiana's portrait. Raymon, in his eagerness to see it,
forgot his scruples, stepped on a chair, removed the pins, and was
amazed to see a full-length portrait of a handsome young man.[24]

This scene, toward which, as I have tried to show, an entire literary tradition has been tending, is remarkable in its complexity. The gesture of tearing
away the doubled gauze veil doubles back upon itself, for in uncovering the
portrait of the other gentleman—here no harmless old man as in *Corinne*, but
rather a most threatening young one—Raymon exposes his own egotism,
even as Sand demonstrates the functioning of what Eve Sedgwick has termed
the "homosocial" bond.[25] Beyond or bound up with male representational
narcissism is an aggressive fascination with the imaginary Other. When Noun
returns, carrying the breakfast tray, Raymon can barely contain the "violent
flame of wrath" (p. 67) that the sight of the portrait kindles in him. He rants:

"Upon my word!" he said to himself, "this dapper young Englishman
enjoys the privilege of being admitted to Madame Delmare's most secret
apartment! His vapid face is always there, looking coldly on at the most
private acts of her life! He watches her, guards her, follows her every
movement, possesses her every hour of the day." (p. 68)

And he goes on to say to Noun that were he in Delmare's place, "I wouldn't
have consented to leave it [the picture] here unless I had cut out the eyes." Not
surprisingly, then, given the violence of Raymon's reaction to the fancied
voyeuristic privileges enjoyed by the man in the portrait, the rivalry between
Raymon and Sir Ralph, the portrait's model, will be entirely ocular, a struggle
over who shall possess the exclusive right not to be gazed at by Indiana but to
gaze at her:

She exchanged a meaning[ful] glance with Raymon but, swift as it was,
Sir Ralph caught it on the wing, and Raymon was unable, during the rest
of the evening, to glance at her or address her without encountering
Monsieur Brown's eyes or ears. A feeling of aversion, almost of jealousy,
arose in his heart. (p. 117)

Clearly at these moments, as Leslie Rabine as phrased it, "the heroine is the
space within which Ralph and Raymon look at each other."[26]

In the earlier versions of the portrait scene, the possibility of a misreading is carefully inscribed. Both Mme de La Fayette and Mme de Staël do allow the male protagonist and the male reader who identifies with him some measure of narcissistic gratification, even as they condemn the specularity of male desire and its representations. Sand's rescripting of this scene allows the resisting male reader no recourse to the comforts of misprision. In the event that the meaning of the portrait scene should have escaped the reader, male or female, it is doubled by another scene that takes place in Indiana's bedroom. This time it is Indiana who, giving in to Raymon's insistent pleas, has invited him to a midnight rendezvous in her room. Alerted by Ralph, Indiana has begun to suspect the truth about Raymon's affair with Noun and the part he played in driving the pregnant and abandoned Noun to commit suicide by drowning. Racked by doubts as to Raymon's guilt, Indiana is suddenly inspired to devise "a strange and delicate test against which Raymon could not be on his guard" (p. 161). As Raymon approaches Indiana, she points to a "mass of black hair" (p. 162) she holds in her hands. At first, believing that the hair is Indiana's, Raymon is beside himself with joy:

> "O Indiana!" cried Raymon, "you know well that you will be lovelier than ever to me henceforth. Give it to me. I do not choose to regret the absence from your head of that glorious hair which I admired every day, and which now I can kiss every day without restraint. Give it to me, so that it can never leave me." (p. 163)

But when he takes "that luxurious mass" of hair into his own hands, Raymon realizes that it is not shorn from the scalp of the living Indiana but rather from the corpse of the dead Noun. Upon which, he faints away. When he comes to, he exclaims:

> "You have inflicted a horrible wound on me," he said, "a wound which it is not in your power to cure. You will never restore the confidence I had in your heart; that is evident to me. You have shown me how vindictive and cruel your heart can be." (p. 164)

The diabolical trap set for Raymon works in ways unforeseen by Indiana, though not, of course, by Sand. The sudden and irreversible death of Raymon's love for Indiana is caused less by the confirmation of his heartless seduction of Noun than by the supplementary revision of his fetishism. Once again, as in our earlier examples, male narcissism and fetishism are shown to be inextricably linked; to unmask the one is to unmask the other, and to unmask both is to attack the very foundations of the representational system elaborated by patriarchal society. Or, perhaps more important: to attack representation is to attack patriarchy and its distributions of power. For it is a central intuition of postmodernist thought that "representation stands for the interests of power."[27] An impassioned condemnation of the barbarous "laws which still govern woman's existence in wedlock, in the family and in society,"[28] Indiana has long been recognized as the most feminist of Sand's early feminist fiction, so it is surely no accident that in this novel the subversive intent of the portrait scene, so artfully camouflaged in the works of La Fayette and Staël, should be stripped of its protective veil and revealed in something like its truth.

At this juncture several questions arise, two of which I will raise only in passing: the first concerns the reasons for the difference between the French and the English traditions in women's writing. To begin to answer this question one would have to risk venturing onto the slippery terrain of national character, to speculate on the historical, social, and economic reasons why French culture seems more self-consciously visual than the English. This I have neither the inclination nor the competence to do. The second question concerns not national but sexual difference and could be formulated as follows: what features distinguish exposures of male narcissism in men's writings from those in women's writings? While I am not yet prepared to answer that important question, the implication of the preceding analysis is that that difference is bound up with the recurrence of the portrait scene in women's fiction, that is, with the persistent linkage in female-authored texts between representations of men and representations of representation. Ultimately what is at stake in women's representations of the specularity of male desire is representation itself. This brings me to a third question and one that I will attempt to answer: what becomes of the portrait scene in French women's writing of the twentieth century? Does it simply disappear, suggesting that it is historicizable, bound up with a social organization that, being neither natural nor eternal, has changed significantly over the years? The portrait scene recurs, but it does so in a guise so new and unfamiliar that it is at first unrecognizable. It recurs in, of all places, an early novel by Nathalie Sarraute, aptly titled Portrait of a Man Unknown. What makes this example so compelling from my perspective is that over the years Sarraute has consistently and vigorously denied the impact of gender on (her) writing. The following response to a journal questionnaire on the fictional inscription of sexual difference is typical:

On the level on which the interior dramas I strive to bring to light are produced, there is, I am firmly convinced, no difference between men and women, just as there is none in their respiratory or circulatory systems. . . .

Consequently, I have never asked myself if [the text] had qualities or defects said to be masculine or feminine.

I think these distinctions are based on prejudices, on pure conventions. They are unverifiable assertions which rest only on a very small number of examples, examples where the male or the female author claims to possess certain qualities he believes proper to his sex.[29]

Sarraute's refusal to be read as a woman writer extends far beyond her public statements about her own work. In *Portrait of a Man Unknown* it takes the form of a denial of female intertextuality; in a novel replete with literary allusions—for example, to *War and Peace*, *The Notebooks of Malte Laurids Brigge*, and *Madame Bovary*—one would be hard pressed to find any reference to a literary foremother; if there exists any conscious link between *Portrait* and the tradition we have been tracing, all material evidence of it has been completely expunged.[30] To further complicate my effort to appropriate Sarraute's novel for my argument, *Portrait* is a first-person narrative whose narrator is male and whose story, to the extent he tells one, is a deliberate rewriting of Balzac's *Eugénie Grandet*, entirely focused on the father-daughter struggle to the complete and significant exclusion of the mother and Charles, the love-object. Though the novel does end with the daughter's engagement to be married, Sarraute writes from beyond the erotics of the conventional marriage plot in which the previous portrait scenes function. Consequently, what I will nevertheless call the portrait scene takes place not in a woman's boudoir but in the very public space of a museum somewhere in Holland. I want now to compare Sand's description of the portrait of Sir Ralph, an example of academic portraiture of the school of Ingres or better Gainsborough, with Sarraute's description of a Dutch painting in the school of Frans Hals or Rembrandt:

The peaceable baronet was represented in hunting costume . . . and surrounded by his dogs, the beautiful pointer Ophelia in the foreground, because of the fine silver-gray tone of her silky coat and the purity of her Scotch blood. Sir Ralph had a hunting-horn in one hand and in the other the rein of a superb, dapple-gray English hunter, who filled almost the whole background of the picture. It was an admirably executed portrait, a genuine family picture with all its perfection of detail, all its puerile niceties of resemblance, all its bourgeois minutiae;

a picture to make a nurse weep, dogs bark and a tailor faint with joy. (p. 67)

The lines of the face, the lace jabot and waistcoat, as also the hands, seemed to present the kind of fragmentary, uncertain outlines that the hesitant fingers of a blind man might come upon haltingly, feeling his way. It was as though all effort, all doubt, all anxiety had been overtaken by a sudden catastrophe, and had remained congealed in action, like corpses that have petrified in the position they were in when death overtook them. The eyes alone seemed to have escaped the catastrophe and achieved fulfillment. It was as though they had attracted and concentrated in themselves all the intensity, all the life that was lacking in the still formless dislocated features. (p. 84)[31]

What we have here are two instances or stages of what I call "female iconoclasm," a peculiarly feminine form of antirepresentationalism.[32] Sand's description of the portrait of a true English gentleman is a witty send-up of a sex, a class, a nation, and, above all, an aesthetic ideal: bourgeois realism. The butt of the humor is clearly the male human figure, here singularly diminished by being sandwiched between the foregrounded canine and the backgrounded equine figure, and further by being reduced to a mere clothes-horse. And yet, however clever the pastiche, by definition the portrait of Sir Ralph obeys the very convention it mocks.[33]

The same cannot be said of the portrait of a man unknown. The extraordinary disfiguration of the anonymous gentleman bodies forth the radical assault on representation Sarraute undertakes in what Sartre, in his preface to Portrait, describes as her "antinovel." Visiting an exhibit with the novel's female protagonist later in the novel, the narrator elaborates on the aesthetic ideal embodied in his favorite painting:

"I believe that rather than the most perfectly finished works I prefer those in which complete mastery has not been attained . . . in which one still feels, just beneath the surface, a sort of anxious groping . . . a certain doubt . . . a mental anguish. . . . " I was beginning to sputter more and more . . . "before the immensity . . . the elusiveness of the material world . . . that escapes us just when we think we have got hold of it . . . the goal that's never attained . . . the insufficiency of the means at our disposal." (p. 201)

That the painting of the man unknown represents en abîme Sarraute's fictional universe with its celebrated tropismes—those multiple, minute stirrings that lie midway between the inchoate formlessness of the semiotic and the rigid armature of the symbolic—is hardly cause for surprise, given the relentlessly self-reflexive nature of the modernistic new novel. Further, one might argue that there is nothing particularly feminine about Sarraute's attack on the figure in an era when figurative art was giving way to abstraction. And yet the terms in which Sarraute's attack is formulated resonates with feminist critiques of representation. The main thrust of Sarraute's assault on traditional modes of figuration is significantly double: the visual and the whole. The morcelizing of the masculine imago works here to dethrone the visual from its hegemony over representation in favor of the tactile. And the promotion of the tactile in the arts leads inevitably to an end to mastery.

Sarraute's deconstruction of masculine representation does not end here. As the narrator stands transfixed before the portrait of the one he calls "The Man with the Waistcoat," he experiences a lyrical moment of total identification with the figure in the painting:

> And little by little, I became aware that a timid note, an almost forgotten strain from long ago, had sounded within me, at first, hesitantly. And it seemed to me, as I stood there before him lost, dissolved in him, that this faltering note, this timid response he had awakened in me, penetrated him and reverberated inside him, that he seized it and gave it back to me increased and magnified as though by an amplifier; it began to rise from him and from me, louder and louder, a song filled with hope that lifted me up and bore me along. (p. 85)

Though the narrator's ecstatic fusion with his alter imago calls to mind the Duke of Nemours's *jouissance*, it arises from a curious form of mutual resonance that bypasses the specular in favor of the vocal. And, as though to seal the end of the reign of the specular, the operatic merging of the two male figures—with its vestigial male narcissism—is brutally undercut by the narrator's description of his reflection:

> As I trotted along beside her, I avoided looking at the fellow "beyond his prime," with the bedraggled air and short legs, balding and slightly pot-bellied. But occasionally, I was unable to avoid him. He sprang forth from a mirror just opposite me, as we crossed the street. Never had my weary lids, my dull eyes, my sagging cheeks, appeared to me so pitilessly, as at that moment, beside her reflection, in that garish light. (p. 198)

Unsupported by an adoring female gaze—the narrator's female companion registers no surprise on catching sight of his sorry figure in the glass: "She had seen me like that for a long time," he remarks ruefully—the male figure appears here in its un- or de-idealized form, in its all-too-human contingency. The mirror has turned on Narcissus.

I began this piece by evoking an exhibit titled "Women's Images of Men," suggesting that what would follow would deal by analogy with "images of men" in women's writing, as though feminist criticism were somehow condemned to revert always to its origins, the now largely discredited pioneering work on "images of women" in men's writings. If I have hoped to demonstrate anything in the course of this essay it is that one of the major differences between men's and women's writing, at least in France, is that *there are, so to speak, no "images of men" in women's writing* because that writing is marked from the outset by a profound suspicion of the image and its grounding phallicism. Rarefaction, multiplication, pastiche, and disfiguration are some of the operations to which the image, the male image that is, is subjected in French women's fiction from La Fayette to Sarraute. My final question then becomes: can there be misandry where there are no unproblematized images, where representation is from its very inception in crisis? For cannot it be said that misogyny, like all forms of discrimination, relies on the power of the subject in power to fix the Other in a static image, a stereotype, or better yet a cliché? And can it not be further said that the ability of the subject in power to do so derives from his own possession of a secure, larger-than-life self-image? If the answer to these questions is affirmative—and that, of course, is a rather big if—then we can better understand why it is that for women writers, for whom the mirror has for centuries remained empty, the representation of men is bound up with the death of the image of man.

Triste Amérique: Atala and the Post-Revolutionary Construction of Woman

Historians and art historians have in recent years begun to recognize the extraordinary significance of the prevalence of feminine civic allegory in the iconography produced by the French Revolution. As Lynn Hunt writes: "The appearance of feminine allegorization was momentous for it became associated with the Republic ever after."[1] Though, as Hunt beautifully documents, the figure of Marianne, emblem of Liberty and of the French Republic, did not immediately impose itself as the unique, consensual icon of national sovereignty, from the time of its first appearance in 1792 it became an increasingly powerful visual source of legitimation for the successive revolutionary regimes that ruled France and eventually, after periods of eclipse and contestation, the official symbol of the state.[2]

Curiously, however, literary critics and historians—myself included—have been slow to draw the consequences of this important iconographic shift for the representation of women in nineteenth-century French fiction. And yet, arguably the most lasting effect of the French Revolution on nineteenth-century French representations of women from Chateaubriand's virginal Atala to Zola's courtesan Nana may well have been the powerful revolutionary conflation of the feminine and the state, the tendency for representations of woman in postabsolutist France to be collapsed with the stabilization and destabilization of the new social order instituted by 1789.

So heavily politicized and so insistently genderized is representation in the wake of the Revolution that the feminine subject in post-Revolutionary French fiction from early romanticism through naturalism becomes fully intelligible only when viewed in light of the historical circumstances which presided over its construction. Because of the widespread feminization of Republican iconography, in France the nineteenth-century heroine, in contradistinction to her eighteenth-century predecessor, is always inhabited by the uncanny shadow of the state, whose very laws serve to silence and oppress her. This allegorical specter, sometimes muted, sometimes boldly foregrounded, encumbers the female protagonist in the nineteenth-century French novel with an ideological charge that neither pre-Revolutionary female protagonists in French novels nor female protagonists in other nineteenth-century European literatures carry to quite the same degree, though of course feminine civic allegory is both an ancient and a pervasive phenomenon. Throughout the century, the representation of woman in France will be trapped between two excesses which stem from the matrix from which it emerges: the disembodiment inherent in allegorism and the hyperembodiment characteristic of naturalism, which are in fact two sides of the same representational coin, as demonstrated by the synchronous putrefaction of Nana's corpse and the decline and fall of the Second Empire in the final chapter of *Nana*.[3] Bearing in mind that the relationship between woman and representation is always saturated with history, I want in what follows to consider through a specific example the modalities of that relationship in the immediate aftermath of the French Revolution.

I

Two fictional scenes delimit the space in which I want to inscribe my reflections on the relationship between women, representation, and the French Revolution in nineteenth-century French fiction. The first scene is drawn from the opening pages of one of the major feminocentric narratives of the eighteenth century, *Manon Lescaut* (1 7 3 1). The first-person narrator is the Marquis de Renoncour, the man of quality within whose memoirs *Manon Lescaut* is embedded. By way of the framing of Des Grieux's first-person narrative of his love for Manon, Renoncour recounts his first sighting of the tragic pair in the town of Pacy. Manon, condemned to exile in America, is part of a group of twelve women being transported under guard to Le Havre:

> Parmi les douze filles qui étaient enchaînées six à six par le milieu du corps, il y en avait une dont l'air et la figure étaient si peu conformes à sa condition, qu'en tout autre état je l'eusse prise pour une personne du premier rang. Sa tristesse et la saleté de son linge et de ses habits l'enlaidissaient si peu, que sa vue m'inspira du respect et de la pitié. Elle tâchait néanmoins de se tourner, autant que sa chaîne pouvait le permettre, pour dérober son visage aux yeux des spectateurs.

> Amongst the twelve women who were chained together by the waist in two rows of six was one whose face and bearing were so out of keeping

with her present situation that in any other setting I would have taken her for a lady of the gentler birth. She was in abject misery and her clothes were filthy, but all that had so little effect on her beauty that I felt nothing but pity and respect for her. She was trying to turn away as much as the chains would allow, so as to hide her face from us onlookers, and this effort at concealment was so natural that it seemed to come from feelings of modesty.[4]

Suspending for a moment any commentary on this remarkable tableau, I want to turn now to my second scene, this one drawn from Chateaubriand's *Atala*, whose publication date of 1801 makes it the most immediately post-Revolutionary fiction published in France and which is still retained, however grudgingly, in the canon. We are now in the new world, indeed among its native inhabitants. The speaker is Chactas, an aged and blind Natchez Indian; the story, his youthful love for Atala, a fair young Indian maiden. Taken prisoner by the tribe to which Atala belongs, Chactas has been tied down Gulliver-like prior to his being put to death. In his sleep he dreams he is being freed. Upon awakening he finds he is not dreaming:

A la clarté de la lune . . . j'entrevois une grande figure blanche penchée sur moi et occupée à dénouer silencieusement mes liens. . . . Une seule corde restait, mais il paraissait impossible de la couper sans toucher un guerrier qui la couvrait tout entière de son corps. Atala y porte la main, le guerrier s'éveille à demi et se dresse sur son séant. Atala reste immobile et le regarde. L'Indien croit voir l'Esprit des ruines; il se recouche en fermant les yeux et en invoquant son Manitou. Le lien est brisé. Je me lève; je suis ma libératrice.

By the light of a moonbeam filtering between two clouds, I made out a large white figure leaning over me, silently untying my bonds. . . . A single rope still remained, but it seemed impossible to cut it without touching a warrior who was covering its whole length with his body. Atala placed her hand on it. The warrior half awakened and sat up. Atala remained motionless, watching him. The Indian thought he was looking at the Spirit of the Ruins and lay down again, closing his eyes and invoking his Manitou. The bond was broken. I stood up and followed my deliverer.[5]

Suffused with eroticism, each of these tableaus enacts a different fantasmatic scenario of bondage. Permeated by an erotics of female vulnerability, the eighteenth-century text represents the titillating pathos of a woman in chains.

The emphasis here is on the marks of class and the redemptive virtues of modesty. Soiled, exposed, bound, Manon is a woman in distress. Entirely bound over to the exchange system that makes her a mere commodity, Manon's chains can be lightened only by bribing her jailers. A radical paradigm shift marks the scene from *Atala*. Grandiose, ghostly, garbed in white, Atala is represented as a near-mythic figure of power and cunning. In Chactas's captivity narrative, the captive is male and his liberator a liberatrix. In what appears to be a striking instance of role reversal, in this enactment of the bondage fantasy, the male protagonist is reduced to the passivity of an object, the helplessness of an infant. Disempowered by the multiple bonds pinning him to the ground, Chactas, the brave Indian warrior, awaits deliverance at the hands of an all-powerful female. Furthermore, in this beyond of the European market economy, money is uncoupled from liberation, and class differences wither away.

The paired readings of the bondage scenes from *Manon* and *Atala* I have just presented are, of course, tendentious, informed by the assumption that in some manner still to be determined the reslotting of the female protagonist as liberatrix is, so to speak, bound up with the events of the French Revolution. Bracketing for the moment the endlessly vexed question of the relationship between Text and Event—which is precisely what is at stake in this essay—a couple of thorny methodological questions present themselves: first, the juxtaposition I have just staged is rigged. An entirely different intertextual relationship between these same two texts might be constructed to entail a less optimistic conclusion regarding the effect of the Revolution on the representation of women. Indeed, if we were to read jointly the death scenes of Manon and Atala—and we will—we would have to conclude that the syntax of the female literary text continues undisturbed from the Age of Enlightenment to the Age of Napoleon. The presumption of progress, of some sort of liberation of and for women fostered by the macronarrative of the Revolution, is denied by the seemingly ritualistic sacrifice of the eternal female protagonist, as well, of course, as by the historical record. And then there is the second problem: granting the heuristic value of my admittedly selective double reading, the question arises: why *Manon Lescaut*, why *Atala*? The question, I hasten to note, is not: is this comparison legitimate? For at least ever since Sainte-Beuve the intertextual relationship of *Manon* and *Atala* has been a critical commonplace of the writing, meager as it is, on *Atala*.[6] The question I am raising is somewhat different: what grounds are there for attributing to these two fictional works representative status? In short, one of the main issues this comparison raises is the issue of canonicity. At this point a distinction must be introduced between the cases of *Manon Lescaut* and *Atala*, for whereas *Manon* has long occupied a secure position in the canon—which is, of course, subject to change—*Atala* has not.

II

A brief review of some of the circumstances surrounding the genesis, publication, and critical reception of *Atala* is necessary in order to understand the uniquely liminal position it occupies in standard histories of French literature. Begun in 1792, during or shortly after Chateaubriand's voyage to America, *Atala* was originally conceived of as part of a work on the Natchez Indian tribe, the *Natchez*. However, for reasons that remain obscure, in 1801 Chateaubriand decided to publish *Atala* separately, as a sort of prepublication "teaser" for his coming magnum opus, *The Genius of Christianity*, which appeared in 1802. The publication of *Atala* was by all accounts (and not just Chateaubriand's, that master of self-promotion) a major literary event. The exotic tale of doomed love between a Europeanized noble savage and a Christianized Indian maiden made Chateaubriand a celebrity and gave rise to a veritable industry of popular iconography and artifacts. But, for all its spectacular success and popularity, *Atala* was not to be Chateaubriand's main claim to fame as a novelist. That claim rests on *René*, yet another spin-off from Chateaubriand's apologetic work.

Written virtually in tandem with *Atala*, *René* was first published as part of *The Genius*. It was only in 1805 that *Atala* and *René*, presumably in response to popular demand, assumed their definitive literary existences as autonomous yet linked works of fiction. Connected by a double synecdoche via the same master text, actantially conjoined through the character of René, who is Chactas's interlocutor in *Atala* as well as the narrator of the text that bears his name, the literary fates of *Atala* and *René* have been radically different. Whereas *Atala* is generally characterized as having "aged," which is to say it has aged badly—and in many ways it has, but that is hardly the point—*René* has been preserved in the literary histories that constitute the French canon as eternally youthful, the embodiment of literary adolescence. Because of its prestigious posterity—*René* is the founding text of French Romanticism—the androcentric novel has completely eclipsed the feminocentric, now relegated to the nebulous limbo of the transitional work. Viewed as the dying fall of neoclassicism or, at best, pre-Romanticism, *Atala* is never viewed as inaugural, foundational. Primogeniture and contiguity have to date assured its place in the canon, but that place is that of a quaint curio rather than that of a work of major cultural significance. Reproducing the same fratricidal scenario as that played out in both René and Atala, René, the brother-text, has killed Atala, its incestuous female Other.

I use the vocabulary of the nuclear family structure and sibling rivalry advisedly, for it is intrinsic to Chateaubriand's metaphorics of literary paternity. Thus, for example, in his Memoirs, Chateaubriand casts Atala in the role of daughter, indeed devoted, self-sacrificing daughter; like the proverbial Bible, during a military engagement the daughterly manuscript of Atala acts to shield her father from enemy bullets: "A l'affaire de la Plaine, deux balles avaient frappé mon havresac pendant un mouvement de conversion. Atala, en fille dévouée, se plaça entre son père et le plomb ennemi" ("At the business of the plain, two bullets had struck my knapsack during a change of front. Atala, acting as a devoted daughter, placed herself between her father and the enemy shot").[7] Elsewhere in the Memoirs, Chateaubriand describes the perplexity generated among the academicians by Atala's "birth" in these revealing terms: "On ne savait si l'on devait la classer parmi les monstruosités ou parmi les beautés; était-elle Gorgone ou Vénus? Les académiciens assemblés dissertèrent doctement sur son sexe et sa nature" ("They didn't know whether to class her among the monstrosities or the beauties; was she a Gorgon or a Venus? The assembled academicians learnedly held forth on her sex and her nature").[8] The taxonomic undecidability provoked by the text is doubly coded as sexual: in the first instance there seems to be no doubt about the text's sex, but rather about its precise inscription within the mythic paradigm of femininity. In the second, it is the text's very sex that is at issue: the alternative is no longer between Venus and Medusa but between maleness and femaleness, or Atala as Hermaphrodite. The figure of Medusa mediates these two apparently mutually exclusive statements; for if the text is in fact monstrous, more Medusa, then its very sex is thrown into doubt.

Now I will want to argue that it is precisely that doubt, that sexual indeterminacy, that Atala functions to check. And I will want to argue further that the "sexual fix" (Heath) of Atala is inseparable from what I take to be one of the text's major ideological effects: the putting into place of a cultural construction of femininity adequate to the reactionary sexual regime brought into being by the French Revolution. There is, in other words, a sense in which Atala helped pave the way for the Napoleonic Code first promulgated in 1804 and which all historians of women and feminism in nineteenth-century France agree was a disaster for women, tightening the loopholes in the Old Regime legal system so as to subject all women to the same inequitable laws regarding marriage and property rights, depriving women of the fragile gains they had made during the Revolution, setting back women's rights in France by at least a century.[9] At the same time, it should be noted that feminist historians of the French Revolution have argued that the very betrayal of women by the Revolution and the repressive regimes that followed it are perversely largely responsible for the coming into being of modern French feminism.

What *Atala* participates in is the prevalence of allegorism in nineteenth-century French figurations of the Revolution; what *Atala* founds is the tradition of representing woman in nineteenth-century French fiction as sexually stigmatized. Let me develop each of these points in turn. Considering the magnitude and the significance of the French Revolution in ushering in the modern era in France, it is a striking fact of nineteenth-century French cultural production that the Revolution, especially in its mythic form of 1789, is significantly underrepresented in mimetic high art, with the emphasis on the word mimetic.[10] Scenes from the Revolution are, of course, abundantly documented in popular iconography and the bloody battles of the Chouan resistance, memorably depicted in the works of Hugo, Balzac, and Barbey d'Aurevilly, among others. Better yet, French Romanticism, Realism, and Naturalism all draw their impetus from the Revolution: nineteenth-century literature in France is a protracted and therapeutic working through of the trauma of regicide and the shock of democraticization. But the French Revolution—at least in France; the situation in England is quite different—in some very real sense escapes representation, except in the displaced mode of allegory. This tendency to depict the Revolution by displacement is perhaps most famously apparent in the neoclassical History paintings of David. The recourse to a preexisting Greco-Roman, but especially Roman, repertory of images and stories can be explained by what Ronald Paulson has called the "central aesthetic challenge" posed by the French Revolution: "how to represent the unprecedented."[11] As Marx was the first to note in the celebrated opening pages of *The Eighteenth Brumaire of Louis Bonaparte*, from 1789 to 1814 that challenge was met in large part by reappropriating earlier, notably Roman, modes of representation, and as historians like Maurice Agulhon have recently demonstrated, these earlier modes included the predominantly female allegorical figures which have, since antiquity, served to represent civic virtues.[12]

Atala, whose writing spans the revolutionary decade, is, to borrow a phrase from Jane Tompkins, "social criticism written in an allegorical mode,"[13] and that explains in large part why it appears to have "aged" so badly. The aging effect is produced by the misguided application to an allegorical work of the aesthetic standards and readerly expectations grounded in high realism; it is only when one reads *Atala* through the appropriate allegorical lens that its youthful beauty is restored and one can begin to grasp the reasons for its immense popular success. Written largely in exile by an aristocratic French emigré, *Atala* enlists the ready-made generic conventions of travel literature and sterotypical schemata of exotic romance to the ends of consolidating the reaction to the Revolution. And that consolidation takes the form of a spectacular binding or rebinding of female energy, a containment which only makes sense as a response to an equally spectacular explosion of female energy: the active participation of women in the Revolution. Indeed, so terrifying to the male leaders of the French revolution was the invasion of the public sphere by women—and especially lower-class women—that the binding of female energy and the resulting silencing of women follow immediately upon their increasingly threatening attempts to represent themselves in the arena of public debate. As early as 1793, "women were," according to Joan B. Landes, "banned from active *and* passive participation in the political sphere."[14]

The "crisis in representation" (Hunt) of the 1790s was, as Mona Ozouf, Lynn Hunt, and Marie-Hélène Huet have persuasively argued, bound up with a struggle by such figures as Robespierre and David to reclaim the sphere of symbolic representation from the hordes of unruly women unleashed by the Revolution and to realign representation with the male principle from which it had been severed after the beheading of the king: thus David actively promoted the virile effigy of Hercules over the feminine figure of Liberty as a candidate for the seal of the Republic, while Robespierre, with David's expert help, choreographed the Festival of the Supreme Being to stamp out the female-centered cult of Reason in favor of a sublime, suprasensorial ceremony.[15] This last contest for an appropriate secular celebration of the Revolution is of particular pertinence to our reading of *Atala*, for what was at stake in Robespierre's iconoclastic superproduction was the wish not so much to hasten the de-Christianization of France, a purpose already served by the Festival of Reason, but rather, as Huet argues, to avert the perceived threat posed by the triumphant female embodiment of Reason, a fully corporeal female allegory: "La femme et l'image seront de fait inextricablement liées dans la stratégie des partisans du culte de l'Etre suprême, et l'on pourrait voir, dans la détermination dont ils feront preuve pour instaurer un culte 'sublime,' le rejet conjugué de l'idole et du féminin" ("Woman and the image are in fact inextricably linked in the strategy of the partisans of the cult of the Supreme Being, and one might see in the determination they will display in order to institute a 'sublime' cult, the conjoined rejection of the idol and the feminine").[16] The highly successful Festival of Reason, held in the Cathedral of Notre-Dame on November 10, 1793 (20 brumaire, Year II), featured, let us recall, an allegory of Reason fully and sensually embodied by an actress, and this was only the most spectacular instance of such a live personification of a civic virtue and, moreover, one generally held to be incompatible with femininity.

Chateaubriand's *Atala* is deeply implicated in the struggle to recontain the female energy briefly unchained by the Revolution and to ward off the dangers represented by a too palpably embodied female cult figure. That Chateaubriand was aware of the active participation of women in the Revolution and that he deplored it is indicated in *Atala* through the depiction of a bloodthirsty, chorus-like group of Indian women, who call for Chactas's condemnation to death, as well, of course, as by the Dickensian passage in his *Mémoires* describing the women of la Halle (sic) knitting in the galleries of the National Assembly, banging their clogs, and foaming at the mouth as they called for the death of the members of the royalist opposition.[17] That Chateaubriand grasped that the most effective way to counter the threat posed by women to the symbolic order involved the decorporealization of feminine allegory is clearly evident from his treatment of the figure of Atala. Which brings me to my second point.

Nineteenth-century French fiction, especially in its hegemonic, realist-naturalist modality, relies heavily, as I have argued elsewhere, on the containment of female sexual energy to propel its narratives forward.[18] Chained, hystericized, and maimed, women's disciplined bodies provide an essential motor for the smooth running of the nineteenth-century textual machine. Atala, whose access to sexuality is barred by the vow her mother made at her birth committing her to virginity, is but the first of a long line of nineteenth-century French heroines denied *jouissance*. This is not to say that the eighteenth-century novel represents a pre-Lapsarian paradise for the female protagonist, nor for that matter that the nineteenth is, in Jane Gallop's words, "beyond the *jouissance* principle":[19] Manon, as we have seen, makes her debut on the scene of representation in chains, and the Marquise de Merteuil in *Dangerous Liaisons* exits the same scene hideously disfigured for her sins. But whereas Sade's heroines are subjected to multiple bodily wounds and suturings for the greater delight of their male lovers, the earth does move for Emma Bovary.

Even if we were able to demonstrate persuasively that the sextual economies of key eighteenth-century texts differ in significant and predictable ways from their nineteenth-century equivalents—say, *Atala*, *Les Diaboliques*, and *Nana*—we would still be confronted by the enormous difficulty of specifying those reified entities, the eighteenth- and nineteenth-century novels. Historicizing the representations of women (but also of men, crowds, etc.) is an infinitely complex task, certainly far more so than I allowed in *Breaking the Chain*. Periodization, then, as well as canonicity—can the two ever really be separated—is here at issue. Earlier I asked what grounds there were for according, indeed claiming, for *Atala* representative status. The question now becomes: wherein lies *Atala's* historical specificity, what an earlier generation of critics called its "originality"? What are the markers of *Atala's* post-Revolutionary production?

III

To begin to answer these questions requires bringing into play a third novel, the text that serves by all accounts as *Atala's* privileged intertext. I am referring to Bernardin de Saint-Pierre's hugely popular *Paul et Virginie* (1778). For Chateaubriand's contemporaries there was little doubt but that *Atala* was (nothing more than) a rewriting of this now little-known text, which was to mark the imaginary nineteenth-century French novelists in a way that few other eighteenth-century novels did, a text Chateaubriand explicitly and significantly comments on in a chapter of *The Genius of Christianity*.[20] Set in the Ile de France (Mauritius), *Paul et Virginie* is the story of two children who are raised together by their mothers, who have sought refuge on this tropical island to escape the injustices of patriarchal society: misogyny, slavery, and violence. In time, however, Virginie leaves this matriarchal paradise to go off to Paris to be educated. Upon her return there is a terrible storm, and the ship that is carrying her home is wrecked. Faced with the choice of taking her clothes off to swim to safety or preserving her modesty and drowning, Virginie does not hesitate: she drowns, her modesty intact.

Two aspects of the novel have garnered the most readerly attention: the bliss of the children's dyadic fraternal relationship—rarely in modern European fiction has the mirror stage been portrayed in more lyrical terms—and the implausibility of the ending. The incest motif is, of course, present in *Atala*, since Chactas's adoptive father, the Spaniard Lopez, is also, as is slowly revealed in the course of the narrative, Atala's biological father. Hence Chactas's somewhat melodramatic exclamation on burying Atala: "Lopez, m'écriai-je alors, vois ton fils inhumer ta fille!" ("'Lopez,' I cried out, 'behold your son interring your daughter'" [p. 122/p. 74]). But in *Atala* sexual difference precedes and precipitates desire; we are from the outset plunged into a degraded world beyond the supposedly idyllic pre-Oedipus. When Chactas first appears in the frame "Prologue," he *is* (at least by analogy) Oedipus: "Une jeune fille l'accompagnait sur les coteaux du Meschacebé, comme Antigone guidait les pas d'Oedipe sur le Cythéron" ("A young girl accompanied him over the slopes along the Mescacebe, just as Antigone once guided the steps of Oedipus over Mount Cytheron" [pp. 43–44/p. 20]).

What is more for the white, European male, Chateaubriand's new world is like Lévi-Strauss's irremediably *triste*: despite the signifiers of exoticism flaunted in the landscape descriptions, the forests of the Louisiana territory are in *Atala* the site of a lost French empire, reciprocal violence, and ontological homelessness. Fleeing the unspecified "passions et [des] malheurs" ("passion and sorrow" [p. 44/p. 20]) that had driven him from Europe (cf. *René*), René finds in America only more of the same, of sameness itself. Dystopia turns out to be a prison house of mirroring, where René cannot escape his specular image. An extended chiasmus figures this negative mirror stage: "Je vois en toi," says Chactas to René, "l'homme civilisé qui s'est fait sauvage; tu vois en moi l'homme sauvage, que le grand Esprit (. . .) a voulu civiliser. Entrés l'un et l'autre dans la carrière de la vie par les deux bouts opposés, tu es venu te reposer à ma place, et j'ai été m'asseoir à la tienne" ("I see in you the civilized man who has become a savage; you see in me the savage whom the Great spirit has . . . chosen to civilize. Having entered life's path from opposite ends, you have now come to rest in my place while I have gone to sit in yours" [p. 47/p. 22]).

Clearly, then, if *Atala* is, in the words of one disgruntled nineteenth-century literary critic, "l'exagération, je n'ose pas dire la charge de *Paul et Virginie*" ("the exaggeration, dare I say the caricature of *Paul et Virginie*"), what *Atala* mimes in the earlier text is not the joy of fraternal fusion, but rather the implausibility of the virtuous ending.[21] Here I want to be quite explicit about the connection between the pre- and the post-Revolutionary texts: in both instances, the mother-daughter dyad precludes the daughter's consummation of her sexual desire, indeed her sexuality *tout court*. The princess of Clèves, the founding victim of the reproduction of mothering in the French novelistic canon, does at least marry and presumably lose her virginity. But in *Atala*, as in *Paul et Virginie*, the intensity of the mother-daughter relationship results in a veritable taboo concerning the daughter's virginity. Atala's secret, the fatal enigma of her femininity—Chactas describes her as "un être incompréhensible" ("an incomprehensible being" [p. 75/p. 41])—is her mother's vow: feeling herself on the verge of succumbing to Chactas's impetuous desire, Atala commits suicide rather than break the promise extracted from her by her dying mother, that she respect the vow her mother made at her birth in exchange for her life.

There is, then, no radical discontinuity between the sexual politics of the two novels: in both cases the daughter is suicided by the author in order to serve a double imperative: the maternal critique of patriarchy—better dead than seduced and abandoned—and, at the same time, patriarchy's censure of female sexual activity—better dead than troubling the homosocial order. And yet, there is to my mind a crucial difference between *Atala* and *Paul et Virginie* which can best be grasped by considering the mother's death-bed speech to her daughter, which surely deserves to be set beside Mme de Chartres's famous last words to the princess of Clèves:

> O mon Atala! je te laisse dans un monde qui n'est pas digne de posséder une chrétienne, au milieu d'idolâtres qui persécutent le Dieu de ton père et le mien, le Dieu qui, après t'avoir donné le jour, te l'a conservé par un miracle. Eh! ma chère enfant, en acceptant le voile des vierges, tu ne fais que renoncer aux soucis de la cabane et aux funestes passions qui ont troublé le sein de ta mère! Viens donc, ma bien aimée, viens; jure sur cette image de la mère du Sauveur, entre les mains de ce saint prêtre et de ta mère expirante, que tu ne me trahiras point à la face du ciel. Songe que je me suis engagée pour toi, afin de te sauver la vie, et que si tu ne tiens ma promesse tu plongeras l'âme de ta mère dans des tourments éternels.

> "My daughter," she said, "you know about the vow I once made for you. Would you have your mother speak falsely? O my Atala! I leave you in a world unworthy of having a Christian woman in the midst of heathens who persecute your father's God and mine, the God who first gave you life and then preserved it by a miracle. Ah, my dear child, when you accept the virgin's veil, you give up only the cares of the cabin and the mortal passions which distressed your mother's bosom. Come, then, beloved daughter, swear upon this image of the Savior's mother, under the hands of the holy priest and before your dying mother, that you will not betray me in the face of Heaven. Remember that I gave my word for you in order to save your life, and if you do not keep my promise, you will plunge you mother's soul in everlasting woe." (p. 100/pp. 58–59)

Maternal discourse in *Atala* does not emanate from the depths of some timeless, transhistorical unconscious, nor does it draw its affective power from the matrix of the pre-Oedipus. The language of the mother is coextensive with that of the Christian apologist; the key words in her vocabulary are persecution, salvation, and damnation. This, then, is what I will not hesitate to call Chateaubriand's brilliant innovation in *Atala*: in the guise of rehabilitating Christianity in the wake of the secularizing trends of eighteenth-century philosophy and the de-Christianization promoted by the Revolution, Chateaubriand fuses to stunning effect the categories of gender and religion. The coupling of the two is mutually beneficent and reinforcing: a threatened Christianity draws renewed strength from being mapped onto sexual difference while a threatening breakdown of sexual hierarchies is averted by sanctifying the cultural construction of femininity. In *Atala*, a work written in the white heat of a historically unprecedented Revolution, we catch a stunningly rare glimpse of anaclisis doing the work of ideology over the body of a woman. To say this is neither to deny nor to paper over the ideological fissures in *Atala*—prominent traces of Chateaubriand's original *roman à thèse* condemning the excesses of Christian dogma do persist in the irony of Atala's unnecessary suicide; the knowledge that she might have been relieved of her vow by higher Church authorities comes too late to save her from death. But, however unorthodox Chateaubriand's apologetic discourse, however much the powerful eroticism of the doomed love story strains against the exigencies of denial—Atala does come vertiginously close to succumbing to temptation—it performs its double ideological function with remarkable efficacy.

The same potent linkage of Christianity and femininity—as well, one might add, as the same dogmatic lapses—are at work in the larger apologetic design of the *Genius*. For, as Stéphane Michaud has pointed out in his study of Mariolatry in nineteenth-century France, Chateaubriand's case for Christianity is grounded in an inherited discourse of naturalized feminine inferiority. The weakness inherent in woman's sex, especially in regard to pleasure, necessitates her faith, while at the same time the goodness and compassion inherent in woman's maternal nature make her a quasi-religious figure on the order of the Virgin Mary: "la religion est en effet un aussi indispensable soutien à sa fragilité qu'une alliée naturelle de sa pudeur et son ignorance" ("Religion is in effect as much an indispensable support for her frailty as a natural ally for her modesty and her ignorance").[22]

Let us return now as promised to the death, or rather burial scenes, in *Manon Lescaut* and *Atala*. First *Manon*:

> Je rompis mon épée pour m'en servir à creuser, mais j'en tirais moins de secours que de mes mains. J'ouvris une large fosse, j'y plaçai l'idole de mon coeur, après avoir pris soin de l'envelopper de tous mes habits pour empêcher le sable de la toucher. Je ne la mis dans cet état qu'après l'avoir embrassée mille fois avec toute l'ardeur du plus parfait amour. Je m'assis encore auprès d'elle. Je la considérais longtemps. Je ne pouvais me résoudre à fermer sa fosse.

> I broke my sword so as to use it for digging, but it was not as useful as my hands. I opened a wide trench and into it I committed the idol of my

Anne-Louis Girodet-Trioson, *The Funeral of Atala*, Musée du Louvre, © PHOTO R.M.N.

heart, having first wrapped her in all my clothes lest the sand should touch her. But first I kissed her a thousand times with all the tenderness of perfect love. I could not bring myself to close her grave, but sat still for a long time contemplating her. (p. 213/p. 188)

Because the section of *Atala* titled "The Funeral" is more protracted than the shockingly brief section of *Manon* devoted to Manon's sudden death and unceremonious burial, I want to compare the scene of Manon's burial with an icon indelibly engraved on every French child's conscience, the painting invariably reproduced in literary manuals to illustrate the excerpt from *Atala* describing the dead Atala, Girodet's 1808 painting, "Atala carried to the grave."[23]

This scene does not in fact correspond to any single passage in the text, but rather synoptically and idiosyncratically interprets the entire section; for in this complex representation Girodet is, it should be noted, promoting his own homoeroticism even as he lends striking visual immediacy to Chateaubriand's more homosocially inflected apologetic design.[24] In the strikingly immediate foreground there are not two but three figures: to the left a prostrate and highly idealized Chactas embraces Atala's legs; in the center the highlighted, virginally white body of Atala hangs suspended over the dark gaping hole of the freshly dug grave; and to the right, holding up Atala's upper body, stands the bent, hooded, and patriarchally bearded père Aubry. Corresponding to the three figures, three crosses are arrayed in full view: in the foreground on the horizontal plane and ostentatiously placed near the grave, a curiously cross-shaped shovel is bled over the edge of the painting; just over Atala's right breast, a fragment of the cross she holds in her demurely folded hands can be made out; and finally, in the background, a cross rises vertically in the gash of open sky glimpsed through the woodsy grotto opening.[25]

Whether read from right to left or from top to bottom, the painting tells the same story: in sharp contrast with Manon's remarkably secular burial, Atala's is a pieta. The ritualistic death of the female protagonist is here powerfully reconfigured through the ostentatious display of the full panoply of Christian symbolism: in death, Atala syncretizes the attributes of both the Virgin and Christ. Here again the comparison with *Paul et Virginie* serves to confirm the thesis I am putting forward, for if Manon is denied a decent Christian burial, and Atala virtually canonized in death—"nous passerions la nuit en prières auprès du corps de cette sainte" ("we resolved to spend the night in prayer beside the body of the saintly maid" [p. 119/p. 72])— Virginie, whom Chateaubriand not surprisingly insists on describing as a "Christian virgin," is given a ceremonial burial, but the ceremony is, pace Chateaubriand, resolutely and exotically pagan:

> Lorsqu'elle fut arrivée au lieu de sa sépulture, des négresses de Madagascar et des Cafres de Mozambique déposèrent autour d'elle des paniers de fruits, et suspendirent des pièces d'étoffes aux arbres voisins, suivant l'usage de leur pays; des Indiennes du Bengale et de la côte Malabre apportèrent des cages pleines d'oiseaux, auxquelles elles donnèrent la liberté sur son corps: tant la perte d'un objet aimable intéresse toutes les nations, et tant est grand le pouvoir de la vertu malheureuse, puisqu'elle réunit toutes les religions autour de son tombeau.

> When she had reached her burial-place, black women from Madagascar and Kafirs from Mozambique laid baskets of fruits around her and hung rolls of cloth on neighboring trees in keeping with the customs of their countries; Indian women from Bengal and the coast of Malabar brought cages full of birds which they set free over her body. So affecting is the loss of a fair object to all nations and so great is the power of unhappy virtue, since it brings together all religions around its grave.[26]

Though both Virginie and Atala die for virtue, the contrast between the two virgins' burials could not be greater: Virginie's burial is a colorful, life-affirming, and above all ecumenical affair officiated at by an ethnically diverse group of women, whereas Atala's is, as we have already seen, a gloomy rite presided over by two men whose very real cultural differences are overridden by the homogenizing and allegorizing discourse of Christian apologetics: "Quiconque eût ignoré que cette jeune fille avait joui de la lumière, aurait pu la prendre pour la statue de la Virginité endormie" ("Whoever was unaware that this maid had once enjoyed the light of day might have taken her for a statue of sleeping virginity" [p. 120/p. 72]).

By making of the lifeless corpse of the young Indian maiden an allegory of Virginity, Chateaubriand successfully manages to capitalize on the legitimating power of feminine allegory, while voiding the feminine form of female corporeality and desire and erasing from it the marks of racial difference. The allegorization of woman, a sort of degree zero of female representation, can only be brought about through a violent act of suppression of all particularities, not to mention of life. And, once again, Zola's hyperembodied Nana confirms the rule: during her last appearance on stage before disappearing from Paris and returning there only to die, Nana is cast in an entirely silent role, effectively silenced the better to be allegorized.[27]

IV

Recently I saw a fascinating video documentary, *Mother Ireland*, produced by the Derry Film and Video Collective, which explores the various uses to which the allegorization of Ireland as Woman or Mother has been put and the effects that this allegorization have had on "real Irish women" in their nationalist and/or feminist political struggles and activities. As Annie Goldson, the documentary's editor, points out in her commentary on the video:

> On the one hand, it can be said that allegory is oppressive for women, denying them power. Feminists cogently argue that the representation of gender within culture contributes to the process of aligning an object, woman, with an image, Woman, and bringing her under social control. . . . On the other hand, as is apparent in *Mother Ireland*, many women admire and derive strength from allegorical representations. These symbolized female images can affirm women in their choices and political struggles, not only as role models, but also as a symbol of the general good in which they, as half of humanity, are deeply implicated.[28]

Though it is difficult to evaluate the effects of the allegorical representations of women produced by the French Revolution on the lives of the "real women" of nineteenth-century France, we can at least raise the question: how did post-Revolutionary women writers in France cope with the allegorical imperative? Were female allegories disempowering or empowering for them? Not surprisingly for nineteenth-century women and more especially feminist authors[29]—I am thinking chiefly of Staël and Sand—this representational constraint posed special difficulties while at the same time offering unsuspected if limited opportunities for subversion. Staël's *Corinne, or Italy* (1807) poignantly testifies to the complexities of post-Revolutionary feminine allegorization for the feminist writer: the relationship between Corinne and Italy so enigmatically foregrounded in the novel's title can quite properly be described as allegorical, and, as Madelyn Gutwirth has shown, in portraying Corinne as a modern-day goddess, Staël knowingly appropriates the iconographic attributes of the Nike figure so popular during the first Empire to her own ends.[30] But Corinne's triumph is short-lived, and the feminine allegory is soon recoded in a dysphoric mode: as Corinne's love affair with the Scottish peer, Lord Nelvil, precipitates her from her divine pinnacle to an all too human end, her erotic victimage at Lord Nelvil's hands comes to allegorize in a feminine form the political fate of Italy under Napoleon's regime.

What we might call the *secondary feminine allegory* in *Corinne* suggests why the first cannot hold, cannot be sustained: it is because primary feminine allegory is grounded in the idealization of woman, which is to say in the denial of the contingencies of her body and its history, the erasure of her lived experience under bourgeois and imperialist patriarchy. If feminine allegorization served in the dominant male culture to consolidate the power of the state and the newly enfranchised middle class, for post-Revolutionary French women writers such as Staël but also Sand (see *Lélia*), allegory could never be but a failed form of representation, a representation of a Revolution that failed them.[31]

Before the Castle: Women, Commodities, and Modernity in Au Bonheur des Dames

A poor, plain, but modest and plucky young orphan arrives before a sort of castle ruled by a master richly endowed with charm and power. In this castle, a veritable labyrinth full of traps, the young woman must face a series of trials and endure all manner of moral and physical suffering. Among the trials she must face in this terrifying place is a series of traumatic encounters with other women, including a first wife who haunts the place and a wealthy, beautiful, and powerful rival who is apparently loved by the master. At one point, worn down by her suffering, the young woman leaves this damned and fascinating place for a sort of exile in the wilderness. In the end she returns to the castle and, having resisted the master's advances, ends up mastering him and becoming the mistress of the castle.

I have just retraced the initiatory trajectory of the female protagonist of Charlotte Brontë's *Jane Eyre*, but the story of Jane Eyre is also that of Denise Baudu, the heroine of Emile Zola's *Au Bonheur des Dames (The Ladies' Paradise)*. *Jane Eyre* is not only the paradigm of the female *bildungsroman*, it is also the paradigmatic example of an Anglo-American literary genre which specifically targets a female audience, the "gothic." One need only perform a few slight transpositions—replace Mr. Rochester's manor (Thornfield) by Octave Mouret's department store ("Au Bonheur des Dames"), the young governess Jane Eyre by the young saleswoman Denise Baudu, the little ward Adèle by the two young brothers (Jean and Pépé)—to reveal in Zola's novel the most stereotypical narrative schemata of this most stereotypical genre and further to classify this novel among the gothic novels. It is only a matter of noting the characteristic elements of the genre, the very young, innocent, and virginal heroine, the seductive hero, and the identification of the young woman with a first wife who died under mysterious circumstances (perhaps at the hands of her husband), to recover in degraded form the clichés of the genre. It is not, however, so easy to distinguish the gothic genre from the genre known as the "romance," which also draws its inspiration from Jane Eyre, or from the sentimental novel, whose prototype is Samuel Richardson's Pamela. Beneath the features of Denise and Octave one can make out those of that eminently romantic couple, Jane and Rochester, but also the older and more bourgeois lineaments of Pamela and her master and future husband, M. B. Nevertheless, for convenience's sake, I will group these three genres as well as Au Bonheur des Dames under the rubric "gothic."[1]

The demonstration of the presence in this futurist novel (or at least turned toward the future) of a plot and a set of characters drawn from genres which have continued to exert their fascination over the general audience, and especially the mass female readership, from the dawn of modernity to our own postmodernity is easily accomplished. Therein lies neither the difficulty, nor the interest of the comparison I have just made. They are located elsewhere: the question that confronts us is to know why—and my assumption is that Zola is writing a gothic novel unwittingly—this updating of the roman noir as well as the sentimental novel occurs. And this question raises another: how does Zola inflect the stereotypes and renew the laws of a genre he seems to reinvent?

If it is easy to make out behind the shiny facade of the department store the terrifying architectonics of the gothic château, this does not in any way signify that the transposition Zola effects is not decisive, not to say brilliant. Because, as a great number of recent studies have shown, the gothic novel is particularly well suited to representing the entrance of women onto the scene of modernity. As Eve Sedgwick remarks: "There has been a history of useful critical attempts to look to the Gothic for exploration of the position of women in relation to the changing shapes of patriarchal domination."[2] In its darkest version, the gothic—I am thinking here of Horace Walpole's The Castle of Otranto or Ann Radcliffe's The Mysteries of Udolpho—came into being at the moment when in England the industrial Revolution and the rise of the bourgeoisie determined the separation of male and female spheres. According to Kate Ellis, the author of a recent book on the gothic, the principal stake of this novelistic genre is precisely the domestic hearth, the home whose idealization goes hand in hand with the exclusion of bourgeois women from the world of labor and their great confinement between the walls of the apartment, indeed of the bourgeois house.[3] But if, as the saying goes, "A man's home is his castle," the same does not hold for women, or rather, for them, the home sweet home turns out to be a very special kind of castle—a haunted one. The castle in the gothic novel would then be a nightmarish representation of the domestic sphere that women are charged with ridding of all dangers and whose perverse mores they are assigned to purify, those vestiges of an aristocratic order in complete decline, the very sphere where they are to ground their power. Paradoxically, they will have to conquer at great cost this house-castle to which they are anyhow confined. For the female protagonist it is the site of trial and triumph; as Ellen Moers remarks, from Ann Radcliffe on, the gothic is "a novel in which the central figure is a young woman who is simultaneously persecuted victim and courageous heroine."[4]

It is not hard to see just how the department store as represented by Zola functions like an oversized bourgeois home: there is the reassuring proliferation of living rooms, the dream-like multiplication of lingerie, the fabulous extension of the patriarchal figure's power. It is also not hard to see how Denise's role will be to humanize this place, to align the store's domestic vocation with the new, allegedly feminine moral qualities. What is more, and this is another aspect of the genre's ideological work, idealizing the house is a way of promoting the family, and everything is designed here to reinforce the bourgeois family—and not simply through the attention Mouret devotes to children and their mothers. At the outset, it is true, the department store is denounced as a threat to the family, and traditional patriarchal commerce, represented by the Baudu family, which will be the new regime's principle victim.[5] But in the end, Octave must submit to Denise in order to perpetuate his line, to keep the business in the family, to restore the family, but in a form more adequate to triumphant capitalism. That is one of the meanings of the legend of the first wife, Mme Hédouin, whose blood irrigates the store's foundations and whose portrait functions as a family portrait in the castle's furnishings. As Michelle Perrot reminds us in the section of *A History of Private Life* titled "The Family Triumphant": "Business history is primarily a family history," and above all, "The founders of large department stores raised the 'happy household' to the pinnacle of honor."[6] The threat constituted by this place of temptation and perdition, where women's sexual appetites run wild, must be checked by a moralization of equal strength, a domestication of masculine sexuality.

The rise of the gothic novel corresponds to a critical moment in the history of the relationships between men and women in a modern Europe in the throes of industrialization, just as its eclipse corresponds to a period where these relationships seem to achieve stability under the hegemony of a bourgeois and patriarchal regime. It follows that all updating of this genre corresponds to a new crisis in these relationships; but in this particular instance it is not the one that one thinks it is, because if up to now I have emphasized all that makes the department store function like a disproportionately enlarged bourgeois home, I would like now to emphasize the specificity of the department store, all that distinguishes it and even opposes it to the home where the rituals of private life unfold.

Indeed, if Zola spontaneously recreates the schemas of this worn-out genre, it is to mark another mutation, to speak of another crisis, to allow anxieties to surface other than those of the inventors of the genre, preoccupied as they were by the passage of a social order dominated by the aristocracy to a bourgeois social order. What differentiates the department store—home from the castle-house is, first and foremost, that the department store is the place where the industrial revolution with its mass production of objects culminates: what is emphasized in the department store is not the confinement of women to the bourgeois home, but rather the invasion of this home by the world of merchandise, and especially the novelties produced by the fashion system.[7] The mutation that is made visible here is the transformation of the good wife and mother into a good consumer. But that is not all (and I shall return to this point): there is something else. It is through the door of the department store that women set out to conquer public space. Elaine Abelson points out: "In the asymmetry of the Victorian world shopping becomes a woman's natural public sphere."[8] One could then speak of the department store as a transitional space, which finally opens the way to the liberation of women.

But what women? Up to now I have spoken of women in general; it is now time to distinguish clearly—as Zola does—upper-class women, the clients, from lower-class women, the saleswomen. In point of fact there is no neat overlap either between the clientele and the upper classes or between the store's employees and the lower classes, since there are women of modest means in the crowd of customers, and the saleswomen especially constitute "a vague nameless class, something between a working girl and a middle-class lady" (p. 138). In this regard one might speak of a sort of third class, as one does or used to do of a third sex, or still, according to Zola, of a sort of neutral class, for the loss of social markers goes hand in hand with an ambiguous, louche sexual status: "The worst of all was their neutral, badly-defined position, between the shop-woman and the lady. Thrown in the midst of luxury, often without any previous instruction, they formed a singular, nameless class" (p. 276). What nevertheless tends to reinforce the difference between these two large social categories represented by Denise and Mme Desforges, is that for the bourgeois lady the department store constitutes a protected public space at the heart of the metropolis, whereas for the lower-middle-class woman that Denise is, there is but a slight difference between the aggressions she endures in the street and those of which she is a victim at her workplace. As Griselda Pollock has shown, the urban space of modernity is laid out on two grids; modernity appears in the spaces where the differences of class and gender intersect:

> The spaces of modernity are where class and gender interface in critical ways, in that they are the spaces of sexual exchange. The significant spaces of modernity are neither simply those of masculinity, nor are they those of femininity which are as much the spaces of modernity for being the negative of the streets and bars. They are, as the canonical works indicate, the marginal or interstitial spaces where the fields of the masculine and feminine intersect and structure sexuality within a classed order.[9]

Consequently one could say that whereas bourgeois women find in the department store the equivalent of the passages dear to the flâneurs, those emblematic figures of male modernity, that is, a protected space midway between the house and the street, the same does not hold true for the women belonging to other classes, for whom the department store is but another version of the street: be she inside or outside, by the very fact of her subaltern social status Denise is constantly prey to the masculine gaze and desire. Pursued as she is, both in the street and her room by an omnipresent voyeurism, for Denise the department store offers no asylum. There are no passages for the poor woman; in Second Empire Paris, but also Third Republic Paris, a woman who does not enjoy the status of a bourgeoise is prohibited from "flânerie."

> Then, her neighbor, the baker, had shown a disposition to annoy her; he never came home till the morning, and would lay in wait for her, as she went to fetch her water; he even made holes in the wall to watch her washing herself, so that she was obliged to hang her clothes against the wall. But she suffered still more from the annoyances of the street, the continual persecution of the passers-by . . . the men pursued her to the very end of the dark passage. . . . (p. 163)

And Denise, longing to escape the looks of all these men . . . (p. 46)

They smiled. Denise had turned very pale, she felt ashamed at being thus turned into a machine, which they were examining and joking about freely . . . she felt herself violated, exposed to all their looks, without defence. (pp. 102–103)

. . . she felt herself disrobed by all these men. (p. 261)

Like so many other female protagonists in Zola, like her unfortunate cousin, Geneviève Baudu, Denise is stripped bare by the materialist and sexist society that surrounds her. The stripping of women also affects characters like Renée in *La Curée*. For though she only circulates in protected spaces which shelter her from the male gaze, the bourgeois woman does not, for all that, escape the eroticization of the space of modernity, which invades everything, which transforms everything that is for sale into an object of desire, and all that is desirable into an object of exchange. That is the significance of kleptomania, a new, almost exclusively female perversion whose rise accompanies the development of the department store.[10] Now, what fascinates the clinicians and jurists of the period is that this new perversion—which is the female equivalent of male fetishism—is reserved not just for women, but especially for bourgeois women. It is precisely because the kleptomaniac does not steal out of economic necessity that she is distinct from the average shoplifter, that her theft is a matter for the clinic and not for the court. Kleptomania is a gratuitous, disinterested act; thus Mme Boves "stole for the pleasure of stealing, as one loves for the pleasure of loving" (p. 374). Kleptomania for the bourgeoise is equivalent to prostitution for the woman of the people: of course one steals for pleasure, whereas the other sells herself out of need; one acts in secret, while the other exhibits herself in public; one escapes the law, while the other is harshly subject to it. Both are, however, victims of the same ideology of gender, which reduces women to their anatomical destiny, since the pathology of the department-store shoplifters is gynecological in nature: pregnancy, menstruation, and menopause are considered by Zola as well as by the scientific experts as the principal pathologizing factors of this perversion, this misdemeanor.

Neither a woman who sells herself nor a woman who steals, neither a prostitute nor a kleptomaniac, because of her honesty[11] Denise seems to evade the system, to escape the straitjacket of female sexual identity, if not of the hold of the invasive male gaze. In fact, Denise will be but the exception that confirms the rule: her story is that of a coming to Femininity, a revalorization of the myth of the "eternal feminine." And that is perhaps the case for all the heroines of this novelistic genre, whence the fascination it exerts on its female readers: in other words, it is not solely because these novels satisfy desires, fulfill regressive female fantasies, but also because they make femininity itself seductive—they enact feminization[12]—that they enjoy such success with women. The story of Denise will be that of the transformation of a "little savage" or of "an impossible girl" into a desiring and desirable woman. How does this transformation occur, and is it really a transformation? Wouldn't it be more accurate to speak of a construction? This is precisely the doubt that pervades Zola's novel, for in this tale of feminization, that is, of Denise's progressive narcissization, the novelist seems to hesitate between two logically incompatible positions: on the one hand it is as if Denise's femininity were essential and needed only a catalyst to come to light; on the other hand, it is as if this femininity were a pure construction, an effect produced by her entry into the department store, Mouret's greatest success:

> He treated her like a child, with more pity than kindness, his curiosity in matters feminine simply awakened by the troubling, womanly charm which he felt *springing up* in this poor and awkward child. (p. 108; emphasis added)

> But under these rumours which gradually *awoke* the woman in her . . . (p. 120; emphasis added)

> He paid no more attention to her now, only addressing a few words to her from time to time, to give her a few hints about her toilet, and to joke with her, as an *impossible girl, a little savage almost like a boy, of whom he would never make a coquette, notwithstanding all his knowledge of women.* (p. 120; emphasis added)

> Was this little savage going to *turn out* a pretty girl? (p. 135; emphasis added)

> Her ideas were ripening, a woman's grace was developing out of the *savage child* newly arrived from Valognes. (p. 176; emphasis added)

At the end of the nineteenth century, the gothic novel serves to reveal the extreme fragility of sexual difference, indeed of femininity, which turns out in the end to be but an object of consumption like any other that one purchases in the department store and that one can return like an uncomfortable or ill-fitting garment. In the bazaar that the great industrial city has become, at the very moment when women begin to launch out to conquer their place in the public sphere, femininity (like the masculinity which depends on it) must constantly be reinvented, adorned with new attractions, for fear that the universal equivalent that circulates everywhere will dissolve the differences that structure bourgeois society, and that the fiction of a natural order of heterosexuality (as of an immutable economic order) will be laid bare.

Endpiece

Depression in the Nineties

I n the marketplace of ideas there is no room and no time for mourning and melancholia. Mourning is viewed as somehow shameful, not to say retrograde. Furthermore, in the age of postmodernist "waning of affect,"[1] those who wish to bring back affects such as depression are not viewed as very good company, unless of course their name happens to be Julia Kristeva.[2] I want in what follows to transgress this taboo on mourning and speak of depression, even death. Clearly there is a lot to be depressed about in these twilight days of the bloodiest of centuries, especially when one is, as I am, of a melancholic disposition. But I have no intention to invoke either Prozac or Zoloft or even the substantial clinical and autobiographical literature of and on depression. My aim is rather to speak of depression as a condition internal to academia, if indeed such a notion of academia as having an inside neatly marked off from an outside makes sense in this age of tabloid theory. Perhaps it never did. I want to speak as someone who used to write, and write with a certain gusto, about gender and fiction, but who was sidelined by illness for a couple of years and woke up like a female Rip van Winkle to find herself plunged into a state of deep confusion over both terms *gender* and *narrative*. I want to focus here on what I have found professionally depressing about the nineties: we, the now middle-aged feminist critics of the seventies and eighties, have simultaneously lost the two pillars of feminist criticism as we knew it: narrative and gender, which is precisely why we are being called upon to remap them. The old mapping, or mapping of gender onto narrative, which assumed both the stability of gender and its privilege as a category of difference on the one hand, and the centrality of narrative as a mode of cultural expression on the other, no longer holds.

My contention is that the current work on gender has contributed little to our understanding of narrative, which flourished most recently in the age of structural poetics and psychoanalysis as exemplified by *Reading for the Plot*, by Peter Brooks, who, of course, had no use for gender. If narrativity has been replaced by performativity in queer theory, it is in part because traditional teleological narrative is viewed as irremediably heterosexist. Coming at it from another angle, in the era of cultural studies, the novel has lost its integrity, its spatiality, its defining temporality: Foucault, whose writings have been so central both to queer theory and cultural studies, offers no protocol for reading fiction, no theory of narrative. One may, following Foucault, study the discourse on various pathologies[3] in nineteenth-century French fiction and medical texts, but in the process fiction loses its distinctive formal properties and is reduced to a series of scenes. At a time when the grand narratives have been pronounced dead, it is in fact the narratives of fiction which have vanished in the chop shop, where people go to furnish themselves with spare narrative parts.

In the current array of approaches, only one seems wedded to narrative and that is postcolonialist criticism, as evidenced by Homi Bhabha's *Nation and Narration* and Edward Said's *Culture and Imperialism*, where Said writes:

> narrative is crucial to my argument here, my basic point being that stories are at the heart of what explorers and novelists say about strange regions of the world; they also become the method colonized people use to assert their own identity and the existence of their own history. . . . The grand narratives of emancipation and enlightenment mobilized people in the colonial world to rise up and throw off imperial subjection; in the process, many Europeans and Americans were also stirred by these stories and their protagonists, and they too fought for new narratives of equality and human community.[4]

The crucial link that is established here is not so much between narrative and imperialism, but between narrative and enlightenment; emancipation is the key word here, and it resonates significantly with this declaration of principles in the jointly authored "Editor's Note," which introduces *Materialist Feminism*, a recent issue of *South Atlantic Quarterly* edited by Toril Moi and Janice Radway:

> Narratives of liberation have inspired feminists everywhere to work for historical change. We believe that feminist narratives of liberation can—and do—inform different feminist projects without unifying them under the sign of a single, coercive identity, community, or name. Yet all feminist narratives of liberation still have one thing in common: the

assumption that the aim of feminism is not to preserve feminism in the name of some putative body or group of "women," but to abolish patriarchy.[5]

What these preliminary remarks suggest is that what may ultimately be at stake in the concurrent troubling of both gender and narrative is the vexed question of the Enlightenment legacy. I can only gesture in that direction, however, because I want to evoke from the perspective of depression two discourses that combined to provide critics with what are, to my mind, as yet unsurpassed devices for reading and theorizing narratives: I refer to deconstruction and psychoanalysis. I offer this brief reading of Mme de Staël's Corinne as an allegory of the death of feminist criticism, the very one I mourn.

My initial claim is outlandish: because of the disparity between the chronology of events and the narrative organization of the material, when Corinne first appears in the novel that bears her name, she is already dead, a victim of patriarchy, the ghost of gender. In other words, Corinne is neither, as the narrator suggests, a mere retelling of the archetypal story of Sheherazade, who enlists narrative in the deferral of death, nor, by the same token, a reworking of what Peter Brooks has called Freud's masterplot, the dawdlings and detours of the death-driven Beyond the Pleasure Principle.[6] Death in Corinne is not the telos to be avoided but the disaster that has already occurred, which sets the narrative in motion and brings it finally to its foreordained conclusion, the physical enactment of a symbolic death.

From the very first page of the novel the prominence of death in this deeply melancholic early romantic novel is made clear, but it is not, as one might expect, the heroine's, or any other woman's for that matter, but that of the hero's father. When we first encounter Oswald Lord Nelvil, he is on a journey to Italy for medical reasons: "The most personal of all griefs, the loss of a father, had provoked his illness."[7] Implicit in this phrase is a maxim which goes something like: his father's death is man's greatest sorrow. When, as is the case for Oswald, that irreparable loss is overlayed with guilt, then the disease is, as we in time discover, incurable. Afflicted with a bad case of what Margaret Waller has wittily called "the male malady" (a.k.a. the mâle de siècle),[8] Oswald is a severely depressed Oedipus. It is in this state that he encounters Corinne, who is at the very pinnacle of her success. I am referring, of course, to the celebrated scene of her crowning at the Capitol, to which I shall return. From that moment on, Corinne takes it upon herself to cure the unhappy Oswald. This is tourism as therapy: she will cure him by making him see Italy and its beauties, for, like Oedipus at Colonnus, Oswald in Italy is blind, sightless: "Oswald crossed the Marches and the Papal States as far as Rome without noticing anything"; "he took no notice whatever of the ancient places traversed by Corinne's chariot" (C, p. 22).

But above all, to see Italy is to see Corinne; the cure for Oswald's undone grief-work is gazing at Corinne. Gazing at Corinne is a moral imperative for Oswald, for as the prince Castel-Forte enjoins him: "Behold Corinne."

What does it mean to "behold" Corinne? Corinne, when Oswald first sees her, is the picture of health; at the height of her powers she is the most animated of heroines. It is this animation that I want to hold up to scrutiny, for it is illusory; the solar Corinne conceals a cold lunar landscape. Hers is the peculiar effulgence of a star long-dead, twinkling in a galaxy far away. We are here in the temporality of the always already, and in this strange temporality the reading of the novel that would have Corinne waste away as a result of Oswald's craven abandonment is a partial reading that is too ready to accept conventional causality as its organizing principle, that is too quick to charge the male protagonist—absent a male author—with murder. It forgets one of the crucial lessons of Lacan's mirror stage, the impossibility of representing the body in pieces except from the perspective of the body as whole. The disjointed body of the infant can only be reconstructed from the vantage point of an imaginary identity. Corinne must reach the pinnacle of success for her underlying inexistence to become visible. Stardom—and Corinne, the performance artist, is nothing if not a star—is ghostly, a state of haunting.

Let us recall that when Corinne at last provides the key to the enigma of her identity, her missing patronym, she makes the following crucial avowal: after her father Lord Edgermond's death in England, she is driven into exile by her stepmother, who strikes the following bargain with her: " . . . should you decide on a course of action that will dishonor you in public opinion, you owe it to your family to change your name and pass for dead" (C, p. 267).

If by virtue of its history Italy is the land of ruins and crumbling tomb-stones, England by virtue of its rigid ideology of separate spheres is at least for women the "land of the living dead" (MM, pp. 76–79).[9] English society is a cemetery where a brilliant public woman like Corinne can only be buried alive, racked by nightmares—"perchance to dream." To leave England is to rise, Lazarus-like, from the dead, yet at the same time to leave England is to leave behind more than the lifeless letters that make up one's patronym; rather one leaves one's mortal envelope; to return to Italy is to (re)enter the land of the living but in spectral form. The extraordinary Corinne that Oswald sees is, then, posthumous, not literally a dead female body, but a dead female soul: "It is as if I were a shade still wanting to remain on earth when the light of day, the approach of the living, compel it to disappear," she writes when she is wasting away (C, p. 371). She does not become a ghost because she was abandoned; rather, she was abandoned precisely because of her ghostliness.

The death of feminist criticism, of what has been characterized, following Alice Jardine, as gynesis, has placed some of us early feminist critics in a common postmodern predicament: we are, as it were, haunted by our own past work, caught up in a spectral moment. What Derrida has called the "logic of spectrality"[10] affects us as it affected Corinne. Gender is now being mapped onto other narratives, deprivileged as a form of difference, when it is not being abandoned altogether as what Joan Scott called, not so long ago, a "useful category of . . . analysis."[11] It is no accident that a number of early gynocritics have moved in the direction of personal memoirs and/or holocaust studies, two modes of critical writing that fulfill the need for narratives that redeem the past. If feminist literary criticism is to have a future—and that is a big if—if it is to rise from its death, then gender, however reconfigured, must remain an essential component of our study of narrative, and narrative, however contested by currently dominant forms of criticism, must be retained lest storytelling be lost as an essential meaning-giving and, I will risk the word, universal means of making sense of one's hopes and desires, one's ideals and one's despair, not to say one's depression.

French Feminism Is a Universalism

In the course of writing this essay I have incurred some very special debts. First and foremost to Barbara Herrnstein-Smith, colleague and neighbor, who read an early draft of this essay with exemplary rigor and generosity, even though I would venture to say she disagreed with every word in it, including, to borrow a phrase from Mary MacCarthy, "if, and, and but." My second debt is to Ellen Rooney, who provided the original occasion for this essay, albeit a sad one: the first Roger H. Henkle Memorial Lecture at Brown University, Spring 1992. My third is to my very supportive students and somewhat more critical colleagues at the School of Criticism and Theory, Summer 1994. Toril Moi read the piece in its penultimate form with her customary sharpness and decisiveness. Evelyn Enders and Ieme van der Poel provided remarkably civilized forums in which to present the short version of this essay. And throughout its many avatars, Linda Orr promoted this text with admirable collegiality and friendship.

1   Max Horkheimer and Theodor W. Adorno, *Dialectic of Enlightenment*, trans. Joan Cumming (New York: Continuum, 1993).

2   See Julia Kristeva, *Strangers to Ourselves*, trans. Leon S. Roudiez (New York: Columbia University Press, 1994), and Ernesto Laclau, "Universalism, Particularism, and the Question of Identity," *October* 61, Special Issue, *The Identity in Question* (Summer 1992): 87. See also Marc Shell, *Children of the Earth: Literature, Politics and Nationhood* (New York: Oxford University Press, 1993).

3   For a representative selection of essays written on the interface between feminism and postmodernism, see Linda J. Nicholson, ed., *Feminism / Postmodernism* (New York: Routledge, 1990). See also Linda Alcoff and Elizabeth Potter, eds., *Feminist Epistemologies* (New York: Routledge, 1993).

Note that I am fully aware that my use of these terms, especially *the universal* and *universalism*, will seem to some readers excessively slippery. To a large extent, that slipperiness is inevitable: at least since Kant—*toujours lui*—universalism is both an aesthetic value and a political category. Furthermore, as Ernesto Laclau elegantly demonstrates in "Subject of Politics, Politics of the Subject," *differences* 7, no. 1 (1995): (forthcoming), the universal is an "empty signifier," an empty place, which is filled by changing and contesting "concrete particulars."

4 Pierre Bourdieu, "Pour un corporatisme de l'universel," *Les Règles de l'art: Genèse et structure du champ littéraire* (Paris: Seuil, 1992), p. 467.

5 For a historian's view of this French "missionary universalism," see K. Steven Vincent, "National Consciousness, Nationalism, and Exclusion: Reflections on the French Case," *Historical Reflections / Réflexions Historiques* 19, no. 3 (1993): 1–17.

6 Tzvetan Todorov, *On Human Diversity: Nationalism, Racism, and Exoticism in French Thought,* trans. Catherine Porter (Cambridge: Harvard University Press, 1994), pp. 1–12.

7 One of the responses of nationalistic cultural critics caught up in the veritable "crisis of the universal" that has in recent years permeated French political and philosophical discourses is to project their own universalism onto the United States, as though French and American universalisms were simply mirror images of each other. Thus, in his introduction to the French translation of Robert Hughes's recent book, Pascal Brukner writes: "She (America) is a particular culture which seeks to pass itself off as universal civilization" (*La Culture gnangnan* [Paris: arléa, 1994], p. 9).

8 Pierre Bourdieu, "Deux impérialismes de l'universel," in *L'Amérique des Français,* ed. Christine Fauré and Tom Bishop (Paris: Editions Bourin, 1992), p. 150. All translations are mine except where otherwise noted.

9 Paul Valéry, *French Thought and Art,* as cited by Jacques Derrida in *The Other Heading: Reflections on Today's Europe,* trans. Pascale-Anne Brault (Bloomington: Indiana University Press, 1992), p. 74.

10 Léopold Sédar Senghor, *Liberté 1: Négritude et humanisme* (Paris: Seuil, 1964), p. 98. My thanks to Keith Walker for bringing this quotation to my attention. The translation is his.

11 Toril Moi, *Simone de Beauvoir: The Making of an Intellectual Woman* (Oxford: Blackwell, 1994), p. 195.

12 Simone de Beauvoir, *The Second Sex,* trans. H. M. Parshley (New York: Vintage, 1974), p. 793.

13 In an article that covers much of the same ground as I do in these introductory remarks, Pauline Johnson argues that the feminist repudiation of the Enlightenment is based on an inadequate, indeed erroneous, understanding of that universalizing philosophy, one that fails to distinguish between two forms of enlightenment feminism, that of Mary Astell and that of Mary Wollstonecraft: "The argument is that current attempts to sever feminism's ideological ties with the Enlightenment rest on a basic misinterpretation of the character and spirit of Enlightenment" ("Feminism and the Enlightenment," *Radical Philosophy* 63 [Spring 1993]: 3–4). On feminism's fraught relationship to universality, see also Anne Phillips's fine article, "Universal Pretensions in Political Thought," in *Destabilizing Theory: Contemporary Feminist Debates,* ed. Michèle Barrett and Anne Phillips (Stanford: Stanford University Press, 1992), pp. 10–30, and Iris Young, "Impartiality and the Civic Public: Some Implications of the Feminist Critiques of Moral and Political Theory," in *Feminism as Critique: On the Politics of Gender,* ed. Seyla Benhabib and Drucilla Cornell (Minneapolis: University of Minnesota Press, 1986), pp. 56–76.

14 For more on the historical relationship between French feminism and the Enlightenment, see Joan W. Scott, "Universalism and the History of Feminism," *differences* 7, no. 1 (1995). This article is adapted from her *"Women Who Have Only Paradoxes to Offer": French Feminists, 1789–1944* (Boston: Harvard University Press, forthcoming 1995).

15 I take this cautious assertion by one of the editors of the co-edited anthology, *Feminism Beside Itself,* ed. Diane Elam and Robyn Wiegman, to represent this position: "It may be necessary to reexamine the terms in which we want to describe the work that feminism has to do, for while it is apparent that there is still a great deal of work to be done, it is by no means

evident that the Enlightenment provides the only language in which that work can be discussed" ("Contingencies," right column, p. 5).

16   Monique Wittig, "Homo Sum," in *The Straight Mind and Other Essays* (Boston: Beacon, 1992), p. 46.

17   Rosi Braidotti, "On the Female Feminist Subject, or: From 'She-self' to 'She-other,'" in *Beyond Equality and Difference: Citizenship, Feminist Politics and Female Subjectivity*, ed. Gisella Bock and Susan James (London: Routledge, 1988), p. 190.

18   Ernesto Laclau, "Universalism," p. 87. For my purposes, this is by far the most significant contribution to the rethinking of the particularism-universalism paradigm in the special issue in which it appears, and while I cannot take on board its Hegelian historicization of their relationship from the ancients through Christianity to the present in all its complexity, I shall draw on it heavily throughout what follows.

19   Joan Scott, "Multiculturalism and the Politics of Identity," *October* 61 (Summer 1992): 14–15.

20   A similar point is made by David Palumbo-Liu, who asks: "Should we abandon [the] Universal at precisely the moment more and more marginalized peoples are accessing it positively and contestively" ("Universalisms and Minority Culture," *differences* 7, no. 1 [Spring 1995]). What many of those who might otherwise wish to jettison the universal and its encumbering baggage in the name of a general abandonment of the Enlightenment are confronted with is that those very constituencies in whose name they condemn the Universal espouse it whether in a new or even unregenerate form. See, for example, Jacqueline Rose, who, in a subtle and nuanced article on the African novelist Bessie Head, concludes that "*universality is not yet a dispensable term*" ("On the 'Universality' of Madness: Bessie Head's *A Question of Power*," *Critical Inquiry* 20 [Spring 1994]: 402). The reason why the universal cannot simply be relegated to the dustheap of history is that it is crucial to Bessie Head's writing: "That movement from the personal, to the historical, to the universal is, I think, central to Bessie Head's writing" (p. 411).

21   Barbara Christian, *Black Feminist Criticism: Perspectives on Black Women Writers* (Berkeley: Pergamon Press, 1985), p. 160. Note that Christian leapfrogs over the assertion of the claim of African American women to universality to a different, more humanist claim: African American women writers deserve to be recognized for their humanity.

22   Patricia J. Williams, *The Alchemy of Race and Rights: Diary of a Law Professor* (Cambridge: Harvard University Press, 1991), p. 164.

23   Moi, *Simone de Beauvoir*, pp. 191–192.

24   Nancy Fraser and Linda J. Nicholson, "Social Criticism without Philosophy," in *Feminism/Postmodernism*, ed. Linda J. Nicholson, (New York: Routledge, 1990).

25   Elizabeth Grosz, "Sexual Difference and the Problem of Essentialism," reprinted in *The Essential Difference*, ed. Naomi Schor and Elizabeth Weed (Bloomington: University of Indiana Press, 1994), p. 85.

26   Important distinctions must be made between the status of the universal as an aesthetic category among African American intellectuals and African nationalist or nativist intellectuals. For the nativists, according to Anthony Appiah, universalism is to be rejected because it is (rightly) perceived as an imperative fraudulently imposed from the outside, but at the same time nativism is to be rejected because it posits (falsely) the separability of the inside and the outside, whereas the two are in fact tightly coiled up together: modern African literature—and here I follow Appiah's no doubt deliberate use of the universalizing singular—is always already entangled with European modernity, including the abstract uni-

versals of the Enlightenment. More telling still is Appiah's repeated demonstration of the ways that nativist particularism "is itself covertly universalist," in that it accepts and reproduces the ways that European and American academics frame the debates over literary value and literary theory (Anthony Appiah, In My Father's House: Africa in the Philosophy of Culture [Oxford: Oxford University Press, 1992], p. 60). For another view of the same issues see James Snead, "European Pedigrees/African Contagions: Nationality, Narrative, and Communality in Tutuola, Achebe, and Reed," in Nation and Narration, ed. Homi K. Bhabha (New York: Routledge, 1990), pp. 231–249.

27   Judith Butler, Gender Trouble: Feminism and the Subversion of Identity (New York: Routledge, 1990), p. 3.

28   Phillips, "Universal Pretensions," p. 13.

29   See Diana Fuss on "politics" as the essence of feminism in Essentially Speaking: Feminism, Nature and Difference (New York: Routledge, 1989), pp. 36–37.

30   Denise Riley, Am I that Name? Feminism and the Category of 'Women' in History (Minneapolis: University of Minnesota Press, 1988), p. 112.

31   Butler, Gender, p. 15.

32   This is not the place to delve into Foucault's relationship to the Enlightenment, but see Geoffrey Galt Harpham, "So . . . What Is Enlightenment? An Inquisition into Modernity," Critical Inquiry 20, no. 3 (Spring 1994), esp. pp. 524–535.

33   Judith Butler's essay, "Critically Queer," was originally published in GLQ: A Journal of Lesbian and Gay Studies 1, no. 1 (1993): pp. 17–32, and is reprinted in slightly revised form in Bodies that Matter: On the Discursive Limits of "Sex" (New York: Routledge, 1993). The next citations are drawn from the earlier version of the text.

34   Bodies that Matter, p. 229. See also Butler in October, where she again backtracks, moving to more of an "as if" position: "My own view is that it is imperative to assert identities at the same time that it is crucial to interrogate the exclusionary operations by which they are constituted" (p. 109).

35   Judith Butler, "Contingent Foundations," in Feminists Theorize the Political, ed. Judith Butler and Joan W. Scott (New York: Routledge, 1992), p. 7.

36   Nancy K. Miller, Getting Personal: Feminist Occasions and Other Autobiographical Acts (New York: Routledge, 1992), p. 126.

37   Ellie Bulkin, "An interview with Adrienne Rich," as quoted by Bonnie Zimmerman, in The New Feminist Criticism, ed. Elaine Showalter (New York: Pantheon, 1985), p. 219.

38   Cf. Cornel West, "The New Cultural Politics of Difference," in Out There: Marginalization and Contemporary Culture, ed. Russell Ferguson et al. (New York: New Museum of Contemporary Art, 1990): "Distinctive features of the new cultural politics of difference are to trash the monolithic and homogeneous in the name of diversity, multiplicity and heterogeneity; to reject the abstract, general and universal in light of the concrete, specific and particular; and to historicize, contextualize and pluralize by highlighting the contingent, provisional, variable, tentative, shifting and changing" (p. 19). See also by West, "Diverse New World," in Debating P. C., ed. Paul Berman (New York: Laurel, 1992), pp. 326–332.

39   The participants were Joan Scott, Judith Butler, Cornel West, Chantal Mouffe, Ernesto Laclau, Homi Bhabha, Jacques Rancière, Andreas Huyssen, Stanley Aronowitz, and E. E. Smith. Butler's paper, however, is not included in the proceedings, although her comments in the discussion are recorded.

40   In Gender Trouble, Judith Butler is a notable exception to this rule in that her training as a philosopher does not seem to entail any felt need on her part to rethink the universal,

which is relentlessly targeted for destruction whether as an attribute of feminist identity politics, of essentialism (p. 14), Wittig's neohumanism, or Lacan and Lévi-Strauss's structuralism. And yet she notes: "To claim that a law [incest taboo] is universal is not to claim that it operates as a dominant framework within which social relations takes place. Indeed, to claim the universal presence of a law in social life is in no way to claim that it exists in every aspect of the social form under consideration; minimally, it means that it exists and operates somewhere in every social form" (p. 76).

41 Michael Walzer, "Two Kinds of Universalism," in *The Tanner Lectures on Human Values* 11 1990, ed. Grethe B. Peterson (Salt Lake City: University of Utah Press, 1990), p. 509.

42 Cf. Paul Gilroy on the significance of Hegel for "intellectuals formed by the black Atlantic" (*The Black Atlantic: Modernity and Double Consciousness* [Cambridge: Harvard University Press, 1993], p. 54).

43 Luce Irigaray, *J'aime à toi: Esquisse d'une félicité dans l'histoire* (Paris: Grasset, 1992), p. 31.

44 Margaret Whitford, *Luce Irigaray: Philosophy in the Feminine* (London: Routledge, 1991), p. 3.

45 For more on the Rousseau-Hegel connection, see Carole Pateman, *The Disorder of Women: Democracy, Feminism and Political Theory* (Stanford: Stanford University Press, 1989).

46 Luce Irigaray, *Sexes and Genealogies*, trans. Gillian C. Gill (New York: Columbia University Press, 1993), p. 147.

47 Irigaray, *J'aime*, p. 65.

48 Ibid., p. 45.

49 See Jacques Derrida, *Glas*, trans. John P. Leavey Jr. and Richard Rand (Lincoln: University of Nebraska Press, 1984), for his enlightening comment on this passage: "A stranger to the city as such, the woman guards an immediate relationship to the universal. She remains glued, limed in the natural, in sensibility. The man, on the contrary, dissociates and mediatizes as a member of the city, a universal actor . . . " (p. 164).

50 G.W.F. Hegel, *Phenomenology of Spirit*, trans. A. V. Miller (Oxford: Oxford University Press, 1977), pp. 274–275.

51 Irigaray, *J'aime*, p. 45.

52 Gayatri Spivak, "French Feminism Revisited: Ethics and Politics," in *Feminists Theorize the Political*, ed. Judith Butler and Joan Scott (New York: Routledge, 1992), p. 80.

53 Ibid., p. 75.

54 Irigaray, *J'aime*, pp. 84–85.

55 Ibid., p. 72. Cf. Phillips's congruent statement: "Woman can be encompassed on an equality with men only if sexual difference is first of all acknowledged" ("Universal Pretensions," p. 12).

56 Irigaray, *J'aime*, p. 85.

57 For more on Irigaray's linguistics see *Le Langage des déments, Parler n'est jamais neutre*, and "L'ordre sexuel du discours" in *Le sexe linguistique*, Luce Irigaray, ed.

58 Irigaray, *Sexes and Genealogies*, p. 138.

59 Irigaray, *J'aime*, p. 112.

60 Braidotti, "On the Female Feminist Subject," p. 185.

61 On the link between Beauvoir and Wittig, see Linda Zerilli, "The Trojan Horse of Universalism," *Social Text*, nos. 25–26 (1990). This very pertinent and congruent article came to my attention some time after I had drafted my own section on Wittig; I have tried nevertheless to incorporate some of its insights where opportune.

62 Ibid., pp. 162, 168.

63 Ibid., p. 149.

64 Miller, *Getting Personal*, p. 91.

65 Edward Said, "Nationalism, Human Rights, and Interpretation," *Raritan* 12, no. 3 (Winter 1993): 45.

66 Cornel West, "A Matter of Life and Death," *October* 61 (Spring 1992): 22–23.

67 Alessandro Ferrara, "Universalisms: Procedural, Contextualist, and Prudential," *Philosophy and Social Criticism* 14, nos. 3/4 (1988): 243.

68 Seyla Benhabib, *Situating the Self: Gender, Community and Postmodernism in Contemporary Ethics* (New York: Routledge, 1992).

69 Had I the time and the necessary expertise, this would be the place to address the question of pluralism—not to say liberalism, tolerance, and cosmopolitism—which often comes up at this point in the discussion and is an ism in need of some careful reevaluation.

70 For a recent example of this French inhospitability to cultural differences, especially differences emanating from its non-European, non-Christian communities, see the brouhaha that came to be known as "l'affaire du voile" (the veil affair). See Françoise Lionnet, "Identity, Sexuality, and Criminality: 'Universal Rights' and the Debate around the Practice of Female Excision in France," *Contemporary French Civilization* 16, no. 2 (Fall 1992): 294–307.

Dreaming Dissymmetry: Barthes, Foucault, and Sexual Difference

1 Ann Snitow, Christine Stansell, and Sharon Thompson, eds., *Powers of Desire: The Politics of Sexuality* (New York: Monthly Review Press, 1983), p. 9.

2 Ibid., p. 10.

3 Ibid. As valuable as this point is, in her article "Feminism, Criticism, and Foucault," *New German Critique* 27 (Fall 1982): 3–30, Biddy Martin reminds us that "Foucault's deconstructive methodology provides an immanent critique of such a search for *the* authentic female voice or *the* sexuality, a warning against the commitment to any confessional mode as necessarily liberating, and a challenge to the notion that simply speaking or writing frees us in any simple way from patriarchy or phallocentrism" (p. 15).

4 Roland Barthes, *Roland Barthes by Roland Barthes*, trans. Richard Howard (New York: Hill and Wang, 1977), p. 74.

5 I am thinking of Claudine Herrmann, who, in her book *The Tongue Snatchers* (trans. Nancy Kline [Lincoln: University of Nebraska Press, 1989]) catches out Barthes's subtle reinscription of cultural stereotypes of femininity; see pp. 13–15.

6 On the question of the relationship between feminist *jouissance* and Barthes, see Jane Gallop, "Beyond the *Jouissance* Principle," *Representations* 7 (1984): 110–115.

7 Stephen Heath, "Barthes on Love," *Sub-Stance* 37/38 (1983): 105. Not all readers of *A Lover's Discourse* share Heath's view that that discourse operates in a sexual limbo. Writing in *Christopher Street*, Richard Sennett asserts: "I do not wish to leave you with the impression that *A Lover's Discourse* is a neutered book. It is clearly about love between men" (p. 27).

8 Jane Gallop, "The Perverse Body," in *Thinking Through the Body* (New York: Columbia University Press, 1988), pp. 100–118.

9 John Sturrock, "Roland Barthes," in *Structuralism and Since: From Lévi-Strauss to Derrida*, ed. John Sturrock (Oxford: Oxford University Press, 1979), p. 73. See also p. 53, where Sturrock traces Barthes's lifelong crusade against essentialism to the origins of his thought in Sartrean existentialism, which may indeed be the original modern French philosophical discourse of indifference.

10   Sarrasine's misprision relies on a triad of "enthymemes" or "imperfect syllogisms," what Barthes calls "the three proofs": narcissistic, psychological, and aesthetic. Example: "all women are timid; La Zambinella is timid; therefore La Zambinella is a woman" (Roland Barthes, S/Z, trans. Richard Miller [New York: Hill and Wang, 1974], p. 148).

11   Stephen Heath, *Vertige du déplacement* (Paris: Fayard, 1974), p. 20. All translations are mine except where otherwise noted.

12   Ibid., p. 36. Cf. the almost identical analysis Barthes offers of the dramatis personae in *Sur Racine*: "The division of the Racinian world into strong and weak, into tyrants and captives, covers in a sense the division of the sexes: it is their situation in the relation of force that orchestrates [*verse*] some characters as virile and others as feminine, without concern for their biological sexes. . . . Here we find a first sketch of Racinian fatality: a simple relation, in origin purely circumstantial (captivity or tyranny), is converted into a biological datum; situation is converted into sex, chance into essence" (from *On Racine*, trans. Richard Howard, in *A Barthes Reader*, ed. Susan Sontag [New York: Hill and Wang, 1982], p. 180). Here sexual difference is subordinated to positionality within a power structure; sexual difference is not primary, not a given, but is rather the consequence of the position a subject occupies in a configuration of power. Masculinity does not guarantee power; it is the possession of power that produces masculinity. Femininity, by the same token, is the sex of the powerless, irrespective of their biological sex.

13   Kaja Silverman, *The Subject of Semiotics* (New York: Oxford University Press, 1983), p. 272.

14   Barthes, *Roland Barthes*, p. 133. In her brilliant reading of Barthes's reading of Balzac's *Sarrasine*, Barbara Johnson has shown that by fetishizing castration, Barthes, unlike Balzac, reduces the tale to a mere "reversal" of the readerly/writerly paradigm, failing to account for Balzac's more radical deconstruction of the difference within the readerly: "Balzac's text does not operate a simple *reversal* of the readerly hierarchy: Balzac does not proclaim castration as the truth behind the readerly's blindness in as unequivocal a way as Barthes' own unequivocality would lead one to believe" ("The Critical Difference," *Diacritics* 8, no. 2 [Summer 1978]: 8).

15   Roland Barthes, "Masculin, Féminin, Neutre," in *Echanges et communications: Mélanges offerts à Claude Lévi-Strauss à l'occasion de son 60ème anniversaire*, ed. Jean Pouillon and Pierre Maranda, 2 vols. (The Hague: Mouton, 1970), 2:899.

16   In his *De Rerum Naturae*, Lucretius writes: "While the first bodies are being carried downwards by their own weight in a straight line through the void, at times quite uncertain and uncertain places [*sic*], they swerve a little from their course, just so much as you might call a change of motion. For if they were not apt to incline, all would fall downwards like raindrops through the profound void, no collision would take place and no blow would be caused among the first-beginnings: thus nature would never have produced anything" (trans. W. H.D. Rouse, Loeb Classical Library [Cambridge: Harvard University Press, 1975], p. 113, as quoted by Joan de Jean in her article, "*La Nouvelle Héloïse*, or the Case for Pedagogical Deviation," *Yale French Studies* 63 [1982]: 98–116). Bloom's appropriation of the term in *The Anxiety of Influence* (New York: Oxford University Press, 1973) is typical of its recent usage: for him it is synonymous with "misprision," the felicitous misreading by a poet of his strong predecessor. Cf. Shoshana Felman, "De la nature des choses ou de l'écart à l'équilibre," *Critique* 380 (January 1979): 3–15.

17   Roland Barthes, *The Fashion System*, trans. Matthew Ward and Richard Howard (New York: Hill and Wang, 1983), p. ix.

18   Michel Foucault, *Power / Knowledge: Selected Interviews and Other Writings* 1972–1977, ed. Colin Gordon, trans. Gordon et al. (New York: Pantheon Books, 1980), pp. 219–220. Foucault goes on to contrast the desexualization of the women's movement with the fixation on sexuality in the gay rights movement.

19   Michel Foucault, *Herculine Barbin*, trans. Richard McDougall (New York: Pantheon Books, 1980), p. xiii.

20   But is this the only possible way to read Herculine's story? Herculine, Foucault notes, did not write her memoirs as a man because she never adjusted to her belated masculine identity. Rather like a wild child who cannot acquire human speech, Herculine-Abel could not learn to speak as a man, because, of course, masculinity is not just an anatomical fact, it is also the product of socialization. Nevertheless there are places in the memoirs where the narrator grapples with his dilemma by focusing on the signs of his difference from his fellow students, and in so doing Herculine-Abel reinscribes one of the most stereotypical cultural differences between the sexes. He writes of his early school days:

> My progress was rapid, and more than once it aroused the astonishment of my excellent teachers.
> It was not the same for handicrafts, for which I showed the deepest aversion and greatest incapacity.
> The times my companions employed in making those little masterpieces intended to decorate a drawing room or dress up a younger brother, I myself spent reading. History, ancient and modern, was my favorite passion. (p. 8)

According to the dominant cultural code, women are naturally drawn to that lower order of the arts, handicrafts; patience and meticulous attention to details are some of woman's most time-honored virtues. The products of women's artistic endeavors are destined to brighten up the home and please the family. To men belongs the world of public adventure and bold actions, even if only in the realm of fantasy. In short, what I am suggesting is that despite her sexual indeterminacy, Herculine Barbin was what we would call an essentialist.

21   Barthes, *Roland Barthes*, p. 133.

22   Michel Foucault, *The Use of Pleasure*, trans. Robert Hurley (New York: Pantheon Books, 1985), pp. 5–6.

23   Michel Foucault, *The Care of the Self*, trans. Robert Hurley (New York: Pantheon Books, 1986), p. 149.

24   Myra Jehlen, "Against Human Wholeness: A Suggestion for a Feminist Epistemology" (unpublished paper presented to the Columbia University Seminar on Women and Society).

25   The references here are to: Luce Irigaray, *This Sex Which Is Not One*, trans. Catherine Porter with Carolyn Burke (Ithaca: Cornell University Press, 1985), p. 76; Annette Kolodny, "Dancing through the Minefields: Some Observations on the Theory, Practice, and Politics of a Feminist Literary Criticism," *Feminist Studies* 6 (Spring 1980): 1–25; Laura Mulvey, "Visual Pleasure and Narrative Cinema," *Screen* 6 (Autumn 1975): 6–18; Mary Ann Doane, "Film and Masquerade: Theorising the Female Spectator," *Screen* 23 (September / October 1982): 74–87; Teresa de Lauretis, *Alice Doesn't: Feminism, Semiotics, Cinema* (Bloomington: Indiana University Press, 1984), esp. pp. 142–144; Sandra Gilbert and Susan Gubar, *The Madwoman in the Attic* (New Haven: Yale University Press, 1979), from p. 73 passim (interestingly, *palimpsest* is indexed under duplicity); Sarah Kofman, *The Enigma of Woman: Woman in Freud's Writings*, trans. Catherine Porter (Ithaca: Cornell University Press, 1985); Elizabeth L. Berg, "The Third Woman," *Diacritics* 12 (Summer 1982): 11–20; Naomi Schor,

"Female Fetishism: The Case of George Sand" and "Reading Double: Sand's Difference," in *The Poetics of Gender*, ed. Nancy K. Miller (New York: Columbia University Press, 1986); Jane Gallop, "Annie Leclerc Writing a Letter, with Vermeer," *October* 33 (1985): 103–118, reprinted in *The Poetics of Gender*; Biddy Martin, "Feminism, Criticism, and Foucault," 13.

26 Simone de Beauvoir, *The Second Sex*, trans. H. M. Parshley (New York: Vintage, 1974).

27 Hélène Cixous, "Sorties," trans. Ann Liddle, in *New French Feminisms*, ed. Elaine Marks and Isabelle de Courtivron (Amherst: The University of Massachusetts Press, 1980), p. 97.

This Essentialism Which Is Not One:
Coming to Grips with Irigaray

This essay is the revised text of a paper I delivered at a conference held at the University of Alabama, at Tuscaloosa, titled "Our Academic Contract: The Conflict of the Faculties in America." This conference has since achieved footnote status in the history of poststructuralism because it was on the occasion of this gathering that the scandal of Paul de Man's wartime journalism broke in the United States. I wish to thank Richard Rand for having invited me to participate in this event and Jacques Derrida for his response to my remarks, as well as for all his other gifts. I also wish to thank the members of my Brown feminist reading group—Christina Crosby, Mary Ann Doane, Coppélia Kahn, Karen Newman, and Ellen Rooney—as well as Elizabeth Weed, Nancy K. Miller, and Kaja Silverman for their various forms of support and criticism.

1 Jacques Derrida, "Women in the Beehive: A Seminar with Jacques Derrida," in *Men in Feminism*, ed. Alice Jardine and Paul Smith (New York: Methuen, 1987), p. 190. When it was originally published in the Brown student journal, *subjects/objects* [(Spring 1984): 5–19], in keeping with Derrida's wishes, the transcript of the seminar was prefaced by a cautionary disclaimer (reprinted in *Men in Feminism*), which I want to echo, emphasizing the text's undecidable status, "somewhere between speech and writing," "authorized but authorless" (p. 189). All references will be to the reprinted version of the text.

2 Ibid., p. 190.

3 Ibid., p. 191.

4 Ibid., p. 190.

5 Ibid., pp. 191–192; emphasis added.

6 I refer here in turn to *Between Psychoanalysis and Feminism*, ed. Teresa Brennan (London: Routledge, 1989), and Diana Fuss, *Essentially Speaking: Feminism, Nature and Difference* (New York: Routledge, 1989), which started out as a dissertation at Brown University. The keynote to this new deal for essentialism was perhaps sounded in the footnote to a paper given at a major feminist conference by Mary Russo, who writes: "The dangers of essentialism in posing the female body, whether in relation to representation or to 'women's history' have been well stated, so well stated, in fact, that *anti-essentialism may well be the greatest inhibition to work in cultural theory and politics at the moment, and must be displaced*" (*Feminist Studies/Critical Studies*, ed. Teresa de Lauretis [Bloomington: Indiana University Press, 1986], p. 228; emphasis added).

7 William J. Reese, *Dictionary of Philosophy and Religion: Eastern and Western Thought* (New Jersey: Humanities Press, 1980), pp. 81, 80.

8 Repeatedly in the course of an interview with James Creech, Peggy Kamuf, and Jane Todd, Derrida insists on the plural of deconstruction: "I don't think that there is something like

one deconstruction"; " . . . it is difficult to define the *one* deconstruction [*la* déconstruction]. . . . Personally I would even say that its best interests are served by keeping that heterogeneity." ("Deconstruction in America: An Interview with Jacques Derrida," *Critical Exchange* 17 [Winter 1985]: 4, 6). Finally, he concludes it is more accurate to speak of deconstructions than a singular deconstruction.

9   Simone de Beauvoir, *The Second Sex*, trans. H. M. Parshely (New York: Knopf, 1970), 1:249.

10 Jacques Lacan, *Feminine Sexuality: Jacques Lacan and the école freudienne*, ed. Juliet Mitchell and Jacqueline Rose, trans. Jacqueline Rose (New York: Norton, 1982), p. 144.

11. Teresa de Lauretis, ed., *Alice Doesn't: Feminism, Semiotics, Cinema* (Bloomington: Indiana University Press, 1984); de Lauretis, *Feminist Studies / Critical Studies*.

12 There is an extreme form of anti-essentialism, a candidate for a fifth critique, that argues that the replacement of woman by women does not solve but merely displaces the problem of essentialism. This is the position represented by Denise Riley, who suggests in a chapter titled "Does Sex Have a History?": " . . . not only 'woman' but also 'women' is troublesome . . . we can't bracket off either 'Woman,' whose capital letter alerts us to her dangers, or the more modest lower-case 'woman,' while leaving unexamined the ordinary, innocent-sounding 'women'" (*Am I That Name? Feminism and the Category of "Women" in History* [Minneapolis: University of Minnesota Press, 1988], p. 1). Cf. Donna Haraway, who, in her "A Manifesto for Cyborgs: Science, Technology, and Socialist Feminism in the 1980s" remarks: "It is no accident that woman *disintegrates* into women in our time" (*Socialist Review* 80 [March-April 1985]: 79; emphasis added). This is perhaps the place to comment on a critique whose conspicuous absence will surely surprise some: a *modern* Marxist critique of essentialism. I emphasize the word *modern* because, of course, Beauvoir's critique of essentialism in *The Second Sex* is heavily indebted to the Marxism she then espoused. Though the writings of Louis Althusser and Pierre Macherey, to cite the major Marxist theoreticians contemporaneous with Lacan and Derrida, inform some pioneering studies of female-authored fictions, they have not, to my knowledge, generated a critique of essentialism distinct from the critiques already outlined. This seeming absence or failure of a strong recent Marxist critique of essentialism is all the more surprising as the critique of essentialism was at the outset clearly appropriated by Beauvoir (and others) from Marxism. If Riley's book and Haraway's articles are at this point in time the only articulation we have of a postmodernist Marxist critique of essentialism, then it might be said that for them the essentialist is one who has not read history.

13 Ironically, in rejecting the ideal of a universal subject in favor of a subject marked by the feminine, Irigaray has, like other bourgeois white feminists, only managed to relocate universality, to institute a new hegemony. The question that arises is: how to theorize a subjectivity that does not reinscribe the universal, that does not constitute itself by simultaneously excluding and incorporating others?

14 For Irigaray on Beauvoir, see "A Personal Note: Equal or Different," in *Je, tu, nous: Toward a Culture of Difference*, trans. Alison Martin (New York: Routledge, 1993), pp. 9–14. Unfortunately, this text appeared too late to be taken into account in this article. It sets forth in unusually personal terms the differences between Beauvoir's feminism of equality and Irigaray's feminism of difference.

15 Beauvoir, *The Second Sex*, p. xvi.

16 Irigaray, *Speculum of the Other Woman*, trans. Gillian C. Gill (Ithaca: Cornell University Press, 1985), p. 133.

17 Beauvoir, *The Second Sex*, p. xxviii.

18   Ibid., p. 675.

19   Irigaray, "L'Ordre sexuel du discours," *Langages* 85 (March 1987): 83.

20   Nancy K. Miller, "Changing the Subject: Authorship, Writing, and the Reader," in de Lauretis, *Feminist Studies / Critical Studies*, pp. 102–120.

21   Irigaray, *Passions élémentaires* (Paris: Minuit, 1982), p. 101.

22   Irigaray, *Le Corps-à-corps avec la mère* (Montréal: pleine lune, 1981), pp. 63–64.

23   Irigaray, *Parler n'est jamais neutre*, p. 9.

24   Irigaray, *Le Corps*, pp. 63–64.

25   Beauvoir, *The Second Sex*, p. 671.

26   Mary Louise Pratt, "Scratches on the Face of the Country: Or, What Mr. Barrow Saw in the Land of the Bushmen," in *"Race," Writing, and Difference*, ed. Henry Louis Gates, Jr. (Chicago: University of Chicago Press, 1986), p. 139.

27   Beauvoir, *The Second Sex*, p. 667.

28   Irigaray's most explicit rejection of essentialism occurs in the "Veiled Lips" section of *Marine Lover of Friedrich Nietzsche* (trans. Gillian Gill [New York: Columbia University Press, 1991]), where she writes: "She does not set herself up as *one*, as a (single) female unit. She is not closed up or around [*se referme sur ou dans*] one single truth or essence. The essence of a truth remains foreign to her. She neither has nor is a being" (p. 86). Irigaray's best defense against essentialism is the defiant plurality of the feminine; there can be no essence in a conceptual system that is by definition anti-unitary.

29   Toril Moi, *Sexual / Textual Politics* (London: Methuen, 1985), p. 139.

30   Irigaray, *Marine Lover*, p. 118.

31   Irigaray, *This Sex Which Is Not One*, trans. Catherine Porter with Carolyn Burke (Ithaca: Cornell University Press, 1985), p. 76.

32   Mary Ann Doane, *The Desire to Desire: The Woman's Film of the 1940's* (Bloomington: Indiana University Press, 1987), p. 182.

33   See Paul Ricoeur, "Mimesis and Representation," *Annals of Scholarship* 2 (1981): 15–32. Irigaray gives this polysemy full play, reminding us, for example, in a passage of *This Sex* that in Plato mimesis is double: "there is *mimesis* as production, which would lie more in the realm of music, and there is the *mimesis* that would be already caught up in a process of *initiation, specularization, adequation* and *reproduction*. It is the second form that is privileged throughout the history of philosophy. . . . The first form seems always to have been repressed. . . . Yet it is doubtless in the direction of, and on the basis of, that first *mimesis* that the possibility of women's writing may come about" (p. 131). The question is, to paraphrase Yeats: how can you tell mimesis from mimesis?

34   Irigaray, *Le Corps*, p. 29.

35   Derrida, *Positions*, trans. Alan Bass (Chicago: University of Chicago Press), p. 71.

36   Irigaray, *This Sex*, p. 111.

37   Doane, *Desire*, p. 104; emphasis added.

38   Irigaray, *Passions*, p. 18.

39   Ibid., p. 28.

40   Irigaray, *This Sex*, p. 116.

41   Ibid., p. 140.

42   Irigaray, *Le Corps*, p. 49.

43   Irigaray, *L'Oubli de l'air chez Martin Heidegger* (Paris: Minuit, 1983), p. 36.

44   In a brilliantly turned defense of Irigaray against her anti-essentialist critics, Jane Gallop cautions us against "too literal a reading of Irigarayan anatomy" ("Lip Service," in *Thinking*

Through the Body [New York: Columbia University Press, 1988], p. 94). For example, when Irigaray speaks of the plural lips of the female sex, the word she uses, "lèvres," is a catachresis, an obligatory metaphor that effectively short-circuits the referential reading of the text: "Irigaray embodies female sexuality in that which, at this moment in the history of the language, is always figurative, can never be simply taken as the thing itself" (p. 98). As brilliant as are Gallop's arguments against a naively referential reading of the Irigarayan textual body, in the end she recognizes that "the gesture of a troubled but nonetheless insistent referentiality" is essential to Irigaray's project of constructing a "non-phallomorphic sexuality" (p. 99).

45   It is no accident that one of the most thoughtful and balanced recent articles on Irigaray is one which is based on a reading of her complete works, and not, as are many (though not all) of the highly critical analyses, merely on the works currently available in translation; see Margaret Whitford, "Luce Irigaray and the Female Imaginary: Speaking as a Woman," *Radical Philosophy* 43 (1986): 3–8.

46   On this point I would want to qualify Whitford's assessment of the place of science in Irigaray's discourse: "Her account of Western culture runs something like this. Our society is dominated by a destructive *imaginary* (whose apotheosis is the ideology of science elevated to the status of a privileged truth)" ("Luce Irigaray and the Female Imaginary," p. 5). My claim is that while condemning the imperialism of a neutered science, a science cut off from the life-giving female body, and which threatens us with "multiple forms of destruction of the universe" (Luce Irigaray, *Ethique de la différence sexuelle* [Paris: Minuit, 1984], p. 13; cf. the pronounced ecological strain in Luce Irigaray, "Equal to Whom?" trans. Robert L. Mazzola, *differences* 1, no. 2 [Summer 1989]: 59–76), Irigaray continues to look to science as a locus of "privileged truth."

47   Irigaray, *Parler n'est jamais neutre* (Paris: Minuit, 1985), pp. 290–291; see also p. 289.

48   Ibid., p. 291.

49   Irigaray, "Is the Subject of Science Sexed?" trans. Edith Oberle, *Cultural Critique* 1 (1985): 81; emphasis added. The reference here is to the Nobel Prize–winning research by Ilya Prigogine on dissipative structures. For more on the theories of Prigogine, whose influence on Irigaray has been significant, see Prigogine and Stengers, *La Nouvelle alliance: Métamorphose de la science* (Paris: Gallimard, 1979). Shortly after I first presented this paper, I received a letter from Katherine Hayles telling me that, working out of the perspective of the relationship of modern literature and science, she had been struck "by certain parallels between the new scientific paradigms and contemporary feminist theory," notably that of Irigaray. I am most grateful to her for this precious confirmation of my argument.

50   Irigaray, "Is the Subject of Science Sexed?" p. 86; emphasis added.

51   Moi, *Sexual / Textual*, p. 131.

52   Irigaray, *Speculum*, p. 186.

53   Ibid., p. 183.

54   Irigaray, *Ethique*, p. 75.

55   Ibid., p. 81.

56   Ibid., p. 84.

57   Irigaray, *L'Oubli*, p. 10.

58   Irigaray, *Parler n'est jamais neutre*, p. 74.

59   Ibid., p. 73.

60   Ibid., pp. 74–75.

61   Derrida, "Devant la loi," trans. Avital Ronell, in *Kafka and the Contemporary Critical Performance: Centenary Readings*, ed. Alan Udoff (Bloomington: Indiana University Press, 1987), p. 139.

62   The question of gender is raised by Derrida in his reading, but not as regards the "two protagonists." For Derrida what is problematic is the gender of the law, in German *das Gesetz* (neutral), in French *la loi* (feminine) ("Devant," p. 142).

Thème et Version

1   Gustave Flaubert, *Bouvard et Pécuchet* (Paris: Garnier-Flammarion, 1966), p. 377. "Au collège, prouve l'application, comme la version prouve l'intelligence. Mais dans le monde il faut rire des forts en thème." The translation is mine.

2   François Grosjean, *Life with Two Languages: An Introduction to Bilingualism* (Cambridge: Harvard University Press, 1982), p. 232.

3   Alvino E. Fantini, *Language Acquisition of a Bilingual Child: A Sociolinguistic Perspective (To Age Ten)* (San Diego: College-Hill Press, 1985), p. 14.

4   Jane Gallop, *Feminism and Psychoanalysis: The Daughter's Seduction* (London: Macmillan, 1982), p. xi.

5   Jane Gallop, *Thinking through the Body* (New York: Columbia University Press, 1988), p. 122.

6   Jane Gallop, *Around 1981: Academic Feminist Literary Theory* (New York: Routledge, 1992), p. 67.

7   Alice Jardine, *Gynesis: Configurations of Woman and Modernity* (Ithaca: Cornell University Press, 1985), p. 13.

The Righting of French Studies: Homosociality and the Killing of "La pensée 68"

The title of this essay alludes to the book by Jean-Luc Ferry and Alain Renaut, which signaled the coming of age of a generation of *new* new philosophers who rejected the great thinkers of the previous generation, the generation of '68. A version of this essay was delivered in 1991 before the MLA in the session titled, "Do We Have Anything in General to Talk about Now that We've Become So Very Particular?"

1   It would appear that the veritable lock held by the ENS, where the great French master thinkers of the twentieth century (including Sartre, Foucault, and Derrida) were trained, over literary studies both in France and abroad is now being loosened and is being displaced by other Grandes Ecoles, including the unlikely Ecole Polytechnique.

2   Gerald Graff, *Professing Literature: An Institutional History* (Chicago: University of Chicago Press, 1987), p. 2.

3   Commenting on the current interest in postcolonialism, one of my eminent and respected colleagues recently opined that Europe was dead, which seems an astonishing statement in view of recent (political) and future (economic) developments in that part of the world, which represents a population of 325 million people and constitutes the world's second largest economic block.

4   As a daughter of refugees and a first-generation American, I glory in America's openness to all those fleeing persecution, or even just underemployment, in their native countries. It goes without saying that Departments of National Literature have benefitted and will continue to benefit enormously from these open-handed (though of course not disinterested) liberal immigration policies, but as a native-born (though French-educated)

professor of French I am deeply disturbed by the instances of crude anti-Americanism among my foreign colleagues.

5   Jean-Marie Apostolidès, "On Paul de Man's War," *Critical Inquiry* 15, no. 4 (1989): 763.

6   Jacques Derrida, "Biodegradable: Seven Diary Fragments," *Critical Inquiry* 15, no. 4 (1989): 832.

7   A scrupulous male colleague (Philip Lewis) who read this piece suggested that I tone down my vocabulary here; "obsession with feminism" strikes him as an instance of rhetorical inflation. Let me aggravate matters by adding another piece of evidence to my dossier. Probably the most scurrilous attack on French feminist literary criticism I know of appeared in the 1989 issue of the *Stanford French Review*. The article, whose eloquent title is "Clèves Goes to Business School: A Review of DeJean and Miller" is an astonishingly mean-spirited and incoherent piece of writing that taxes Miller and DeJean's pathbreaking readings of Mme de La Fayette's *La Princesse de Clèves* with being opportunistic readings, serving in some sense their own ambitions. It relies on many of the same polemical strategies as those used by Apostolidès, including the tell-tale tarring of deconstruction with the same brush as feminism; thus DeJean is accused of an "eclectic infusion of Derridean motifs" (p. 260). The author of this attack on ideology, eclecticism, and opportunism, Odile Hullot-Kentor, gave this paper as her "job talk" at Stanford; needless to say, she got the job.

8   Compagnon's equation of this shrinkage with the expansion of the Marguerite Duras empire—as though this were a strictly feminist/American phenomenon—has understandably touched a nerve in some American French departments: hence the call for papers that appeared in the Spring 1992 MLA newsletter for a special session wittily titled: " 'Honey, They Shrunk the Canon!' Antoine Compagnon and the Durassification of French Literature in the US." One assumes that had Compagnon been writing in the fifties and sixties, he would have accused his American colleagues of the Sartrification or the Camusization of the canon. My own tastes run to the nonfeminist Sarraute rather than Duras—whose inflated reputation is a symptom of an international fascination with female sexuality, madness, and short sentences—but convincing American undergraduates, even in the élite institutions in which I have taught, to read the stylistically and semantically complex Sarraute instead of the apparently simple and juicy Duras is a losing battle.

9   As Compagnon, author of the cleverly titled *La Troisième République des lettres* (Paris: Seuil, 1983), might do well to note, Pavel expresses some reservations in regard to the notion of a new "republic of letters": "While a system based on classical liberalism is preferable to the domination of the feudal lords of the 1960s, liberalism has its own predicaments, and the use of the purely political metaphor 'the republic of letters' should not induce us to forget that intellectual activities can also be described as symbolic *economies* (as in the work of Pierre Bourdieu)" (p. 31).

10   Thomas G. Pavel, "Le rejet des classiques," *Le Messager européen* 5 (1991): 12.

11   Brett, Patricia. "To French Scholars, 'le Politiquement Correct' Is a Symptom of America's Social Breakdown," *The Chronicle of Higher Education*, 17 June 1992, p. A38; emphasis added.

12   "Appel: L'Avenir de la langue française," *Le Monde*, 11 July 1992, p. 5.

Lanson's Library

This text was originally written for a colloquium held at Yale University in October 1993 on the occasion of the imminent centenary of the publication of Lanson's history of French literature. My thanks to Denis Hollier for having invited me to participate in that event. I also wish to express my gratitude to the organizers of the Columbia French Literature Conference of 1994 for having invited me to deliver this text as the conference's keynote address.

1 Pierre Nora, "La nation-mémoire," in Les Lieux de mémoire, II, La Nation, 3, ed. Pierre Nora (Paris: Gallimard, 1986), p. 568. All translations are mine except where otherwise noted.

2 Ernst-Robert Curtius, Essai sur la France, trans. J. Benoist-Méchin (Paris: l'aube, 1990), pp. 27–28.

3 "De la nation ethnique à la nation citoyenne" [Rudolf von Thadden, Jeanne et Pierre Kaltenbach], Le Monde, 3 July 1993, p. 7.

4 Curtius, Essai sur la France, pp. 28–29.

5 Daniel Milo, "Les Classiques scolaires," in Les Lieux de mémoire, II, La Nation, 3, p. 528.

6 Milo, "Les Classiques," p. 517.

7 Ibid., p. 534. That the university occupied in Britain and the United States the space occupied by primary and especially secondary schools in France in the nineteenth century does not change the basic givens of Milo's comparison; the same differences that earlier characterized French schools and Anglo-Saxon universities between French and American institutions of higher learning well into the twentieth century. See, e.g., Claude Allègre, L'âge des savoirs: Pour une renaissance de l'université (Paris: Gallimard, 1993), esp. chaps. 1 and 2.

8 Milo, "Les Classiques," p. 546.

9 Judith Butler, Gender Trouble: Feminism and the Subversion of Identity (New York: Routledge, 1990), p. 4.

10 Marc Shell, Children of the Earth: Literature, Politics, and Nationhood (New York: Oxford University Press, 1993), pp. 20, 22.

11 Michael Geyer, "Multiculturalism," Critical Inquiry 19 (Spring 1993): 521.

12 Kristin Ross, "The World Literature and Cultural Studies Program," Critical Inquiry 19, no. 4 (1993): "Our foremost problem (and, I think, the most vital question facing the humanities in the 1990s) was how to come to terms with emergent cultures within the U.S., as well as with those non-Euro-American cultures, Islamic for example, that have traditionally existed within a university in a realm of splendid isolation" (p. 667).

13 Fredric Jameson, Postmodernism, or, The Cultural Logic of Late Capitalism (Durham: Duke University Press, 1991), p. 2.

14 Gerald Graff, Professing Literature: An Institutional History (Chicago: University of Chicago Press, 1987), p. 214.

15 Nora, La Nation, 3, p. 319. The allusion is to the work by Paul Bénichou bearing that title.

16 Denis Hollier, "French Customs, Literary Borders," October 49 (Summer 1989): 52.

17 Raymond Williams, Marxism and Literature (Oxford: Oxford University Press, 1990), pp. 45–54, esp. p. 46: "In its modern form the concept of 'literature' did not emerge earlier than the eighteenth century and was not fully developed until the nineteenth century." See also pp. 51–52 for Williams on national literatures.

Female Fetishism: The Case of George Sand

1 Luce Irigaray, This Sex Which Is Not One, trans. Catherine Porter with Carolyn Burke (Ithaca: Cornell University Press, 1985).

2   E.g., paranoia in my "Female Paranoia: The Case for Feminist Psychoanalytic Criticism," *Yale French Studies* 62 (1981): 204–219, reprinted in *Breaking the Chain: Women, Theory, and French Realist Fiction* (New York: Columbia University Press, 1985), pp. 149–162.

3   George Sand, *Valentine* (Paris: Michel Lévy, 1869), pp. 303–304; *Valentine*, trans. George Burnham Ives (Chicago: Academy Press, Limited, 1978), p. 306. All quotations from Sand will be in English, but page references to corresponding French editions will also be provided and will precede the page references to the translations.

4   The theoretical consequences of this traditional view are far reaching. For example, Mary Ann Doane demonstrates that the task of theorizing the female spectator is complicated by the female spectator's presumed inability to assume the distancing built into the male spectator's fetishistic position: "In a sense, the male spectator is destined to be a fetishist, balancing knowledge and belief. The female, on the other hand, must find it extremely difficult, if not impossible, to assume the position of fetishist" ("Film and the Masquerade: Theorising the Female Spectator," *Screen* 23 [September/October 1982]: 80).

The question of female fetishism—why it does not exist and what its clinical specificity would be if it did—is one that has elicited only sporadic interest in the literature of psychoanalysis. In the remarkably complete "Bibliography" included in the special issue on *Perversion* of the *Revue Française de psychanalyse*, volume 47 (1983), André Luissier lists four references to case studies of female fetishism: (1) G. A. Dudley (1954), (2) Ilse Barande (1962), (3) G. Zavitzianos (1971), and (4) G. Bonnet (1977). To this list one should add an article which appears in the same special issue as the bibliography: François Sirois (1983). While all these articles reiterate the rarity of cases of female fetishism, all are case studies of female patients exhibiting sexual perversions on the order of fetishism. The major theoretical stumbling block for these analysts is the Freudian equation: fetish = maternal penis (see below). G. A. Dudley attempts to circumvent this obstacle by de-phallusizing the fetish altogether, arguing that the "fetish may . . . be a substitute for other infantile objects besides the penis" ("A Rare Case of Female Fetishism," *International Journal of Sexology* 8 [1954]: 33). G. Zavitzianos, on the other hand, concludes that in the case of his female fetishist patient, "the fetish symbolized not the maternal penis (as is the case in male fetishism), but the *penis of the father*" ("Fetishism and Exhibitionism in the Female and Their Relationship to Psychopathology and Kleptomania," *International Journal of Psycho-Analysis* 52 [1971]: 302). While taking Zavitzianos's hypothesis into account, Bonnet displaces the problem by rereading Freud via Lacan and introducing the crucial Lacanian distinction between *having* and *being* the phallus. For G. Bonnet, "the female fetish . . . is inscribed in both the problematics of having and not being" ("Fétichisme et exhibitionnisme chez un sujet féminin," *Psychanalyse à l'université* 2 [1977]: 244). The female fetishist, according to Bonnet, is less concerned with having/not having the penis than with being/not being the maternal phallus. Ultimately, at least in the case study presented, the female fetishist is more "fetished" (fétichée) than fetishizing. The female fetishist is a woman who responds to her mother's desire by wanting to be the (missing, absent) phallus. This theoretically sophisticated and innovative case study has interesting implications for the case of George Sand because it involves an Oedipal configuration bearing some resemblance to Sand's: an absent father—Sand's father died when she was four years old, and the patient's parents were divorced when she was small—and a possessive mother who uses her daughter as a phallic substitute. For an earlier Lacanian approach to the question of female fetishism, see Piera Aulagnier-Spairani, Jean Clavreul, et al., *Le Désir et la perversion* (Paris: Seuil, 1967).

5   Nancy K. Miller, "Writing (from) the Feminine: George Sand and the Novel of Female

Pastoral," in *The Representation of Women in Fiction: Selected Papers from the English Institute 1981*, ed. Carolyn Heilbrun and Margaret Higonnet (Baltimore: Johns Hopkins University Press, 1983), p. 137.

6   Sand, *Mauprat* (Paris: Garnier-Flammarion, 1969), p. 127; *Mauprat*, trans. Stanley Young (Chicago: Academy Press Limited, 1977), p. 141.

7   Sigmund Freud, "Fetishism," in *The Standard Edition of the Complete Psychological Works*, vol. 21, ed. James Strachey, trans. James Strachey et al. (London: Hogarth Press, 1953–1974), pp. 154.

8   Sarah Kofman, *The Enigma of Woman: Woman in Freud's Writings*, trans. Catherine Porter (Ithaca: Cornell University Press, 1985).

9   Freud, "Some Psychological Consequences of the Anatomical Distinction between the Sexes," in *Sexuality and the Psychology of Love*, ed. Philip Rieff (New York: Collier, 1963), p. 188.

10   Charles Baudelaire, *Oeuvres complètes* (Paris: Bibliothèque de la Pléiade, 1961), p. 1272.

11   Sand, *Lélia* (Paris: Garnier, 1960), p. 158; *Lélia*, trans. Maria Espinosa (Bloomington: Indiana University Press, 1978), pp. 103–104.

12   On the relationship between Derridean undecidability and (female) fetishism, see Sarah Kofman, "Ça cloche," trans. Caren Kaplan, in *Derrida and Deconstruction*, ed. Hugh J. Silverman (New York: Routledge, 1989), pp. 108–138. The very first question to arise during the discussion that follows Kofman's presentation is: "Does the generalized fetishism of *Glas* allow a female fetishism?" to which Kofman responds: "A generalized fetishism, defined as a generalized oscillation, does not exclude a female fetishism, since it implies the generalization of the feminine and the end of the privileging of the phallus, which ceases to be a fetish" (p. 112).

13   Elizabeth L. Berg, "The Third Woman," *Diacritics* 12 (Summer 1982): 13.

14   See Peggy Kamuf, "Replacing Feminist Criticism," *Diacritics* 12 (1982): 42–47; and Nancy K. Miller, "The Text's Heroine," *Diacritics* 12 (1982): 48–53.

15   Alice Jardine, "Pre-Texts for the Transatlantic Feminist," *Yale French Studies* 62 (1981): 220–236.

16   Elaine Showalter, "Feminist Criticism in the Wilderness," *Critical Inquiry* 8 (1981): 204.

17   Eileen Boyd Sivert, "Lélia and Feminism," *Yale French Studies* 62 (1981): 59. This slippage might usefully be compared to the "ontological slipperiness" Leo Bersani sees at work in Emily Brontë's *Wuthering Heights* and Lautréamont's *Les Chants de Maldoror* (*A Future for Astyanax: Character and Desire in Literature* [Boston: Little, Brown and Co., 1976], p. 198). Bersani makes no distinction between male-authored and female-authored fictions of "depersonalized desire"; nevertheless, the question of the *femininity of undifferentiated characterization* must be raised if only because of the work carried out by such theoreticians of the object-relations school as Nancy Chodorow, who asserts that "separation and individuation remain particularly female developmental issues," rooted in women's mothering (*The Reproduction of Mothering: Psychoanalysis and the Sociology of Gender* [Berkeley: University of California Press, 1978], p. 110). The difficult question then becomes: how does one articulate the bisextuality of female fetishism and the metamorphoses of the "deconstructed self" on the one hand, and the perverse oscillation of female fetishism and the indissolubility of the mother/daughter dyad on the other?

18   The interpretation I am alluding to here is the one elaborated by Leslie Rabine, according to whom the pure Indiana and the fallen Noun are complementary figures ("George Sand and the Myth of Femininity," *Women and Literature* 4, no. 2 [1976]: 2–17).

19   Sand, *Indiana* (Paris: Michel Lévy, 1862), pp. 95–96; *Indiana*, trans. George Burnham Ives (Chicago: Academy Press, Limited, 1978), p. 164.

20   Roland Barthes, *Sade/Fourier/Loyola*, trans. Richard Miller (Berkeley: University of California Press, 1989). Barthes describes his book as: "the book of Logothetes, founders of languages" (p. 3).

Fetishism and Its Ironies

1   Fredric Jameson, "Postmodernism, or, the Cultural Logic of Late Capitalism," *New Left Review* 146 (July-August 1984): 61–62.

2   Jonathan Culler, "The Uses of *Madame Bovary*," in *Flaubert and Postmodernism*, ed. Naomi Schor and Henry Majewski (Lincoln: University of Nebraska Press, 1984), p. 5.

3   "La vue de votre pied me trouble" (Gustave Flaubert, *L'éducation sentimentale* [Paris: Garnier-Flammarion, 1969], p. 440; *Sentimental Education*, trans. Robert Baldick [Harmondsworth, England: Penguin, 1964], p. 414).

4   Shoshana Felman, *Writing and Madness: (Literature/Philosophy/Psychoanalysis)*, trans. Martha Noel Evans (Ithaca: Cornell University Press, 1985), p. 81.

5   Michal Peled Ginsburg, *Flaubert Writing: A Study in Narrative Strategies* (Stanford: Stanford University Press, 1986), p. 1.

6   "Ce n'est point un roman ni un drame avec un plan fixe, ou une seule idée préméditée, avec des jalons pour faire serpenter la pensée dans des allées tirées au cordeau" (Gustave Flaubert, *Mémoires d'un fou*, in *Oeuvres complètes* [Paris: Seuil, 1964], 1: 230, hereafter abbreviated *MF*).

7   "Je vais mettre sur le papier tout ce qui me viendra à la tête, mes idées avec mes souvenirs, mes impressions, mes rêves, mes caprices, tout ce qui passe dans la pensée et dans l'âme" (ibid.).

8   Ibid., p. 236; emphasis added.

9   "Il y a des choses insignifiantes qui m'ont frappé fortement et que je garderai toujours comme l'empreinte d'un fer rouge, quoiqu'elles soient banales et niaises" (ibid., p. 235).

10   On Freud's screen memories, see chapter 4 in Naomi Schor, *Reading in Detail: Aesthetics and the Feminine* (New York: Methuen, 1987), pp. 65–78.

11   "Nous prolongions souvent nos visites assez tard le soir, réunis autour de la vieille maîtresse, dans une grande salle couverte de dalles blanches, devant une vaste cheminée en marbre. Je vois encore sa tabatière d'or pleine du meilleur tabac d'Espagne, son carlin au longs poils blancs, et son petit pied mignon, enveloppé dans un joli soulier à haut talon orné d'une rose noire" (*MF*, p. 236).

12   "Qu'il y a longtemps de tout cela! La maîtresse est morte, ses carlins aussi, sa tabatière est dans la poche du notaire, le château sert de fabrique, et le pauvre soulier a été jeté à la rivière" (ibid., p. 236).

13   "Ce jour-là, une charmante pelisse rouge avec des raies noires était restée sur le rivage. La marée montait, le rivage était festonné d'écume; déjà un flot plus fort avait mouillé les franges de soie de ce manteau. Je l'ôtais pour le placer au loin; l'étoffe était moelleuse et légère, c'était un manteau de femme" (ibid., p. 236).

14   "Un long châle à bandes violettes était placé derrière son dos; sur le bordage de cuivre: Elle avait dû, bien des fois, au milieu de la mer, durant les soirs humides, en envelopper sa taille, s'en couvrir les pieds, dormir dedans! Mais, entraîné par les franges, il glissait peu à peu, il allait tomber dans l'eau; Frédéric fit un bond et le rattrapa" (ibid., p. 236).

15   Susan Rubin Suleiman, "Pornography, Transgression, and the Avant-Garde: Bataille's Story

of the Eye," in *The Poetics of Gender*, ed. Nancy K. Miller (New York: Columbia University Press, 1986), pp. 126–127.

16   D. C. Muecke, *Irony and the Ironic* (London: Methuen, 1970), p. 7.

17   Warning Rainer, "Irony and the 'Order of Discourse' in Flaubert," trans. Michael Morton, *New Literary History* 13, no. 2 (1982): 255.

18   Naomi Schor, "Female Fetishism: The Case of George Sand," this volume.

19   The responsible feminist irony I am calling for here would seem to bear some sort of resemblance to what Wayne Booth has termed "stable irony," a form of irony whose ultimate meaning—in contrast to that of the unstable irony of modernity—can be reconstructed (*A Rhetoric of Irony* [Chicago: University of Chicago Press, 1974]). This resemblance is, however, at best only partial: Booth's agenda in promoting stable irony is fundamentally conservative (see Susan Suleiman, "'Interpreting Ironies," *Diacritics* 6 [Summer 1976]: 15–21), and mine is not. Politically engaged feminist irony would retain the destabilizing effects of modernist irony while rejecting its misogynistic libidinal economy. Arguing for a radical discontinuity between modernist and postmodernist texts, in *Irony / Humor: Critical Paradigms* (Baltimore: Johns Hopkins University Press, 1988), Candace Long reserves the term *irony* for the (relatively) stable irony of modernism and rebaptizes what is (mistakenly) referred to as postmodernist irony, humor. Lang would, then, contest my initial assumption that modernist irony persists in postmodernism; however, as she wryly concedes: "I rather doubt if my proposal for a less misleading terminology will have the slightest effect on general usage" (p. 4). I shall, then, stick to general usage while recognizing that part of the problem in defining feminist irony (as well as female fetishism) is the inadequacy of an ancient terminology when applied to new cultural phenomena.

20   Donna Haraway, "A Manifesto for Cyborgs: Science, Technology, and Socialist Feminism in the 1980s," *Socialist Review* 80 (March-April 1985): 65.

21   Nancy K. Miller, "Changing the Subject: Authorship, Writing, and the Reader," in *Feminist Studies / Critical Studies*, ed. Teresa de Lauretis (Bloomington: Indiana University Press, 1986), p. 119 n. 18, and see p. 114.

22   Warning, "Irony," pp. 264–265.

23   Muecke, *Irony*, p. 33.

The Portrait of a Gentleman: Representing Men in (French) Women's Writing

This essay is gratefully dedicated to the students in my course on French women's writing from the seventeenth century to the present at Brown University, Fall 1984, and the University of California, Berkeley, Spring 1986. Special thanks to Carolyn Duffy for bringing to my attention the text quoted in the epigraph. Lombarda was a woman troubadour of the thirteenth century. The text is drawn from part 2 of her *tenson* with Barnat Arnaut d'Armagnac.

1   Sarah Kent and Jacqueline Morreau, preface to *Women's Images of Men* (London: Writers and Readers Publishing, 1985), p. 1.

2   Sarah Kent, "Looking Back," in ibid., p. 62.

3   Ibid., p. 72.

4   A very recent exception to this rule is Jane Miller's *Women Writing about Men* (New York: Pantheon, 1986). Though our approaches to the topic could not be more different—at no point does Miller problematize the very issue of representation—a disclaimer she makes in

her introduction does point to an odd resonance between our analyses: "My book will be a disappointment, I expect, for anyone hoping for a gallery neatly hung with the portraits women have painted of men" (p. 3). Indeed, despite a typological organization largely informed by the categories of kinship—chapter headings include "Fathers and Gentlemen," "Brothers," and "Sons"—Miller's book frustrates any expectation of an exhaustive taxonomy of male imagoes in (Anglo-American) women's writing. Unfortunately, it also disappoints in other ways, notably by its lack of theoretical rigor. Nevertheless, it is a pioneering study of the ways in which women's disempowerment in modern Western societies translates into their writing about men.

5   Janis Glasgow, Une Esthétique de comparaison: Balzac et George Sand (Paris: A. G. Nizet, 1977), pp. 44–45. Translations in the text are mine except where otherwise noted. The awareness of a special handicap in portraying men is shared by other women writers. Charlotte Brontë, for example, writes to a friend: "In delineating male characters, I labour under disadvantages; intuition and theory will not adequately supply the place of observation and experience. When I write about women, I am sure of my ground—in the other case I am not so sure" (quoted by Miller in Women Writing about Men, p. 39). Writing about the same issues some one hundred years later, Virginia Woolf is, if anything, more pessimistic in her conclusions than Sand: "It remains obvious . . . that a man is terribly hampered and partial in his knowledge of women, as a woman is in her knowledge of men" (A Room of One's Own [New York: Harcourt, Brace and World, Inc., 1957], p. 87).

6   K. K. Ruthven, Feminist Literary Studies: An Introduction (Cambridge: Cambridge University Press, 1984), p. 86. The recent polemic over the representation of the male protagonists in Alice Walker's The Color Purple—though it is, of course, immensely complicated by the tension between racism and sexism—provides a telling current example of the violence unleashed by women artists' attacks on male privilege. See, for example, Mel Watkins, "Sexism, Racism and Black Women Writers," The New York Times Book Review, 15 June 1986.

7   On the subject of misogyny through the ages, see Katherine M. Rogers, The Troublesome Helpmate: A History of Misogyny in Literature (Seattle: University of Washington Press, 1966).

8   Woolf, A Room of One's Own, p. 94.

9   Ibid., p. 35.

10   The references here are in turn to Nancy K. Miller, "Emphasis Added: Plots and Plausibilities in Women's Fiction," in The New Feminist Criticism, ed. Elaine Showalter (New York: Pantheon, 1985), pp. 339–360; Peggy Kamuf, "A Mother's Will," in Fictions of Feminine Desire (Lincoln: University of Nebraska Press, 1982), pp. 67–96; Marianne Hirsch, "A Mother's Discourse: Incorporation and Repetition in La Princesse de Clèves," Yale French Studies 62 (1982): 67–87; Joan DeJean, "Lafayette's Ellipses: The Privileges of Anonymity," PMLA 99 (October 1984): 884–902. The connection between The Princesse de Clèves and Indiana is the subject of an article by Mario Maurin, "Un Modèle d'Indiana," French Review 50 (1976): 317–320. Noting the numerous echoes of The Princesse in Indiana, including the portrait scenes, Maurin concludes: "It is not implausible . . . that at the point of inaugurating an independent career as a novelist, George Sand should have unconsciously placed herself under the patronage of her illustrious predecessor" (p. 320).

11   Nancy K. Miller, "Parables and Politics: Feminist Criticism in 1986," Paragraph 8 (October 1986): 46.

12   Mme de La Fayette, The Princesse de Clèves, trans. Nancy Mitford (Harmondsworth, England: Penguin, 1982), p. 164; emphasis added. Page numbers given in the text refer to this edition; citations in French refer to La Princesse de Clèves (Paris: Garnier-Flammarion, 1966).

13 Jean Fabre, as quoted by Kamuf in "A Mother's Will," p. 68. Kamuf's reading interestingly likens narratorial and maternal omniscience.

14 Nancy K. Miller, "Emphasis Added," p. 350.

15 Michel Butor, "Sur La Princesse de Clèves," in Répertoire I (Paris: Minuit, 1960), pp. 74–78.

16 W.J.T. Mitchell, Iconology: Image, Text, Ideology (Chicago: University of Chicago Press, 1986), in particular p. 113. Symmetry dictates that elsewhere in the novel the scenario we have been tracing is "reversed," if only to show that it is irreversible. I refer to the scene where the princess sees M. de Nemours steal a portrait of her belonging to her husband. The differences between the two portrait scenes are telling: first, the princess's moral dilemma—should she say something to prevent the theft, thereby publicizing Nemours's love for her or, by silently acquiescing to it, encourage Nemours's passion—arises precisely from her inability to occupy the voyeur's position: she knows that Nemours knows that she has witnessed his appropriative gesture. Even in this instance, the male gaze supersedes and recontains the female. Second, rather than experiencing bliss at witnessing Nemours's desire for her portrait, the princess is embarrassed and "very much upset."

17 Dalia Judovitz, "The Aesthetics of Implausibility: La Princesse de Clèves," MLN 99, no. 5 (1984): 1053.

18 Mme de Staël, Corinne, or, Italy, trans. Avriel H. Goldberger (New Brunswick: Rutgers University Press, 1978), p. 124.

19 Michael Riffaterre, Semiotics of Poetry (Bloomington: Indiana University Press, 1978), pp. 81–114.

20 Charlotte Brontë, Jane Eyre (Edinburgh: J. Grant, 1924), pp. 231–232.

21 A clear distinction must be drawn here between Mme de Staël's ruining of representation and Corinne's more ambivalent relationship to the image, which is clearly bound up with the law of the father she would both transgress and reinscribe. Thus, when the portrait of Oswald's father (the posthumous lawgiver who prohibits the marriage of Oswald and Corinne) is nearly destroyed by water, Corinne restores it. In Corinne, female masochism and mimesis are shown to be inseparable.

22 See notes by Béatrice Didier in her edition of George Sand, Indiana (Paris: Folio, 1984), p. 359. Subsequent references to the French are to this edition.

23 Sainte-Beuve, Les Grands écrivains français: XIXe Siècle, les romanciers (Paris: Garnier, 1927), p. 45.

24 George Sand, Indiana, trans. George Burnham Ives (Chicago: Academy Press Limited, 1978), p. 66. The page references in the text are to this edition.

25 Eve Kosofsky Sedgwick, Between Men: English Literature and Male Homosocial Desire (New York: Columbia University Press, 1985).

26 Leslie Rabine, "George Sand and the Myth of Femininity," Women and Literature 4, no. 2 (1976): 8.

27 Brian Wallis, "What's Wrong with This Picture: An Introduction," in Art after Modernism: Rethinking Representation, ed. Brian Wallis, (New York: The New Museum of Contemporary Art in association with David R. Godine, 1984), p. xv. A central theme of this anthology is the politics of representation, its complicities with all forms of power, especially the patriarchal.

28 Sand, Indiana, "Preface of 1843."

29 Nathalie Sarraute, as quoted in La Quinzaine Littéraire 192 (August 1974): 29.

30 This remark raises the question of the "consciousness" of the tradition I have been tracing. In her early Essai sur les fictions (Paris: Editions Ramsey, 1979), Mme de Staël lists La Princesse among the masterpieces written not so much by women as on women for their moral

instruction (p. 48). As for Sand's affiliation with Staël, this celebrated lyrical evocation of her youthful readings attests to Sand's keen awareness of her great predecessor: "Happy time! oh my Vallée Noire! Oh Corinne!" (*Lettres d'un voyageur* [Paris: Garnier-Flammarion, 1971], p. 207).

31   Nathalie Sarraute, *Portrait of a Man Unknown*, trans. Maria Jolas (New York: G. Braziller, 1958). The page references included in the text are to this edition.

32   The very notion of a "female iconoclasm" is iconoclastic in that, as Mitchell points out, the great iconoclastic discourses of both Lessing and Burke align painting and beauty with the feminine. From a very different perspective, in an essay titled "Iconoclastic Moments: Reading the *Sonnets for Helene*, Writing the *Portuguese Letters*," Elizabeth L. Berg "interrogates a certain feminist need to constitute secure self-representations, otherwise known as "images of women." She argues, iconoclastically, for a shattering of these "univocal images" in favor of a dissolution of all identities, especially the sexual (in Nancy K. Miller, ed., *The Poetics of Gender* [New York: Columbia University Press, 1986], pp. 208–221, esp. p. 218).

33   When, later on in the novel, Raymon's new wife, Laure de Nagy, signs her paintings, she writes "Pastiche" next to the signatures (*Indiana*, p. 286). This crucial word is lost in the translation, which substitutes "copy" (p. 267). Didier reads this scene as a sort of private joke, an ironic allusion to Sand's mentor's (Henri de Latouche) initial dismissal of her novel as a mere pastiche of Balzac. For more on Sand's relationship to the then dominant representational mode embodied by Balzac, see my *George Sand and Idealism* (New York: Columbia University Press, 1993).

Triste Amérique: Atala and the Post-Revolutionary Construction of Woman

1   Lynn Hunt, "Engraving the Republic: Prints and Propaganda in the French Revolution," *History Today* 30 (October 1980): 14.

2   For further details on the gradual emergence of Marianne as the emblem of the Republic, see Lynn Hunt, *Politics, Culture, and Class in the French Revolution* (Berkeley: University of California Press, 1984), esp. pp. 87–119. Hunt's account should be read in conjunction with the now classic work by Maurice Agulhon, *Marianne into Battle: Republican Imagery and Symbolism in France, 1789–1880*, trans. Janet Lloyd (Cambridge: Cambridge University Press, 1981).

3   In an article brought to my attention after I had written this essay, Kaja Silverman in some sense confirms my conflation of disembodied and hyperembodied female figures, by emphasizing the political uses to which images of female nudity were put in France from Delacroix's *Liberty Guiding the People* to Courbet's *Origin of the World*. The diaphanously veiled Nana is the literary equivalent of this recurrent figure of the revolutionary prostitute. See Kaja Silverman, "Liberty, Maternity, Commodification," *New Formations* 5 (Summer 1988): 69–89.

4   Abbé Prévost, *Manon Lescaut*, trans. Leonard Tancock (Harmondsworth, England: Penguin, 1949), p. 26.

5   François René de Chateaubriand, *Atala/René*, trans. Irving Putter (Berkeley: University of California Press, 1967), pp. 37–38.

6   Jules Lemaitre puts the matter this way: "If the two lovers did not meet the old missionary, if Atala succumbed during the storm, and if she later died in the woods . . . the story of Atala could end the same way Manon Lescaut's does" (*Chateaubriand* [Paris: Calmann-Lévy, n.d.], p. 92). All translations are mine except where otherwise noted.

7   Chateaubriand, *Mémoires d'outre-tombe*, vol. 1 (Paris: Flammarion, 1948), p. 414.

8   Chateaubriand, *Mémoires*, vol. 2, p. 20. It is interesting to note that in his eyewitness accounts of the revolution, Chateaubriand refers to Marat's hideous friends as a "series of Medusa's heads" (*Mémoires*, vol. 1, p. 376), and on the very next page describes Danton's companions as "male furies" (p. 377), further confirming the sexual indeterminacy of these figures in his imaginary. Chateaubriand's sexual panic in the face of the revolution of 1792 also confirms Neil Hertz's argument regarding the troping of the threat of political violence as the fear of castration, in "Medusa's Head: Male Hysteria under Political Pressure," *Representations* 4 (Fall 1983): 27–54.

9   On women and the French revolution, my main sources of information are: Claire Moses, *French Feminism in the 19th Century* (Albany: SUNY Press, 1984); Darlene Gay Levy, Harriet Branson Applewhite, Mary Durham Johnson, eds., *Women in Revolutionary Paris, 1789–1795* (Urbana: University of Illinois Press, 1979); Paule-Marie Duhet, ed., *Cahiers de doléances des femmes en 1789 et autres textes* (Paris: des femmes, 1981); Maïte Albistur and Daniel Armogathe, *Histoire du féminisme français*, 2 vols. (Paris: des femmes, 1977); and Joan B. Landes, *Women and the Public Sphere in the Age of the French Revolution* (Ithaca: Cornell University Press, 1988).

   Concerning the convergence of Napoleon's politics of religious restoration and Chateaubriand's Christian apologetics, one need perhaps only recall that the second edition of *The Genius*, published in 1803, was dedicated to "the first Consul, general Bonaparte," and that coincidentally during that same year Chateaubriand received the diplomatic posting in Rome he had ardently coveted. In the words of Victor Giraud, the author of a two-volume study on *Le Christianisme de Chateaubriand* (Paris: Hachette, 1928): "The book and the author squared perfectly with the designs of his [Napoleon's] policy: he asked only to use the one and the other" (vol. 2, p. 154).

10 Because of the extravagant and sweeping nature of this assertion, I was particularly gratified to find confirmation of my analysis in my colleague and fellow conference participant Linda Orr's important new book, *Headless History: Nineteenth-Century French Historiography of the French Revolution* (Ithaca: Cornell University Press, 1990). Noting that "The Revolution is a 'black hole' in French Literature" (p. 17), Orr goes on to say: "So nineteenth-century French histories threw themselves where other writers feared to tread directly" (p. 17). Directly is the key word here, because as Orr remarks in a footnote to this sentence, "Yet almost every nineteenth-century novel and many poems approach indirectly the traumatic space of the French Revolution" (p. 17 n. 25). Another name for this indirect approach is allegory. "*Le rouge et le noir*," writes Orr, "is the allegorical repetition of Revolutionary history in Restoration terms." For those French writers who would somehow engage with the French Revolution, there were, then, two possible narrative modes: the displacements of allegory or the abyss of history.

11 Ronald Paulson, *Representations of Revolution* (1789–1820) (New Haven: Yale University Press, 1983), p. 26.

12 See Ronald Paulson, *Representations*; Karl Marx, *The Eighteenth Brumaire of Louis Bonaparte* (New York: International Publishers, 1972); Agulhon, *Marianne au Combat*; and Lynn Hunt, "Engraving the Republic."

13 Jane Tompkins, *Sensational Designs: The Cultural Work of American Fiction 1790–1860* (New York: Oxford University Press, 1985), p. 103.

14 Landes, *Women*, p. 147.

15 See Hunt, *Politics*; Mona Ozouf, *La Fête révolutionnaire, 1789–1799* (Paris: Gallimard, 1976);

Marie-Hélène Huet, "Le Sacre du Printemps: Essai sur le sublime et la Terreur," *MLN* 103 (1988): 781–799.

16   Huet, "Le Sacre," p. 789.

17   See *Mémoires*, vol. 1, p. 230.

18   Naomi Schor, *Breaking the Chain: Women, Theory, and French Realist Fiction* (New York: Columbia University Press, 1985).

19   Jane Gallop, "Beyond the Jouissance Principle," *Representations* 7 (1984): 110–115.

20   See François René de Chateaubriand, *The Genius of Christianity* (New York: Howard Fertig, 1976), pp. 287–290. What is striking about Chateaubriand's reading of *Paul et Virginie* is his insistence on its Christian dimension: "We may even go still farther and assert that it is religion, in fact, which determines the catastrophe. Virginia dies for the preservation of one of the principal virtues enjoined by Christianity. It would have been absurd to make a Grecian woman die for refusing to expose her person; but the lover of Paul is a Christian virgin, and what would be ridiculous according to an impure notion of heathenism becomes in this instance sublime" (p. 290).

21   On this point I disagree with Naomi Segal when she insists, in *Narcissus and Echo* (Manchester: Manchester University Press, 1988), on reading (and quickly and smartly dispatching) *Atala* as merely a less domesticated, hence less successful incest récit than *René* (pp. 54–57). While the presence of the incest motif in *Atala* is anything but hidden, it strikes me as a trivializing gesture to reduce *Atala* to just another variation on Chateaubriand's incestuous eros, thereby confirming what one had set out to prove: namely that the canon is always right and that *Atala* has no other claim to our attention but as *René*'s "mirror-piece" (p. 54), a singularly (in)apt choice of words in a book devoted to unmasking the workings of male narcissism in the classic French récit.

22   Stéphane Michaud, *Muse et madone: Visages de la femme de la Révolution française aux apparitions de Lourdes* (Paris: Seuil, 1985), p. 31. Michaud's remarks are especially valuable for the continuum they reestablish between the eighteenth-century medical discourse of female debility and the post-Revolutionary misogynistic discourse of Christian apologetics.

23   Interestingly, Girodet, the author of a striking portrait of Chateaubriand, produced yet another prominent icon, the painting of the sleeping Endymion featured in Barthes's *S/Z*, which Chateaubriand acknowledged was a source for his description in *Les Martyrs* of the "sommeil d'Eudore." On Chateaubriand and Girodet, see George Levitine, "Some Unexplored Aspects of the Illustrations of *Atala*: The *surenchères visuelles* of Girodet and Hersent," in *Chateaubriand Today*, ed. Richard Switzer (Madison: University of Wisconsin Press, 1970), pp. 139–145.

24   I owe this important qualification to Carol Ockman, who, during the discussion following my presentation of this material at Williams College, pointed out that the most eroticized figure in Girodet's painting is the muscular, backlit Chactas.

25   Following my presentation of this essay at the "Women and Representation" conference held at Rhode Island College (May 1989), Elizabeth Anne Wolf was kind enough to provide me with an image that presents striking and suggestive similarities with the scene depicted by Girodet. Drawn from de Bausset's *Mémoires du palais intérieur* (1827), the engraving by Chasselat portrays the scene of Josephine and Napoleon's last supper at the Tuileries: as Napoleon stands by the door with his hand on the knob, the prostrate body of Josephine, who has fainted upon hearing of the Emperor's decision to divorce her, is held up by the kneeling Count de Bausset. Though Josephine is no Atala, and Napoleon no Chactas, the homologous positioning of the male figures on either side of the lifeless central figure

of the woman in both images produces a telling visual analogue of the joint Chateau-briand-Napoleon ideological venture.

26   Bernardin de Saint-Pierre, *Paul et Virginie* (Paris: Garnier-Flammarion, 1966), p. 162; *Paul and Virginia*, trans. Andrew Lang (New York: Howard Fertig, 1987), p. 115.

To complete my argument, I would need to bring into play here yet another, and perhaps the most famous, episode of male necrophilia in eighteenth-century French fiction: the dilated and endlessly deferred death of Julie in Rousseau's *Le Nouvelle Héloïse*. While it is true that Julie, like Atala, dies a Christian (Protestant) death, indeed engages in extended theological discussions with her local minister while on her deathbed, Julie, who dies for having saved her small son from drowning, is in the minister's words "a martyr to motherly love" (Jean-Jacques Rousseau, *Julie* [Paris: GF-Flammarion 1967], p. 546). This remark points up a crucial aspect of *Atala* and its ideology of gender which I do not want to neglect: marking a hiatus between the maternalist politics of Rousseau and those of the many nineteenth-century figures who, following Rousseau, in Barthes's words promoted a "sticky ideology of familialism" centered on the mother-woman and grounded in Christian values, in *Atala* there is a blight on maternity, a rejection of domestic values, and a curse on the genealogical imperative. Though *Atala* founds the nineteenth-century French construction of femininity, that construction is not yet here fully in place.

For more on the textual misogyny of the *Natchez* as symptomatized by a denial of mater-nal attributes to its female protagonists, see Pierre Barbéris, *Chateaubriand: une réaction au monde moderne* (Paris: Larousse, 1976), esp. pp. 75–84. Regrettably, Barbéris has to date never produced the study on *Atala* announced in *Chateaubriand*, perhaps because like so many read-ers he reads *Atala* entirely through the thematic grid (incest, love, and prohibition) of *René*.

27   Chateaubriand did not only practice allegory, he theorized it, notably in the chapter of *The Genius of Christianity* titled "Of Allegory" (pp. 303–305). Arguing that allegory is not incompatible with Christianity, Chateaubriand distinguishes between two types of alle-gory, what he calls the moral and the physical. About moral allegory, which he approves of, he has little to say; most of this brief chapter is taken up with physical allegory, which he disapproves of. Physical allegory consists in the personification of natural entities, such as the air, water, and, most disturbingly for Chateaubriand, "mute and motionless objects" such as stones. Chateaubriand's devalorization of this lesser form of allegory is curious: according to him, physical allegory is incompatible with the development of mimetic art; only Christianity favors the truthful description of nature. So long as nature is viewed as inhabited by Nymphs and Naiads, there can never be a properly descriptive poetry.

28   Annie Goldson, "Allegories of Resistance," *Afterimage* 16, no. 10 (May 1989): 18–19.

29   In *Subject to Change: Reading Feminist Writing* (New York: Columbia University Press, 1988), Nancy K. Miller makes an important and necessary distinction between women and feminist writers; see in particular pp. 8–10.

30   Madelyn Gutwirth, *Madame de Staël, Novelist: The Emergence of the Artist as Woman* (Urbana: University of Illinois Press, 1978), pp. 176–181.

31   Cf. My "*Lélia* and the Failures of Allegory," *L'Esprit Créateur* 29 (1989): 76–83.

Before the Castle: Women, Commodities, and Modernity in Au Bonheur des Dames

1   On these three genres and their incarnations in mass culture, see Tania Modleski, *Loving with a Vengeance: Mass-produced Fantasies for Women* (New York: Methuen, 1982).

2   Eve Kosofsky Sedgwick, *Between Men: English Literature and Male Homosocial Desire* (New York: Columbia University Press, 1985), p. 91.

3   Kate Ferguson Ellis, *The Contested Castle: Gothic Novels and the Subversion of Domestic Ideology* (Urbana: University of Illinois Press, 1989). "Focusing on crumbling castles as sites of terror, and on homeless protagonists who wander the face of the earth, the Gothic . . . is preoccupied with the home" (p. ix); "The Gothic novel of the eighteenth century foregrounded the home as fortress, while at the same time exposing its contradictions. Displacing their stories into an imaginary past, its early practitioners appealed to their readers not by providing 'escape' but by encoding, in the language of aristocratic villains, haunted castles, and beleaguered heroines, a struggle to purge the home of license and lust and to establish it as a type of heaven on earth" (pp. xi–xii).

4   Ellen Moers, *Literary Women: The Great Writers* (Garden City: Anchor Press, Doubleday, 1977), p. 139.

5   According to Baudu, the savage economic Darwinism practiced by the department stores leads to the death of the family: "However, Baudu still went on, louder than ever, condemning the people opposite, calling them a pack of savages, murdering each other in their struggle for existence, destroying all his family ties" (Emile Zola, *The Ladies' Paradise* [Berkeley: University of California Press, 1992], p. 24).

6   Michelle Perrot, ed., *From the Fires of Revolution to the Great War*, trans. Arthur Goldhammer, vol. 4 of *A History of Private Life*, ed. Philippe Ariès and George Duby (Cambridge: Harvard University Press, 1990), p. 121.

7   In fact, we don't really see the interiors where the packages sent by the department store end up. It is equally significant that in the scene from chapter 3 that occurs in Mme Desforges's living room, Mme Marty's unwrapping of her latest purchases brings lace into the bourgeois living room, which, more than anything else, arouses covetousness in female clients and thieves of department stores. If, as Rachel Bowlby has shown so well, silk functions as a mirror in which women are reflected, lace seems to give women a pleasure that is more tactile than visual, and which reveals more a type of auto-seduction than auto-speculation. Through lace—which is hardly a serial item, but rather a luxury article—women achieve their narcissism, make love to themselves: "It seemed as if all the seductions of the shop had converged into this supreme temptation, that it was the secluded alcove where the customers were doomed to fall, the corner of perdition where the strongest must succumb. Hands were plunged into the overflowing heaps, retaining an intoxicating trembling from the contact" (p. 234).

8   Elaine S. Abelson, "The Invention of Kleptomania," *Signs* 15, no. 1 (1989): 136.

9   Griselda Pollock, "Modernity and the Spaces of Femininity," in *Vision and Difference: Femininity, Feminism and the Histories of Art* (London: Routledge, 1988), p. 70.

10 See Abel's article cited above; see also Patricia O'Brien, "The Kleptomania Diagnosis: Bourgeois Women and Theft in Late Nineteenth-Century France," *Journal of Social History* 17 (Fall 1983): 65–77, and Paul Dubuisson, "Les Voleuses des Grands Magasins: Etude Clinique et Médico-Légale," *Archives d'Anthropologie Criminelle de Criminologie et de Psychologie Normale et Médico-Légale* 91: 1–20; 94: 341–370.

11 Denise's honesty functions to discredit the misogynous vision represented by Mouret; in this way she draws the following moral from her story: "One ought always to believe a woman to be virtuous, sir. There are numbers who are so, I assure you" (p. 312).

12 Teresa de Lauretis, *Alice Doesn't: Feminism, Semiotics, Cinema* (Bloomington: University of Indiana Press 1984), p. 137.

Depression in the Nineties

Marianne Hirsch provided not only an occasion for this piece—an MLA panel titled, "Remapping Gender and Narrative" (1994), but also helpful feedback that allowed me to clarify some points.

1   Fredric Jameson, "Postmodernism, or, the Cultural Logic of Late Capitalism," *New Left Review* 146 (July-August 1984): 61–62.

2   I am alluding here to Julia Kristeva, *Black Sun: Depression and Melancholia*, trans. Leon S. Roudiez (New York: Columbia University Press, 1989).

3   I am alluding here to Jann Matlock's exemplary *Scenes of Seduction: Prostitution, Hysteria, and Reading Difference in Nineteenth-Century Paris* (New York: Columbia University Press, 1994).

4   Edward W. Said, *Culture and Imperialism* (New York: Vintage, 1993), pp. xii–xiii.

5   Toril Moi and Janice Radway, "Editor's Note," *South Atlantic Quarterly* 93, no. 4, Special Issue, *Materialist Feminism* (1994): 749–750.

6   Peter Brooks, *Reading for the Plot* (Cambridge: Harvard University Press, 1984), p. 90.

7   Mme de Staël, *Corinne, or Italy*, trans. Avriel H. Goldberger (New Brunswick: Rutgers University Press, 1987), p. 3. Subsequent page references will be given within the text under the abbreviation C.

8   Margaret Waller, *The Male Malady: Fictions of Impotence in the French Romantic Novel* (New Brunswick: Rutgers University Press, 1994). Hereafter MM.

9   Cf. Jean Starobinski's congruent description of Corinne as "a living-dead woman" in his article, "Suicide et mélancolie chez Mme de Staël," in *Madame de Staël et l'Europe: Colloque de Coppet* (Paris: Klincksieck, 1970), p. 246. Starobinski's concern is the psychology of Staël and her heroines. The (virtual) abandoned woman is kept alive through the artificial means of a love whose withdrawal determines an "ontological catastrophe" (p. 247).

10   Jacques Derrida, *Specters of Marx: The State of the Debt, the Work of Mourning, and the New International*, trans. Peggy Kamuf (New York: Routledge, 1994), p. 178, n. 3.

11   Joan Scott, "Gender: A Useful Category of Historical Analysis," in *Gender and the Politics of History* (New York: Columbia University Press, 1988), pp. 28–50.

Bibliography

Abelson, Elaine S. "The Invention of Kleptomania." *Signs* 15, no. 1 (1989): 123–143.

Agulhon, Maurice. *Marianne into Battle: Republican Imagery and Symbolism in France, 1789–1880.* Trans. Janet Lloyd. Cambridge: Cambridge University Press, 1981.

Aulagnier-Spairani, Piera, Jean Clavreul, et al. *Le Désir et la perversion.* Paris: Seuil, 1967.

Albistur, Maïte, and Daniel Armogathe. *Histoire du féminisme français.* 2 vols. Paris: des femmes, 1977.

Alcoff, Linda, and Elizabeth Potter, eds. *Feminist Epistemologies.* New York: Routledge, 1993.

Allègre, Claude. *L'âge des savoirs: Pour une renaissance de l'université.* Paris: Gallimard, 1993.

Apostolidès, Jean-Marie. "On Paul de Man's War." *Critical Inquiry* 15, no. 4 (1989): 765–766.

"Appel: L'Avenir de la langue française." *Le Monde,* 11 July 1992, p. 5.

Appiah, Anthony. "The Uncompleted Argument: Du Bois and the Illusion of Race." In *"Race," Writing, and Difference,* ed. Henry Louis Gates, Jr., pp. 21–37. Chicago: University of Chicago Press, 1986.

———. *In My Father's House: Africa in the Philosophy of Culture.* Oxford: Oxford University Press, 1992.

Barbéris, Pierre. *Chateaubriand: une réaction au monde moderne.* Paris: Larousse, 1976.

Barthes, Roland. *The Fashion System.* Trans. Matthew Ward and Richard Howard. New York: Hill and Wang, 1983.

———. "Masculin, Féminin, Neutre." In *Echanges et Communications: Mélanges offerts à Claude Lévi-Strauss à l'occasion de son 60ème anniversaire,* ed. Jean Pouillon and Pierre Maranda. 2 vols. The Hague: Mouton, 1970.

———. *On Racine.* Trans. Richard Howard. In *A Barthes Reader,* ed. Susan Sontag. New York: Hill & Wang, 1982.

———. *Roland Barthes by Roland Barthes.* Trans. Richard Howard. New York: Hill and Wang, 1977.

———. *S/Z.* Trans. Richard Miller. New York: Hill and Wang, 1974.

———. *Sade/Fourier/Loyola.* Trans. Richard Miller. Berkeley: University of California Press, 1989.

Baudelaire, Charles. *Oeuvres complètes.* Paris: Bibliothèque de la Pléiade, 1961.

Beauvoir, Simone de. *The Second Sex.* Trans. H. M. Parshley. New York: Vintage, 1974.

Benhabib, Seyla. *Situating the Self: Gender, Community and Postmodernism in Contemporary Ethics.* New York: Routledge, 1992.

Berg, Elizabeth. "Iconoclastic Moments: Reading the *Sonnets for Helene,* Writing the *Portuguese Letters.*"

In *The Poetics of Gender*, ed. Nancy K. Miller, pp. 208–221. New York: Columbia University Press, 1986.

———. "The Third Woman." *Diacritics* 12 (Summer 1982): 11–20.

Bersani, Leo. *A Future for Astyanax: Character and Desire in Literature*. Boston: Little, Brown and Co., 1976.

Bloom, Leon. *The Anxiety of Influence*. New York: Oxford University Press, 1973.

Bonnet, G. "Fétichisme et exhibitionnisme chez un sujet féminin." *Psychanalyse à l'université* 2 (1977): 231–257.

Booth, Wayne. *A Rhetoric of Irony*. Chicago: University of Chicago Press, 1974.

Bourdieu, Pierre. "Deux impérialismes de l'universel." In *L'Amérique des Français*, ed. Christine Fauré and Tom Bishop. Paris: Editions Bourin, 1992.

———. "Pour un corporatisme de l'universel." In *Les Règles de l'Art: Genèse et Structure du champ littéraire*. Paris: Seuil, 1992.

Braidotti, Rosi. "On the Female Feminist Subject, or: From 'She-self' to 'She-other.' " In *Beyond Equality and Difference: Citizenship, Feminist Politics and Female Subjectivity*, ed. Gisella Bock and Susan James. London: Routledge, 1988.

Brande, Ilse. "Pérette et son 'gai' (d'un cas de phobie d'impulsion et de comportement fétichiste chez une femme)." Mémoire de candidature au titre de Membre adhérent à la Société Pyschanalytique de Paris, 1962.

Brennan, Teresa, ed. *Between Feminism and Psychoanalysis*. London: Routledge, 1989.

Brett, Patricia. "To French Scholars, 'le Politiquement Correct' Is a Symptom of America's Social Breakdown." *The Chronicle of Higher Education*, 17 June 1992, pp. A37–38.

Brontë, Charlotte. *Jane Eyre*. Edinburgh: J. Grant, 1924.

Brooks, Peter. *Reading for the Plot*. Cambridge: Harvard University Press, 1984.

Butler, Judith. *Bodies that Matter: On the Discursive Limits of "Sex."* New York: Routledge, 1993.

———. "Contingent Foundations." In *Feminists Theorize the Political*, ed. Judith Butler and Joan W. Scott. New York: Routledge, 1992.

———. "Critically Queer." *GLQ: A Journal of Lesbian and Gay Studies* 1, no. 1 (1993): 17–32.

———. *Gender Trouble: Feminism and the Subversion of Identity*. New York: Routledge, 1990.

———. "Discussion." *October* 61 (Summer 1992): 108–120.

Butor, Michel. "Sur *La Princesse de Clèves*." In *Répertoire I*. Paris: Minuit, 1960.

Chateaubriand, François René de. *Atala / René*. Trans. Irving Putter. Berkeley: University of California Press, 1967.

———. *The Genius of Christianity*. New York: Howard Fertig, 1976.

———. *Mémoires d'outre-tombe*. Vols. 1, 2. Ed. Maurice Levaillant. Paris: Flammarion, 1949.

Chodorow, Nancy. *The Reproduction of Mothering: Psychoanalysis and the Sociology of Gender*. Berkeley: University of California Press, 1978.

Christian, Barbara. *Black Feminist Criticism: Perspectives on Black Women Writers*. Berkeley: Pergamon Press, 1985.

———. "The Race for Theory." *Cultural Critique* 6 (1987): 51–63.

Cixous, Hélène. "Sorties." Trans. Ann Liddle. In *New French Feminisms*, ed. Elaine Marks and Isabelle de Courtivron. Amherst: University of Massachusetts Press, 1980.

Compagnon, Antoine. "The Diminishing Canon of French Literature in America." *Stanford French Review* 15, nos. 1–2 (1991): 103–115.

Culler, Jonathan. "The Uses of *Madame Bovary*." In *Flaubert and Postmodernism*, ed. Naomi Schor and Henry Majewski. Lincoln: University of Nebraska Press, 1984.

Curtius, Ernst-Robert. *Essai sur la France*. Trans. J. Benoist-Méchin. Paris: l'aube, 1990.

"De la nation ethnique à la nation citoyenne." [Rudolf von Thadden, Jeanne et Pierre Kaltenbach] *Le Monde*, 3 juillet 1993.

de Jean, Joan. "Lafayette's Ellipses: The Privileges of Anonymity." PMLA 99 (October 1984): 884–902.

——. "*La Nouvelle Héloïse*, or the Case for Pedagogical Deviation." *Yale French Studies* 63 (1982): 98–116.

de Lauretis, Teresa. *Alice Doesn't: Feminism, Semiotics, Cinema*. Bloomington: Indiana University Press, 1984.

——, ed. *Feminist Studies / Critical Studies*. Bloomington: Indiana University Press, 1986.

Derrida, Jacques. "Biodegradable: Seven Diary Fragments." *Critical Inquiry* 15, no. 4 (1989): 812–875.

——. "Deconstruction in America: An Interview with Jacques Derrida." *Critical Exchange* 17 (Winter 1985): 1–33.

——. "Devant la loi." Trans. Avital Ronell. In *Kafka and the Contemporary Critical Performance: Centenary Readings*, ed. Alan Udoff, pp. 128–149. Bloomington: Indiana University Press, 1987.

——. *Glas*. Trans. John P. Leavey Jr. and Richard Rand. Lincoln: University of Nebraska Press, 1984.

——. *The Other Heading: Reflections on Today's Europe*. Trans. Pascale-Anne Brault. Bloomington: Indiana University Press, 1992.

——. *Positions*. Trans. Alan Bass. Chicago: University of Chicago Press, 1981.

——. *Specters of Marx: The State of the Debt, the Work of Mourning, and the New National*. Trans. Peggy Kamuf. New York: Routledge, 1994.

——. "Women in the Beehive: A Seminar with Jacques Derrida." In *Men in Feminism*, ed. Alice Jardine and Paul Smith, pp. 189–203. New York: Methuen, 1987.

Doane, Mary Ann. *The Desire to Desire: The Woman's Film of the 1940's*. Bloomington: Indiana University Press, 1987.

——. "Film and Masquerade: Theorising the Female Spectator." *Screen* 23 (September / October 1982): 74–87.

Dubuisson, Paul. "Les Voleuses des Grands Magasins: Etude Clinique et Médico-Légale." *Archives d'Anthropologie Criminelle de Criminologie et de Psychologie Normale et Médico-Légale* 91: 1–20; 94: 341–370.

Dudley, G. A. "A Rare Case of Female Fetishism." *International Journal of Sexology* 8 (1954): 32–34.

Duhet, Paule-Marie, ed. *Cahiers de Doléances des femmes en 1789 et autres textes*. Paris: des femmes, 1981.

Ellis, Kate Ferguson. *The Contested Castle: Gothic Novels and the Subversion of Domestic Ideology*. Urbana: University of Illinois Press, 1989.

Elam, Diane and Robyn Wiegman, eds. *Feminism Beside Itself*. New York: Routledge, 1995.

Fantini, Alvino E. *Language Acquisition of a Bilingual Child: A Sociolinguistic Perspective (To Age Ten)*. San Diego: College-Hill Press, 1985.

Felman, Shoshana. "De la nature des choses ou de l'écart à l'équilibre." *Critique* 380 (January 1979): 3–15.

——. *Writing and Madness: (Literature / Philosophy / Psychoanalysis)*. Trans. Martha Noel Evans. Ithaca: Cornell University Press, 1985.

Ferrara, Alessandro. "Universalisms: Procedural, Contextualist, and Prudential." *Philosophy and Social Criticism* 14, nos. 3 / 4 (1988): 243–269.

Ferry, Jean-Luc and Alan Renant. *La pensée 68: essai sur l'anti-humanisme contemporain*. Paris: Gallimard, 1985.

Flaubert, Gustave. *Bouvard et Pécuchet*. Paris: Garnier-Flammarion, 1966.

——. *L'éducation sentimentale*. Paris: Garnier-Flammarion, 1969.

——. *Mémoires d'un fou*. In *Oeuvres complètes*, vol 1. Paris: Seuil, 1964.

——. *Sentimental Education*. Trans. Robert Baldick. Harmondsworth, England: Penguin, 1964.

Foucault, Michel. *The Care of the Self*. Trans. Robert Hurley. New York: Pantheon Books, 1986.

——. *Herculine Barbin*. Trans. Richard McDougall. New York: Pantheon Books, 1980.

——. *Power / Knowledge: Selected Interviews and Other Writings 1972–1977*. Ed. Colin Gordon, trans. Colin Gordon et al. New York: Pantheon Books, 1980.

——. *The Use of Pleasure*. Trans. Robert Hurley. New York: Pantheon Books, 1985.

Freud, Sigmund. "Fetishism." In *The Standard Edition of the Complete Psychological Works*, ed. James Strachey, trans. James Strachey et al., 21: 149–157. London: Hogarth Press, 1953–1974.

——. "Some Psychological Consequences of the Anatomical Distinction between the Sexes." In *Sexuality and the Psychology of Love*, ed. Philip Rieff, pp. 183–193. New York: Collier, 1963.

Fuss, Diana. *Essentially Speaking: Feminism, Nature and Difference*. New York: Routledge, 1989.

Gallop, Jane. "Annie Leclerc Writing a Letter, with Vermerr." In *The Poetics of Gender*, ed. Nancy K. Miller, pp. 137–156. New York: Columbia University Press, 1986.

——. *Around 1981: Academic Feminist Literary Theory*. New York: Routledge, 1992.

——. "Beyond the Jouissance Principle." *Representations* 7 (1984): 110–115.

——. *Feminism and Psychoanalysis: The Daughter's Seduction*. London: Macmillan, 1982.

——. "Feminist Criticism and the Pleasure of the Text." *North Dakota Quarterly* 54, no. 2 (Spring 1986): 119–132.

——. *Thinking through the Body*. New York: Columbia University Press, 1988.

Geyer, Michael. "Multiculturalism." *Critical Inquiry* 19 (Spring 1993): 499–533.

Gilbert, Sandra, and Susan Gubar. *The Madwoman in the Attic*. New Haven: Yale University Press, 1979.

Gilroy, Paul. *The Black Atlantic: Modernity and Double Consciousness*. Cambridge: Harvard University Press, 1993.

Ginsburg, Michal Peled. *Flaubert Writing: A Study in Narrative Strategies*. Stanford: Stanford University Press, 1986.

Giraud, Victor. *Le Christianisme de Chateaubriand*. Paris: Hachette, 1928.

Glasgow, Janis. *Une Esthétique de comparaison: Balzac et George Sand*. Paris: A. G. Nizet, 1977.

Goldson, Annie. "Allegories of Resistance." *Afterimage* 16, no. 10 (May 1989): 18–19.

Graff, Gerald. *Professing Literature: An Institutional History*. Chicago: University of Chicago Press, 1987.

Grosjean, François. *Life with Two Languages: An Introduction to Bilingualism*. Cambridge: Harvard University Press, 1982.

Grosz, Elizabeth. "Sexual Difference and the Problem of Essentialism." In *The Essential Difference*, ed. Naomi Schor and Elizabeth Weed. Bloomington: University of Indiana Press, 1994.

Gutwirth, Madelyn. *Madame de Staël, Novelist: The Emergence of the Artist as Woman*. Urbana: University of Illinois Press, 1978.

Haraway, Donna. "A Manifesto for Cyborgs: Science, Technology, and Socialist Feminism in the 1980s." *Socialist Review* 80 (March-April 1985): 65–107.

Harpham, Geoffrey Galt. "So . . . What Is Enlightenment? An Inquisition into Modernity." *Critical Inquiry* 20, no. 3 (Spring 1994): 524–556.

Heath, Stephen. "Barthes on Love." *Sub-Stance* 37 / 38 (1983): 100–106.

——. *Vertige du déplacement*. Paris: Fayard, 1974.

Hegel, G.W.F. *Phenomenology of Spirit*. Trans. A. V. Miller. Oxford: Oxford University Press, 1977.

Hermann, Claudine. *Les voleuses de langue*. Paris: des femmes, 1976.

Hertz, Neil. "Medusa's Head: Male Hysteria under Political Pressure." *Representations* 4 (Fall 1983): 27–54.

Hirsch, Marianne, and Evelyn Fox Keller, eds. *Conflicts in Feminism*. New York: Routledge, 1990.

——. "A Mother's Discourse: Incorporation and Repetition in *La Princesse de Clèves*." *Yale French Studies* 62 (1982): 67–87.

Hollier, Denis. "French Customs, Literary Borders." *October* 49 (Summer 1989): 41–52.

hooks, bell. *Ain't I a Woman: Black Women and Feminism*. Boston: South End, 1981.

Horkheimer, Max, and Theodor W. Adorno. *Dialectic of Enlightenment*. Trans. Joan Cumming. New York: Continuum, 1993.

Huet, Marie-Hélène. "Le Sacre du Printemps: Essai sur le sublime et la Terreur." *MLN* 103.4 (1988): 781–799.

Hughes, Robert. *La Culture gnangnan*. Trans. Pascal Brukner. Paris: arléa, 1994.

Hullot-Kentor, Odile. "*Clèves* Goes to Business School: A Review of DeJean and Miller." *Stanford French Review* 13, nos. 2–3 (1989): 251–266.

Hunt, Lynn. "Engraving the Republic: Prints and Propaganda in the French Revolution." *History Today* 30 (October 1980): 11–17.

——. *Politics, Culture, and Class in the French Revolution*. Berkeley: University of California Press, 1984.

Irigaray, Luce. *Le Corps-à-corps avec la mère*. Montréal: pleine lune, 1981.

——. "Equal to Whom?" Trans. Robert L. Mazzola. *differences* 1, no. 2 (Summer 1989): 59–76.

——. *Ethique de la différence sexuelle*. Paris: Minuit, 1984.

——. "Is the Subject of Science Sexed?" Trans. Edith Oberle. *Cultural Critique* 1 (1985): 73–88.

——. *J'aime à toi: Esquisse d'une félicité dans l'histoire*. Paris: Grasset, 1992.

——. *Marine Lover of Friedrich Nietzsche*. Trans. Gillian Gill. New York: Columbia University Press, 1991.

——. *Le Language des déments*. The Hague: Mouton, 1973.

——. "L'Ordre sexuel du discours." *Langages* 85 (March 1987): 81–123.

——. *L'Oubli de l'air chez Martin Heidegger*. Paris: Minuit, 1983.

——. *Parler n'est jamais neutre*. Paris: Minuit, 1985.

——. *Passions élémentaires*. Paris: Minuit, 1982.

——. "A Personal Note: Equal or Different." In *Je, tu, nous: Toward a Culture of Difference*, trans. Alison Martin, pp. 9–14. New York: Routledge, 1993.

——. *Sexes and Genealogies*. Trans. Gillian C. Gill. New York: Columbia University Press, 1993.

——. *Speculum of the Other Woman*. Trans. Gillian C. Gill. Ithaca: Cornell University Press, 1985.

——. *This Sex Which Is Not One*. Trans. Catherine Porter with Carolyn Burke. Ithaca: Cornell University Press, 1985.

Jameson, Fredric. *Postmodernism, or, The Cultural Logic of Late Capitalism*. Durham: Duke University Press, 1991.

——. "Postmodernism, or, The Cultural Logic of Late Capitalism." *New Left Review* 146 (July-August 1984): 53–92.

Jardine, Alice. *Gynesis: Configurations of Woman and Modernity*. Ithaca: Cornell University Press, 1985.

——. "Pre-Texts for the Transatlantic Feminist." *Yale French Studies* 62 (1981): 220–236.

Jehlen, Myra. "Against Human Wholeness: A Suggestion for a Feminist Epistemology." Unpublished paper presented to the Columbia University Seminar on Women and Society.

Johnson, Barbara. "The Critical Difference." *Diacritics* 8, no. 2 (Summer 1978): 2–9.

Johnson, Pauline. "Feminism and the Enlightenment." *Radical Philosophy* 63 (Spring 1993): 3–12.

Judovitz, Dalia. "The Aesthetics of Implausibility: *La Princesse de Clèves*." *Modern Language Notes* 99, no. 5 (1984): 1037–1056.

Kamuf, Peggy. "A Mother's Will." In *Fictions of Feminine Desire*, pp. 67–96. Lincoln: University of Nebraska Press, 1982.

——. "Replacing Feminist Criticism." *Diacritics* 12 (1982): 42–47.

Kent, Sarah. "Looking Back." In *Women's Images of Men*. London: Writers and Readers Publishing, 1985.

Kent, Sarah, and Jacqueline Morreau. Preface to *Women's Images of Men*. London: Writers and Readers Publishing, 1985.

Kofman, Sarah. "Ça cloche." Trans. Caren Kaplan. In *Derrida and Deconstruction*, ed. Hugh J. Silverman, pp. 108–138. New York: Routledge, 1989.

——. *The Enigma of Woman: Woman in Freud's Writings*. Trans. Catherine Porter. Ithaca: Cornell University Press, 1985.

Kolodny, Annette. "Dancing through the Minefields: Some Observations on the Theory, Practice, and Politics of a Feminist Literary Criticism." *Feminist Studies* 6 (Spring 1980): 1–25.

Kristeva, Julia. *Black Sun: Depression and Melancholia*. Trans. Leon S. Roudiez. New York: Columbia University Press, 1989.

——. *Strangers to ourselves*. Trans. Leon S. Roudiez. New York: Columbia University Press, 1994.

Lacan, Jacques. *Feminine Sexuality: Jacques Lacan and the école freudienne*. Ed. Juliet Mitchell and Jacqueline Rose, trans. Jacqueline Rose. New York: Norton, 1982.

Laclau, Ernesto. "Subject of Politics, Politics of the Subject." *differences* 7, no. 1 (Spring 1995): forthcoming.

——. "Universalism, Particularism, and the Question of Identity." *October* 61, Special Issue, *The Identity in Question* (Summer 1992): 83–90.

Lafayette, Mme de. *La Princesse de Clèves*. Paris: Garnier-Flammarion, 1966.

——. *The Princesse de Clèves*. Trans. Nancy Mitford. Harmondsworth, England: Penguin, 1982.

Landes, Joan B. *Women and the Public Sphere in the Age of the French Revolution*. Ithaca: Cornell University Press, 1988.

Lemaitre, Jules. *Chateaubriand*. Paris: Calmann-Lévy, n.d.

Levitine, George. "Some Unexplored Aspects of the Illustrations of *Atala*: The *Surenchères visuelles* of Girodet and Hersent." In *Chateaubriand Today*, ed. Richard Switzer, pp. 139–145. Madison: University of Wisconsin Press, 1970.

Levy, Darlene Gay, Harriet Branson Applewhite, and Mary Durham Johnson, eds. *Women in Revolutionary Paris, 1789–1795*. Urbana: University of Illinois Press, 1979.

Lionnet, Françoise. "Identity, Sexuality, and Criminality: 'Universal Rights' and the Debate around the Practice of Female Excision in France." *Contemporary French Civilization* 16, no. 2 (Fall 1992): 294–307.

Long, Candace. *Irony/Humor: Critical Paradigms*. Baltimore: Johns Hopkins University Press, 1988.

Lucretius. *De Rerum Naturae*. Trans. W.H.D. Rouse. Loeb Classical Library. Cambridge: Harvard University Press, 1975.

Luissier, André. "Bibliography." *Revue Française de Psychanalyse* 47, Special Issue, *Perversion* (1983): 132–142.

Martin, Biddy. "Feminism, Criticism, and Foucault." *New German Critique* 27 (Fall 1982): 3–30.

Marx, Karl. *The Eighteenth Brumaire of Louis Bonaparte*. New York: International Publishers, 1972.

Matlock, Jann. *Scenes of Seduction: Prostitution, Hysteria, and Reading Difference in Nineteenth-Century France*. New York: Columbia University Press, 1994.

Maurin, Mario. "Un Modèle d'*Indiana*." *French Review* 50 (1976): 317–320.

Michaud, Stéphane. *Muse et madone: Visages de la femme de la Révolution française aux apparitions de Lourdes*. Paris: Seuil, 1985.

Miller, Jane. *Women Writing about Men*. New York: Pantheon, 1986.

Miller, Nancy K. "Changing the Subject: Authorship, Writing, and the Reader." In de Lauretis, *Feminist Studies / Critical Studies*, pp. 102–120.

——. "Emphasis Added: Plots and Plausibilities in Women's Fiction." In *The New Feminist Criticism*, ed. Elaine Showalter, pp. 339–360. New York: Pantheon, 1985.

——. *Getting Personal: Feminist Occasions and Other Autobiographical Acts*. New York: Routledge, 1992.

——. "Parables and Politics: Feminist Criticism in 1986." *Paragraph* 8 (October 1986): 40–54.

——. *Subject to Change: Reading Feminist Writing*. New York: Columbia University Press, 1988.

——. "The Text's Heroine." *Diacritics* 12 (1982): 48–53.

——. "Writing (from) the Feminine: George Sand and the Novel of Female Pastoral." In *The Representation of Women in Fiction: Selected Papers from the English Institute 1981*, ed. Carolyn Heilbrun and Margaret Higonnet. Baltimore: Johns Hopkins University Press, 1983.

Milo, Daniel. "Les Classiques scolaires." In *Les Lieux de mémoire, II, La Nation*, 3, ed. Pierre Nora. Paris: Gallimard, 1986.

Mitchell, W.J.T. *Iconology: Image, Text, Ideology*. Chicago: University of Chicago Press, 1986.

Modleski, Tania. *Loving with a Vengeance: Mass-produced Fantasies for Women*. New York: Methuen, 1982.

Moers, Ellen. *Literary Women: The Great Writers*. Garden City: Anchor Press, Doubleday, 1977.

Moi, Toril. *Sexual / Textual Politics*. London: Methuen, 1985.

——. *Simone de Beauvoir: The Making of an Intellectual Woman*. Oxford: Blackwell, 1994.

Moi, Toril and Janice Radway. "Editor's Note." *South Atlantic Quarterly* 93, no. 4, Special Issue, *Materialist Feminism* (1994): 749–750.

Moses, Claire. *French Feminism in the 19th Century*. Albany: SUNY Press, 1984.

Muecke, D. C. *Irony and the Ironic*. London: Methuen, 1970.

Mulvey, Laura. "Visual Pleasure and Narrative Cinema." *Screen* 6 (Autumn 1975): 6–18.

Nicholson, Linda J., ed. *Feminism / Postmodernism*. New York: Routledge, 1990.

Nora, Pierre. "'La nation-mémoire." In *Les Lieux de Mémoire, II, La Nation*, 3, ed. Pierre Nora, Paris: Gallimard, 1986.

O'Brien, Patricia. "The Kleptomania Diagnosis: Bourgeois Women and Theft in Late Nineteenth-Century France." *Journal of Social History* 17 (Fall 1983): 65–77.

Orr, Linda. *Headless History: Nineteenth-Century French Historiography of the French Revolution*. Ithaca: Cornell University Press, 1990.

Ozouf, Mona. *La Fête révolutionnaire, 1789–1799*. Paris: Gallimard, 1976.

Palumbo-Liu, David. "Universalisms and Minority Culture." *differences* 7, no. 1 (Spring 1995): forthcoming.

Pateman, Carole. *The Disorder of Women: Democracy, Feminism and Political Theory*. Stanford: Stanford University Press, 1989.

Paulson, Ronald. *Representations of Revolution (1789–1820)*. New Haven: Yale University Press, 1983.

Pavel, Thomas G. "The Present Debate: News from France." *Diacritics* 19, no. 1 (1989): 17–32.

——. "Le rejet des classiques." *Le Messager européen* 5 (1991): 3–13.

Perrot, Michelle, ed. *From the Fires of Revolution to the Great War*. Trans. Arthur Goldhammer. Vol. 4 of *A History of Private Life*, ed. Philippe Ariès and George Duby. Cambridge: Harvard University Press, 1990.

Phillips, Anne. "Universal Pretensions in Political Thought." In *Destabilizing Theory: Contemporary Feminist Debates*, ed. Michèle Barrett and Anne Phillips. Stanford: Stanford University Press, 1992.

Pollock, Griselda. "Modernity and the Spaces of Femininity." In *Vision and Difference: Femininity, Feminism and the Histories of Art*. London: Routledge, 1988.

Pratt, Mary Louise. "Scratches on the Face of the Country: Or, What Mr. Barrow Saw in the Land of the Bushmen." In *"Race," Writing and Difference,"* ed. Henry Louis Gates Jr., pp. 138–163. Chicago: University of Chicago Press, 1986.

Prevost, Abbé. *Manon Lescaut.* Paris: Folio, 1972.

——. *Manon Lescaut.* Trans. Leonard Tancock. Harmondsworth, England: Penguin, 1949.

Prigogine, Ilya, and Isabelle Stengers. *La Nouvelle Alliance: Métamorphose de la science.* Paris: Gallimard, 1979.

Quinzaine Littéraire, La. "L'écriture a-t-elle un sexe. Questions à des écrivains." *La Quinzaine littéraire* 192 (August 1974): 27–30.

Rabine, Leslie. "George Sand and the Myth of Femininity." *Women and Literature* 4, no. 2 (1976): 2–17.

Rainer, Warning. "Irony and the 'Order of Discourse' in Flaubert." Trans. Michael Morton. *New Literary History* 13, no. 2 (1982): 253–286.

Reese, William J. *Dictionary of Philosophy and Religion: Eastern and Western Thought,* pp. 80–81. New Jersey: Humanities Press, 1980.

Ricoeur, Paul. "Mimesis and Representation." *Annals of Scholarship* 2 (1981): 15–32.

Riffaterre, Michael. *Semiotics of Poetry.* Bloomington: Indiana University Press, 1978.

Riley, Denise. *Am I that Name? Feminism and the Category of 'Women' in History.* Minneapolis: University of Minnesota Press, 1988.

Rogers, Katherine M. *The Troublesome Helpmate: A History of Misogyny in Literature.* Seattle: University of Washington Press, 1966.

Rose, Jacqueline. "On the 'Universality' of Madness: Bessie Head's *A Question of Power.*" *Critical Inquiry* 20 (Spring 1994): 401–418.

Ross, Kristin. "The World Literature and Cultural Studies Program." *Critical Inquiry* 19, no. 4 (1993): 666–676.

Rousseau, Jean-Jacques. *Julie, ou La Nouvelle Héloïse.* Paris: GL-Flammarion, 1967.

Ruthven, K. K. *Feminist Literary Studies: An Introduction.* Cambridge: Cambridge University Press, 1984.

Said, Edward W. *Culture and Imperialism.* New York: Vintage, 1993.

——. "Nationalism, Human Rights, and Interpretation." *Raritan* 12, no. 3 (Winter 1993): 26–51.

Saint-Pierre, Bernardin de. *Paul and Virginia.* Trans. Andrew Lang. New York: Howard Fertig, 1987.

——. *Paul et Virginie.* Paris: Garnier-Flammarion, 1966.

Sainte-Beuve. *Les Grands écrivains français: XIXe Siècle, les romanciers.* Paris: Garnier, 1927.

Sand, George. *Indiana.* Paris: Folio, 1984.

——. *Indiana.* Paris: Michel Lévy, 1862.

——. *Indiana.* Trans. George Burnham Ives. Chicago: Academy Press Limited, 1978.

——. *Lélia.* Paris: Garnier, 1960.

——. *Lélia.* Trans. Maria Espinosa. Bloomington: Indiana University Press, 1978.

——. *Lettres d'un voyageur.* Paris: Garnier-Flammarion, 1971.

——. *Mauprat.* Paris: Garnier-Flammarion, 1969.

——. *Mauprat.* Trans. Stanley Young. Chicago: Academy Press Limited, 1977.

——. *Valentine.* Paris: Michel Lévy, 1869.

——. *Valentine.* Trans. George Burnham Ives. Chicago: Academy Press Limited, 1978.

Sarraute, Nathalie. *Portrait of a Man Unknown.* Trans. Maria Jolas. New York: G. Braziller, 1958.

Schor, Naomi. *Breaking the Chain: Women, Theory, and French Realist Fiction.* New York: Columbia University Press, 1985.

——. "Female Paranoia: The Case for Feminist Psychoanalytic Criticism." *Yale French Studies* 62 (1981): 204–219.

——. *George Sand and Idealism*. New York: Columbia University Press, 1993.

——. "Lélia and the Failures of Allegory." *L'Esprit Créateur* 29 (1989): 76–83.

——. "Reading Double: Sand's Difference." In *The Poetics of Gender*, ed. Nancy K. Miller. New York: Columbia University Press, 1986.

——. *Reading in Detail: Aesthetics and the Feminine*. New York: Methuen, 1987.

Scott, Joan W. "Gender: A Useful Category of Historical Analysis." In *Gender and the Politics of History*. New York: Columbia University Press, 1988.

——. "Multiculturalism and the Politics of Identity." *October* 61 (Summer 1992): 12–19.

Sedgwick, Eve Kosofsky. *Between Men: English Literature and Male Homosocial Desire*. New York: Columbia University Press, 1985.

Segal, Naomi. *Narcissus and Echo*. Manchester: Manchester University Press, 1988.

Senghor, Léopold Sédar. *Liberté 1: Négritude et humanisme*. Paris: Seuil, 1964.

Shell, Marc. *Children of the Earth: Literature, Politics, and Nationhood*. New York: Oxford University Press, 1993.

Showalter, Elaine. "Feminist Criticism in the Wilderness." *Critical Inquiry* 8 (1981): 179–206.

Silverman, Kaja. "Liberty, Maternity, Commodification." *New Formations* 5 (Summer 1988): 69–89.

——. *The Subject of Semiotics*. New York: Oxford University Press, 1983.

Sivert, Eileen Boyd. "Lélia and Feminism." *Yale French Studies* 62 (1981): 45–66.

Snead, James. "European Pedigrees/African Contagions: Nationality, Narrative, and Communality in Tutuola, Achebe, and Reed." In *Nation and Narration*, ed. Homi K. Bhabha, pp. 231–249. New York: Routledge, 1990.

Snitow, Ann, Christine Stansell, and Sharon Thompson, eds. *Powers of Desire: The Politics of Sexuality*. New York: Monthly Review Press, 1983.

Sollers, Philippe. "La Littérature et ses juges." *Le Monde*, 18 October 1991, p. 1.

Spivak, Gayatri. "French Feminism Revisited: Ethics and Politics." In *Feminists Theorize the Political*, ed. Judith Butler and Joan Scott, pp. 54–85. New York: Routledge, 1992.

——. *In Other Worlds*. New York: Methuen, 1987.

Staël, Mme de. *Corinne, or Italy*. Trans. Avriel H. Goldberger. New Brunswick: Rutgers University Press, 1987.

——. *Essai sur les fictions*. Paris: Editions Ramsey, 1979.

Starobinski, Jean. "Suicide et mélancolie chez Mme de Staël." In *Madame de Staël et l'Europe: Colloque de Coppet*. Paris: Klincksieck, 1970.

Sturrock, John. "Roland Barthes." In *Structuralism and Since: From Lévi-Strauss to Derrida*, ed. John Sturrock. Oxford: Oxford University Press, 1979.

Suleiman, Susan. "Interpreting Ironies." *Diacritics* 6 (Summer 1976): 15–21.

——. "Pornography, Transgression, and the Avant-Garde: Bataille's Story of the Eye." In *The Poetics of Gender*, ed. Nancy K. Miller. New York: Columbia University Press, 1986.

——. "(Re)writing the Body." In *The Female Body in Western Culture: Contemporary Perspectives*. Cambridge: Harvard University Press, 1985.

Todorov, Tzvetan. *On Human Diversity: Nationalism, Racism, and Exoticism in French Thought*. Trans. Catherine Porter. Cambridge: Harvard University Press, 1994.

Tompkins, Jane. *Sensational Designs: The Cultural Work of American Fiction 1790–1860*. New York: Oxford University Press, 1985.

Vincent, K. Steven. "National Consciousness, Nationalism, and Exclusion: Reflections on the French Case." *Historical Reflections/Réflexions Historiques* 19, no. 3 (1993): 1–17.

Waller, Margaret. *The Male Malady: Fictions of Impotence in the French Romantic Novel*. New Brunswick: Rutgers University Press, 1994.

Wallis, Brian. "What's Wrong with This Picture: An Introduction." In *Art after Modernism: Rethinking Representation*, ed. Brian Wallis. New York: The New Museum of Contemporary Art in association with David R. Godine, 1984.

Walzer, Michael. "Two Kinds of Universalism." In *The Tanner Lectures on Human Values* 11, 1990, ed. Grethe B. Peterson. Salt Lake City: University of Utah Press, 1990.

Watkins, Mel. "Sexism, Racism and Black Women Writers." *The New York Times Book Review*, 15 June 1986.

West, Cornel. "Diverse New World." In *Debating P. C.*, ed. Paul Berman, pp. 326–332. New York: Laurel, 1992.

——. "A Matter of Life and Death." *October* 61 (Summer 1992): 20–23.

——. "The New Cultural Politics of Difference." In *Out There: Marginalization and Contemporary Cultures*, ed. Russell Ferguson et al. New York: New Museum of Contemporary Art, 1990.

Whitford, Margaret. "Luce Irigaray and the Female Imaginary: Speaking as a Woman." *Radical Philosophy* 43 (1986): 3–8.

——. *Luce Irigaray: Philosophy in the Feminine*. London: Routledge, 1991.

Williams, Patricia J. *The Alchemy of Race and Rights: Diary of a Law Professor*. Cambridge: Harvard University Press, 1991.

Williams, Raymond. *Marxism and Literature*. Oxford: Oxford University Press, 1990.

Wittig, Monique. "Homo Sum." In *The Straight Mind and Other Essays*. Boston: Beacon, 1992.

Woolf, Virginia. *A Room of One's Own*. New York: Harcourt, Brace and World, Inc., 1957.

Young, Iris. "Impartiality and the Civic Public: Some Implications of Feminist Critiques of Moral and Political Theory." In *Feminism as Critique: On the Politics of Gender*, ed. Seyla Benhabib and Drucilla Cornell, pp. 56–76. Minneapolis: University of Minnesota Press, 1986.

Zavitzianos, G. "Fetishism and Exhibitionism in the Female and their Relationship to Psychopathology and Kleptomania." *International Journal of Psycho-Analysis* 52 (1971): 297–305.

Zerilli, Linda. "The Trojan Horse of Universalism." *Social Text*, nos. 25–26 (1990): 146–170.

Zimmerman, Bonnie. *The New Feminist Criticism*. Ed. Elaine Showalter. New York: Pantheon, 1985.

Zola, Emile. *The Ladies' Paradise*. Berkeley: University of California Press, 1992.

Naomi Schor is Professor of Romance Languages and
Literatures at Harvard University. She is the author of many
books including *George Sand and Idealism* and *Reading in Detail:
Aesthetics and the Feminine*. She is also the co-editor of *differences*.

Library of Congress Cataloging-in-Publication Data
Schor, Naomi.
Bad objects : essays popular and unpopular / by Naomi Schor.
Includes bibliographical references and index.
ISBN 0-8223-1681-1 (cl : alk. paper). — ISBN 0-8223-1693-5
(pa : alk. paper)
1. French literature—20th century—History and criticism.
2. French literature—19th century—History and criticism.
3. Feminism in literature. 4. Feminist theory. I. Title.
PQ307.F43S36   1995
801'.95'082—dc20   95-15446CIP